THE RENEWAL OF
LITERATURE

THE RENEWAL OF LITERATURE
Emersonian Reflections

RICHARD POIRIER

RANDOM HOUSE NEW YORK

Grateful acknowledgment is made to the following for permission to reprint previously published material:

Henry Holt and Company: Excerpts from *The Poetry of Robert Frost*, edited by Edward Connery Lathem. Copyright 1923, 1928, © 1969 by Holt, Rinehart and Winston. Copyright 1942, 1951, © 1956 by Robert Frost. Copyright © 1970 by Lesley Frost Ballantine. Reprinted by permission of Henry Holt and Company.

Alfred A. Knopf, Inc.: Excerpts from *The Collected Poems of Wallace Stevens.* Copyright 1954 by Wallace Stevens. Reprinted by permission of Alfred A. Knopf, Inc.

Raritan: Excerpts from "William James and His Cuttlefish" by Anita Kermode reprinted by permission from *Raritan*, Volume I, Number 3, Winter 1982.

Viking Penguin, Inc.: Excerpt from "Street Musicians" from *Houseboat Days* by John Ashbery. Copyright © 1987 by John Ashbery. Reprinted by permission of Viking Penguin, Inc.

Portions of this book are based upon material previously published in somewhat different form in *Daedalus, Nineteenth Century Fiction, Raritan*, and *The London Review of Books*.

Library of Congress Cataloging-in-Publication Data
Poirier, Richard.
The renewal of literature.
1. American literature—History and criticism—
Theory, etc. 2. Emerson, Ralph Waldo, 1803-1882—
Influence. 3. Literature—Philosophy. I. Title.
PS25.P6   1987   801'.95'0973   86-10232
ISBN 0-394-50140-3

Manufactured in the United States of America
Typography and binding design by J. K. Lambert
24689753
First Edition

TO

RICHARD SANTINO

CONTENTS

THE RENEWAL OF
LITERATURE

PROLOGUE:

THE DEED OF WRITING

Writing may be either the record of a deed or a deed. It is
nobler when it is a deed. . . .

Thoreau, Journal, January 7, 1844

O F ALL THE ARTS, literature has been put, I think, in the most
unenviable position. It is the designated place where everyone in every
sort of need or trouble is advised to go looking for something, told he
can find something or recover it, that he ought "to reclaim a legacy,"
as is suggested by the title of a recent study from the National Endowment for the Humanities. Something literature promises to restore has
been adulterated, it is said, by popular culture or diminished by history
or neglected by society or besmirched by ideologues—our aspirations,
our civility, our self-esteem, some knowledge that will redeem the horrors of recent history and remind us of how really good and creative we
can be. Literature is supposed to hold all of this in trust, in a relatively
uncontaminated form.

It will be clear as I go along that I find reclamation projects of this
kind quite fruitless. They are the expression, usually, of some disguised
cultural or social agenda which none of the great writers summoned
from the past could possibly endorse. Still more perplexing is that the
whole venture fails to take account of how literature is troubled within

itself, how much, in fact, it shows the futility of this quest for truth, values, and exaltations.

From the beginning, literature has expressed this same need to find something that is missing, call it "nature" or "reality." So that the nostalgia of literary-cultural zealots is already going begging, so to speak, on the very spot where they look to have it satisfied. The illusion of literature's resourcefulness will not abate, however, despite what literature itself has to say about it, and any diminution of its popularity is the immediate occasion for pronouncements, by those who use it as a cultural and political resource, that a savage torpor is upon us. No one has ever, I think, made similar protestations about a decline of interest in musical recitals or dance recitals or gallery shows, since these involve forms of art neither commonly shared with the general populace nor obliged to use a material—language—which belongs more or less to everyone. Especially when alleged disaffections from literature can be blamed, quite egregiously, on enthusiasms for other entertainment media, the complaints are accompanied by a proportionate insistence that the schools ought to take a hand, that reading is a cure, that cultural salvation itself may be advanced by more assiduous attention to certain revered texts.

Reading for cultural renovation has a long and self-perpetuating history. F. R. Leavis, for example—in his vastly influential magazine *Scrutiny*, published from Downing College, Cambridge University, England, from 1932 to 1953, and in a series of books equally important to the pedagogy of English literary studies—makes no distinction between, on the one hand, his "great traditions" in fiction and poetry and, on the other, the vitalizing, restorative cultural values that, as he often emphatically puts it, are "there," specific to the words on the page. They were "there" all the more because, in the modern world as he posited it, they could be nowhere else. Leavis is an exceptionally brilliant expositor of a cultural-literary position that has been recurrently and widely held, not least by Matthew Arnold, as far back as Spenser's "A Letter of the Authors" to *The Faerie Queene*. He "followed all the antique Poets historicall," Spenser says, so as to choose as his hero King Arthur, a man protected from modern—that is, sixteenth-century—cultural degeneration, "furthest from the daunger of envy, and suspition of present time."

No "present time" has ever, apparently, known itself to be as exemplary as later times assume and need it to be, which may be why, in its literature, life is so often reflected in an "antique mirror."

Whatever might turn out to be the relation of literature to life or to culture, it is impossible to measure just how important or effective the relation is, as I argue in Chapter 3, "Venerable Complications." Relatively few of the vast proliferations of people in the last five hundred years were readers of literature even when they could read at all. Furthermore, from George Chapman, the translator of Homer and author in 1594 of the aptly titled "The Shadow of Night," to Wordsworth in the nineteenth century on to Eliot in the twentieth, writers have warned that it was exactly the cultural necessity and virtue of their work that made it "difficult" to read. "Away, then," wrote Wordsworth in "Essay, Supplementary to the Preface" (1815), "with the senseless iteration of the word *popular,* applied to new works in poetry, as if there were no test of excellence in this first of the fine arts but that all men should run after its productions, as if urged by an appetite, or constrained by a spell!" Poetry can imagine itself like the goblet, hidden in Frost's poem "Directive," and "Under a spell so the wrong ones can't find it,/So can't get saved, as Saint Mark says they mustn't." Meanwhile, canon formation, in response to imagined cultural crises, has taken its cues from Matthew as much as from Mark: "Wide is the gate, and broad is the way, that leadeth to destruction, and many there be which go in thereat; Because strait is the gate, and narrow is the way, which leadeth unto life, and few there be that find it" (7:13–14). Literature is a very restricted passage into life, if it is one at all. It is never even all at once everything that is sometimes literature. English literature, including the "best" of the most sacrosanct authors, changes shape every twenty years or so, and, as we shall see presently, American literature as it is now conceived was until quite recently kept in hiding or repressed.

Literature is so variable a factor in any situation that it is absurd to suppose that it is some sort of thing waiting neutrally to arbitrate real or imagined cultural crises. More likely it creates crises that do not exist for the people who are supposed to feel them most but who somehow refuse to do so. This was especially true, I think, of the Waste Land ethos during the second quarter of this century. Or it is used factionally to promote the social or political interests of a nation or a group, as was English literature by the British in occupied India. It is forever being exploited, most notably by poets and novelists talking about one another. A stunning case in point is in the criticism of T. S. Eliot, notably his defense of Joyce's *Ulysses*. The novel was received in England with facile incomprehension and hostility, and Eliot was courageous in his efforts to champion it in his *Dial* essay of 1923 and in publishing some of its early chapters in *The Egoist* in 1919, when he was assistant editor. If *The Waste Land,* published like *Ulysses* in 1922, is not significantly indebted to the novel, except for phrases here and there, mostly in the "Hades" and "Proteus" episodes, its status owes something to the promotional effort that goes on in Eliot's "Ulysses, Order and Myth." The essay more aptly describes Eliot's methods and ambitions in the poem than Joyce's book. It makes the book sound pretentiously full of cultural malaise, announces that "the novel is dead," and that Joyce has discovered what Eliot calls "the mythical method" by which it is possible to create "a continuous parallel between contemporaneity and antiquity." That Joyce now and again uses such a technique is obvious enough, though it is scarcely central to the work; that it constitutes a "scientific discovery" might surprise readers of Dante or Spenser or Milton. The claim for "method" is, however, merely preliminary to the larger extravagance by which Eliot goes on to make a cause and effect relationship between the writing method he describes—again, essentially his own— and what he considers contemporary conditions: "It is simply a way of controlling, of ordering, of giving a shape and a significance to the immense panorama of futility and anarchy which is contemporary history." Eliot had been much closer to the spirit of *Ulysses* in an earlier "London Letter" dated August 1922, in *The Dial,* where he said, "It is at once the exposure and the burlesque of that of which it is the perfection."

In 1923 he was anxious to justify a "method" more his own, and on historical-cultural grounds that might possibly dissuade readers from discovering, with I. A. Richards, that his poem was as much about sexual sterility as about immense panoramas. His effort to appropriate Joyce was to become still clearer with *After Strange Gods* in 1934, when he said that Joyce was "penetrated with Christian feeling"—Bloom?!—and in the essay of 1930, "Arnold and Pater." He was ready in the 1930's to use Joyce in whatever way suited his own developing career, and to make Joyce's work into a historical justification for what had become his announced conversion to Christian orthodoxies. The essay on Arnold is in fact no more than a reading, with all the Paterian lyricism and enthusiasm and eagerness drained out of it, of the last section of *A Portrait of the Artist as a Young Man*, and I am more, not less, convinced of this by Eliot's failure even to mention Joyce in the essay. Pater, of *Marius the Epicurean*, has not "influenced a single first rate mind of a later generation," says Eliot, ignoring a fact, obvious at least to Emerson and to an Emersonian-Paterian critic like Harold Bloom, that an influence can be an anxious one, including Joyce's on Eliot, and that Joyce is suffused with Pater. Eliot turns anxiety into rejection because it suits his ideology to do so. He is paraphrasing a too solemn reading of the end of *Portrait* and the opening of *Ulysses* when he complains that "the total effect of Arnold's philosophy is to set up Culture in the place of Religion, and to leave Religion to be laid waste by the anarchy of feeling." We are left, that is, with "aesthetic religion," wherein "religion becomes morals, religion becomes art, religion becomes science or philosophy."

My intention is not to attack Eliot, least of all as a poet. Rather, I propose him as a vivid example, and others will follow, of how writers like to endow their own practices with historical inevitability and large consequence. This in turn promotes the notion that in their work the rest of us can recover meanings that would otherwise yield to chaos or to the blandishments of meaningless pleasure. Wordsworth is a compelling illustration because he issues one of the most effective arguments ever made *against* treating literature as a source of adaptable knowledge even while he manages, in the 1800 Preface to *Lyrical Ballads*, to sound superficially as if he were writing in the pages of *The American Scholar* or for one of the innumerable panels that meet every so often to recommend a solution to the plight of the humanities in the age of video:

For a multitude of causes, unknown to former times, are now acting with a combined force to blunt the discriminating powers of the mind, and, unfitting it for all voluntary exertion, to reduce it to a state of almost savage torpor. The most effective of these causes are the great national events which are daily tak-

ing place, and the increasing accumulation of men in cities, where the uniform-
ity of their occupations produces a craving for extraordinary incident, which
the rapid communication of intelligence hourly gratifies. . . . The invaluable
works of our elder writers, I had almost said the works of Shakespeare and Milton, are driven into neglect by . . . this degrading thirst after outrageous stimulation.

Wordsworth is one of the heroes of this book because he does *not*
mean what he appears to mean at the end of this passage. He could not
show—no one has ever been able to show—any connection between the
neglect of "the invaluable works of our elder writers" and the "savage
torpor" of the population, or that the latter would be lessened by more
attention to the former. The difference between Wordsworth and those
who in our own time like to think that such connections do exist is that
he suspects, and they are anxious not to, that the source of degeneration
lies in economic, demographic, and cultural factors that have little to do
with literature or the taste for it. The argument nowadays that "we" are
in trouble because there is trouble in the centers of the culture, like the
universities or literary criticism or the humanities, is merely one more
journalistic-political maneuver designed to obscure the failures in our
political-economic-social arrangements. Wordsworth might not have
looked favorably over the past few decades on popular entertainment or
urban life, but he would most likely have located the trauma of the
sixties, for example, in the war in Vietnam and the fight for racial
equality. He would not have confused the disasters of the period with
what were in fact clumsy responses to them on college campuses or at
rock concerts, whose violence was in any case negligible compared to
what happens regularly at adult festivals of patriotic masculinity like
hockey and soccer games. And in the seventies and eighties, he might
object to feminist ideological protests without blaming them for a decline in those literary standards of civilization which, as it turns out, had
never over the centuries managed to create a more civilized sense of the
equality of women. Debates on all these issues are so flat minded by now
that it is necessary to add that I am *not* in favor of making universities
the center of political protest and that I am convinced that the practice,
as against the theory, of feminist criticism of literature has in many cases

weakened the critical enterprise. But the causes of what is importantly troubling the Western world lie elsewhere.

It would be nice indeed if cultural and social crises could be solved or ameliorated by more and closer readings of the "elder writers," or if the modern age really could, in Eliot's phrase, be "made possible for art" by Joyce's invention of "the mythic method," though it has been around for half a millennium. Besides, life in the twentieth century was made possible for art without the "method," as in Proust, Lawrence, Woolf, Forster, Frost, among many others, while Eliot's own poetry seems to me best read when you forget about the "method" and forget about the "panorama of futility and anarchy which is contemporary history." Most writers, most readers even more so, want to believe in such magnifications of literary method and literary meaning. The belief is essential to the notion that the writing and reading of literature have a culturally redemptive power. I am arguing that this belief cannot be sustained by the actual operations of language in literary texts. Writing that can be called literature tends, it seems to me, to be discernibly on edge about its own rhetorical status, especially when the rhetoric is conspicuously indebted to any of the great, historically rooted institutions, as in the theological-mythological-literary saturations of idiom in *Paradise Lost* or *Ulysses.* Part of the excitement derives from the way such works resist as well as absorb the meanings which their adopted language makes available to them, and to us.

These proposals will require a lot of demonstration and amplification. In the process I will have things to say about a number of writers, English, American, and European, but mainly about Emerson and some of those in his lineage, including Thoreau and Whitman, and, especially, William James, Frost, and Stevens. Why this grouping? First, because, as with a related figure like Wordsworth, they offer a way to think about literature and about life that seems to me a crucial alternative to the dominant modernist and so-called post-modernist ways of thinking. Second, because they still remain insufficiently understood and assimilated, especially within the academic-journalistic practices of Anglo-American criticism in the past several decades, including what has been going on recently under mostly French provenance. And third, because neither temperament nor circumstance induced them to claim that problems

importantly affecting the production of literature have to do primarily
with the burdens of inherited culture, aside from language itself, or with
particular historical crises. They do not transform their difficulties with
language into the cultural-historical heroics usually attributed to modernist writing.

Of course, like writers of any nation or any historical period, they are
committed to the idea of a great national literature—wherein does any
writer have a better chance for immortality?—and, like writers of any
generation, each of these Americans knew, with Emerson in "The
American Scholar," that "genius is always the enemy of genius by over
influence," and that new writers are required to be "new." They necessarily concerned themselves with these matters, but not, I am suggesting, to any exceptional degree, and they mostly avoided the vulgar forms
of literary nationalism. (When, for example, Whitman first addresses
the issue in the opening lines of the 1855 preface to *Leaves of Grass*—
he was only later to become jingoistic in his prose—he does so in a very
relaxed manner: "America does not repel the past," he says, "is not so
impatient as has been supposed.") As for the cultural blankness or
bareness of America, they tend to see it as a cultural opportunity when
it is not an image of more personal deprivations. When negatively
conceived, the denuded landscapes in American writing are frequently
an image not of cultural bareness at all, but of creative-sexual impotence.
As a result, the Emersonian inclination is to locate the problem of
literary production mostly in language rather than in historical circumstance, in the obscure origins of language, and in the mysteries of its
transmissions and transformations.

The linguistic issue for them has something but not a lot to do with
the fact that the language of American literature is not native to America; Whitman goes so far as to concede in the same preface that "the
English language befriends the frank American expression." Far more
important is the feeling that the bequest of language, to British no less
than to American writers, carries with it certain inducements that are
not distinguishable from obligations. As Emerson says of a Gothic cathe-
dral in the essay "History," language "affirms that it was done by us, and
not done by us." Each of us is enjoined to find himself or herself within
the given discourse, but only by a process that resists and promises to
transform it. There is nothing sacred on the far side of language except

the desire that the words should exist. The desire itself will atrophy if its inheritors leave language in the forms in which they have received it or even if they rest content for long with any new forms they may have given it. We need to keep messing up the idiom, as Stevens suggests in a poem I discuss in Chapter 4: "speech," according to "The Creations of Sound," "is not dirty silence/Clarified. It is silence made still dirtier."

LET ME EXPAND further on these propositions. Literature generates its substance, its excitements, its rhetoric, and its plots often with the implicit intention, paradoxically, to get free of them and to restore itself to some preferred state of naturalness, authenticity, and simplicity. The implication is that if any of these actually did or could exist in an uncorrupted state, then literature itself would be unnecessary, a possibility to which I will return later on. Another way to put it, which will help explain why my emphasis on the Emersonians is not merely an American emphasis, is to say that literature implicitly idealizes that condition of bareness, that thinness of social and cultural circumstance, which, according to Henry James and other observers, was supposed to be the special plight of American writers. For Emerson, William James, and Stevens, however, leaving aside for a moment the differences in their lives and social opportunities, "bareness" is, as I have said, very often salutary, something to be sought after, no matter how much Emerson complained that Concord could be a dreary place for any man of talent.

What is the supposed virtue of bareness? That with nothing to depend on, nothing to lean or rely on, the naked and true self can and will emerge, compelled into expression, or that "something" will emerge. To quote one of the most beautiful passages from Stevens's "The Rock":

As if nothingness contained a métier,
A vital assumption, an impermanence
In its permanent cold, an illusion so desired

That the green leaves came and covered the high rock,
That the lilacs came and bloomed, like a blindness cleaned,
Exclaiming bright sight, as it was satisfied,

In a birth of sight. . . .

Emerson can say in "Experience" that "the God [is] the native of these bleak rocks. That need makes in morals the capital virtue of self-trust. We must hold hard to this poverty, however scandalous, and by more vigorous self-recoveries, after the sallies of action, possess our axis more firmly." Poverty allows us, without having to burrow through layers of impediment, to "recover" a self that has been discernible (though he allows that it might also have been lost) in "the sallies of action." Melville, however, posits a very different condition. He envisioned masks, piles, heaps beyond or beneath which there was possibly nothing at all. Ahab imagines that Moby Dick "heaps me," and next to the passage from Emerson should be placed a passage from *Moby-Dick* inspired by Melville's visit in 1849 to the fourteenth- and fifteenth-century Gothic and Renaissance Hotel de Cluny in Paris. Obviously, he has in mind not merely European accumulations on top of some imaginary human essence, but an accumulation more ancient still which can never be gotten past:

Winding far down from within the very heart of this spiked Hotel de Cluny where we here stand—however grand and wonderful, now quit it;—and take your way, ye nobler, sadder souls, to those vast Roman halls of Thermes; where far beneath the fantastic towers of man's upper earth, his root of grandeur, his whole awful essence sits in bearded state; an antique buried beneath antiquities, and throned on torsoes!

The renowned differences between Emerson and Melville are implicit in their contrasting measure of how much waste obscures the "real" self, if there is one, and the unlikelihood, in Melville's case, that the self can ever be liberated from it. And yet the difference between the two writers has been exaggerated, I think; even though the self in Emerson is not "an antique buried beneath antiquities," an endlessly layered invention, it is still no less in danger of being trapped in language, in the conformities which make language possible. This, as I have been implying, is the prior condition which any literature or work of literature discovers for itself. We are dealing here in matters of degree only, and I want to call attention to the impressiveness of a writer like Emerson who, feeling himself unusually liberated from the burdens of antiquity and able to start from a condition of bareness natively his own and without parallel in history, must then recognize that he is a party, though not always or necessarily an anxious one, to the ineluctable condition of all literature: that someone has been there before you and will also be here after you, and that you cannot escape the evidence of this in the language you use. Emerson has his own vision akin to Melville's Hotel de Cluny, though far less despairing. It is, as he says in the *Journals* for June–August 1845, that "literature has been before us wherever we go,"[1] an admission that initiates a long passage about literary prepossession of the continent that will be discussed later on. The "axis" which Emerson would "possess more firmly" is the capacity for actions belied in this passage from *Moby-Dick* (though not, of course, in Melville's own treatment of language), actions by which you might modify this inheritance of language and thus achieve a modification in human consciousness and history.

While it has been simplified, the difference between Emerson and Melville is, then, real and important. It is akin to the difference between the Emersonian heritage and the modernism of Eliot, and it can be located quite specifically: in the word "action" and in the sense of the efficacy of action. "Action" is a key term which American pragmatism, especially William James's version of it, took over from Emerson, along with the word "transition," which is equally central. Both words, as I hope gradually to make clear, point to an alliance of pragmatism with the workings of language in literature, with poetic making. American pragmatism never assumes that in the beginning was the Word or word. It does not deny that God is a necessary functional term; but it refuses to credit the *problem* of logocentrism. It cannot be a problem when, as James says in "Conclusions" to *A Pluralistic Universe*, "our thoughts determine our acts, and our acts redetermine the previous nature of the world."

To further explore some connections between pragmatism and the act of literary troping, the turning of a word, consider the first invention of that creature who eventually would conceive of the word "man." I ask you to suppose that its first invention was its own muteness. Muteness is not something attributable to a rock or a stone, a tree or a beast. For anything to imagine its own muteness it would have to desire not to be mute, to desire already to be other than what it is, to become different and to make a difference. Suppose that the next invention was the sound that erased the muteness, and that this was followed by the invention of other sounds intended to change those first ones and to change also the sounds of nature, as when Frost allows Adam in "Never Again Would Birds' Song Be the Same," to believe "that the birds there in all the garden round/From having heard the daylong voice of Eve/Had added to their own an oversound,/Her tone of meaning but without the words."

But here, in this possible scenario, we encounter a mystery or a missing element. And it is at this point that most people want to fill the gap with the word "soul" or the word "God." And why not? The human desire to make its presence known to itself and to the world, to make a difference to and in the world—must it not, even in its original muteness, have expected that there really *was* something waiting to be discovered, something "inside" that no other creature possessed? Exactly at this point pragmatism reveals its tough-mindedness as against the tender-minded who want to bring into the story a necessary God and a necessary soul. A pragmatist, by which I mean some version of Emerson, might have to use the words "God" or "soul," but would go on to suppose, as I do, that there was in fact really nothing outside to depend on and nothing inside either, nothing except the desire that there should be more than nothing.

That, if I may say so, is why works of art are not required to exist. There is nothing outside of them that requires their existence. If Shakespeare had never existed we would not miss his works, for there would be nothing missing. This is perhaps the most obvious, important, and repressed fact about artistic production. Critics and artists now and again do boast of being compelled by historical necessity or admit to working on assignment, and yet all that compels Shakespeare or Mozart or Rembrandt or Balanchine is that same desire which brought muteness into the act of sound or motion. The difference is that artistic acts have precedents, while that first act did not. An artistic act can take advantage of the vocabularies of prior works of art, but if the result is merely an imitation, then it might as well have remained mute; what it accomplishes will offer no testimony within itself of its need to exist.

And that, I suspect, is why most inferior artists need and like to explain their works as having been historically necessitated.

The desire which produces works of art is variously associated in Emerson with God or Divinity or the soul *in* each of us. His religious vocabulary is in itself part of the problem he sets for himself, or that is set for him by the historical condition of the language of his time. As I argued a moment ago, words like "soul" or "God" or "Divinity" designate for him the very limitations which human desire must always want to transcend. Even to imagine that any word or text could sufficiently locate the source of life or of truth would mean that the desire to create could come to an end in an object sufficient to itself. This, as Emerson sees it, would be a disaster for the human imagination. Thanks in part to his own sometimes confused confrontations with this terminological dilemma, William James was able later on to state the problem more succinctly, though the italics are mine: "language," he says in *Principles of Psychology* ("The Stream of Thought"), "works *against* our perception of truth."

James means that in "the stream of thought," language tends always to give more stress to the substantives than to either the transitions among them or to the feelings that accompany our experiences of them. Without admitting it, he is directly indebted here to Emerson's insistence, in "Montaigne," that "the philosophy we want is one of fluxions and mobility"; he is especially indebted at this same point in *Principles*, when he italicizes the advice, *"Let us call the resting-places the 'substantive parts,' and the places of flight the 'transitive parts,' of the stream of thought."* And he continues, more crucially:

It then appears that the main end of our thinking is at all times the attainment of some other substantive part than the one from which we have just been dislodged. And we may say that the main use of the transitive parts is to lead us from one substantive conclusion to another.

We are kept from settling on any "substantive conclusion." This leads to a stunning recommendation whose enactments are to be found in what Frost will later call "the sound of sense," and in those shifts in American writing generally by which vernacular intonation is allowed to make wry and running commentaries on the "burden" of a passage. "We ought," says James,

to say a feeling of *and*, a feeling of *if*, a feeling of *but*, and a feeling of *by*, quite as readily as we say a feeling of *blue* or a feeling of *cold*. Yet we do not: so inveterate has our habit become of recognizing the existence of the substantive parts alone, that language almost refuses to lend itself to any other use.

Consider: the emphasis on action, on transitions as a valuable form of action, both in Emerson and in James; the need stressed by both of them for movement *away* from substantives or "resting-places" or settled texts; Frost's definition of a poem as only "a momentary stay against confusion," and the virtue attached by Stevens to becoming "an ignorant man again"—these are evidences of a special Emersonian form of skepticism that seems to me worth promoting in the life of the world no less than in the world of books. This Emersonian skepticism is different from the modernist skepticisms about language which accompanied Eliot's several decades of ascendancy, whereby words were found wanting because they did *not* afford "resting-places," did not, that is, allow spirituality to escape disruptive desires. It is different, too, from the extreme form of post-modernist skepticism best espoused by deconstructionist critics like Paul de Man who want to show, repeatedly, how words in a text release themselves from the active control of any presumptive human presence. On the one hand, as against modernist spirituality, the Emersonians want to prevent words from coming to rest and want to dissuade us from hoping that they ever might. On the other, as against deconstructionist theory (which has been known to look to Emerson's pragmatist descendant Charles Sanders Peirce for support) the Emersonian alternative is more complicated. Emerson may sometimes sound deconstructionist himself, as indeed do some of the pre-Socratics. ("Every end," he says in "Nature," "is prospective of some other end, which is also temporary; a round and final success nowhere.") But he insists, as did James after him, that this very same temporariness is instigated and perpetuated by the human will. "Nothing," he says in "Circles," "is secure but life, transition, the energizing spirit."

The most important difference between these various parties is not, however, theoretical. It is temperamental, a symptom of the way various people think, how they feel about life and history, how they carry themselves. It can determine their moods and the confidence with which they handle the currency of life which is called language. Emerson, the father of American pragmatism, practiced what William James was to preach, that

a pragmatist turns his back resolutely and once for all upon a lot of inveterate habits dear to professional philosophers. He turns away from abstraction and insufficiency, from verbal solutions, from bad *a priori* reasons, from fixed principles, closed systems, and pretended absolutes and origins. He turns toward concreteness and adequacy, towards facts, towards action, and towards power (*Pragmatism*, Lecture II).

I shall say much more about the Emersonian vocabulary of "fact," "action," and "power," but an immediate clue to the importance of this pragmatist terminology for literature and for language is in James's characteristic fondness for the word "turn"—as in "turns his back," "turns away," "turns towards." The word suggests an active, not merely reflective, response to the given, and it is synonymous with "trope," as if the "turning" of a word in and by other words is like the twisting or coiling of a strand or thread within and through the other strands that make up a piece of rope. The turning or troping of words is in itself an act of power over meanings already in place; it distorts "verbal solutions," which are thus shown not to be solutions at all. In that sense one could argue, I guess, that a turn or a trope is in itself a "verbal solution." It promises after all to save us from being caught or fixed in a meaning or in that state of conformity which Emerson famously loathed. Notice, however, that it is never any particular trope that matters, but rather the act of troping. James goes on to say in the same lecture that "you must bring out of each word its practical cash-value, set it at work within the stream of your experience. It appears less a solution, then, than a program for more work, and more particularly an indication of the ways in which existing realities may be *changed.*"

"Cash-values," "set it at work," and "more work"—this is exuberantly capitalistic, anti-intellectualist rhetoric with analogues in Emerson, Thoreau, and Frost, especially in their frequent analogies between literary work and other kinds of work, including athletics. The recent term "making it" is a Thoreauvian pun from his chapter in *Walden* called "The Bean Field," and it is meant to suggest the similarities among the making of poetry, the making of a crop, the making of money. As he insists, he wants "to know beans," and he keeps strict account of profit and loss. Not in spite of the actual work and calculation but actually because of them, he discovers that "dabbling like a plastic artist in the dewy and crumbling sand, making the earth say beans instead of grass . . . it was no more beans that I hoed nor I that hoed beans."

It might be concluded from all this that Emersonian pragmatists want to dispose of the past or escape from it; this is a frequent interpretation, and not for that reason any less superficial. In fact the determination to "act" is based, as I have suggested, on the most ancient of possible precedents—the discovery of voice—and it is further supposed by Emersonians that any act, no matter how menial, if intensely enough pursued, begins to blur or even erase the distinction between man and what is not-man, returning us to some imaginably primal state. The "return" may appear to be at the expense of any intervening social or political history, but it can also constitute a knowledgeable judgment upon it. Far from discouraging efforts at recovery or reclamation, Emersonians tend to insist upon them, but only as necessary forms of action, actions which disturb rather than perpetuate the past, which bring us to mystifications not distinguishable from wisdom. The acts are engendering. Every "new inquiry," James admits in *Pragmatism* (Lecture VII), must take account of "previous truths." They are "previous" the way engendering itself can be said to be, or the way love is an emotion we must *learn* to express, or the way a season of a past year predicts a renewal with a difference in the present year. An act in the present may look to the past less for a "resting place" than as an incentive to further creation, the making of further additions to reality.

I have been emphasizing how different is this view of life, literature, and language from the customary reverence for the literary past, a past which is supposed to be a storehouse of values and wisdom, and even more so when imagined as an alternative to some present-day chaos. In the conventional-conservative view, literature is said to promote order precisely because it can include the tensions that threaten to disrupt it and which are instead resolved within it, even to the point where it can be proposed that the desire for salvation is to be found in the desire for degradation (as with Eliot's Christianizing of Baudelaire or in the novels of Catholic violence by François Mauriac, Graham Greene, or Flannery O'Connor). As to this latter form of theatrical spirituality, Emersonians have little or no interest, which may be yet another reason why they have been relatively slighted and depreciated in Anglo-American literary culture for the past century and a half. Emerson has been a pervasive presence, but he has not been allowed to *be* Emerson in the way I am trying here to describe him and his lineage. In furtherance of that effort I need to say a bit more about the relation between Emersonianism, as I conceive of it, and the modernist episode in Anglo-American literary culture.

THAT RELATION involves not only the predominance, over the past sixty years or so, of Eliot as against, say, a combination of Frost or Stevens with William James, but also the peculiar status of American literature itself just at the time, the early 1920's, when modernism most strongly asserted its claims in English. To put it simply, American literature was still up for grabs, as will be confirmed by any glance into the four volumes of the *Cambridge History of American Literature* first published in 1917 and in successive reprintings until as late as 1946. Cambridge wanted to avoid the appearance of exclusion or, for that matter, of critical discrimination, and accordingly subtitled itself "The Life of the American People in Their Writing." On that basis it could, as had the American people themselves, patronize Melville when it bothered even to notice him. Along with Thomas Buchanan Read and Charles Halpine, he is allowed some ten lines in a section on "Poets of the Civil War"; the one paragraph devoted to *Moby-Dick* in a section on fiction concludes that for all its "originality" it is "too irregular, too bizarre, ever to win the widest suffrage." Perhaps assuming that their prophecy had been made inevitable by their characterization, the editors let the judgment stand in all subsequent reprintings for the next thirty years, even though Raymond Weaver's biography of Melville in 1922 had initiated a critical revaluation that has given the book its present status. Up to

1922, *Moby-Dick* had sold fewer than eight thousand copies in the seventy years since its first publication.

Or consider what happens to American literature in the literary reviews and essays of Henry James written between 1868 and 1916, just before the *Cambridge History* and fully collected for the first time in two large volumes of the Library of America. Besides being always in touch with his native scene, and informed by Howells about any of its literary developments, James read everything or heard of everything that passed any sort of muster of English, American, or European literature. Both his omissions and his throw-away references in critical writings, thick with thousands of allusions, are an indication of what readers on both sides of the Atlantic were prepared to hear or were able to recognize. I am talking, remember, not about private appreciations or the exceptional notice here or there, but about the public assumptions that empower figures like James or the editors of the *Cambridge History*. Doubtless many individuals besides Melville recognized "the power of blackness" in Hawthorne and the greatness of *Moby-Dick*, including, by the way, Faulkner, whose brother Murry reported that in 1911 he called it "one of the best books ever written." There is, besides, a study of Emerson in 1915 by Oscar W. Firkin which can hold its own with any later ones. But such things, in the assessment of literary-cultural power, are of no consequence.

Only reverberations count in such an assessment, and it is a fact that by 1920, when modernism began to take charge of Anglo-American literary thinking, American literature simply had not gotten itself together and could not possibly do justice to its Emersonian components. Until quite recently James was not thought to be either envious of his forebear or afraid of being considered provincial by his English hosts when, in his *Hawthorne*, a book published in 1879 in the English Men of Letters Series, he condescended to say that "on his limited scale," Hawthorne was "a master of expression." This was pretty much the consensus view in 1879 and well into the next century. How otherwise explain so fatuous a characterization of the author of *The Scarlet Letter:* that "the good American, of which Hawthorne was so admirable a specimen, was not critical"! Emerson, he said, was "admirable and exquisite," terms of endearment that would keep him on the shelf forever, and there is no escaping even now the attraction of James's mordant superiority when he remarks that the Concord sage "must have had a charm for people living in a society in which introspection, thanks to the want of other entertainment, played almost the part of a social resource." In the nearly three thousand pages of James's collected criticism, references to writers and works abounding on every one of them, he refers to Melville exactly once and *en passant*, when describing a "repose as mild and easy as an Indian summer in the woods, of Herman Melville, of George William Curtis, of 'Ik Marvel.' " An enthusiasm for Poe, he maintains, is "a mark of a decidedly primitive stage of reflection," and Whitman's poetry is "spurious." Many years later he would modify this latter opinion, though not in print. Edith Wharton reported that after he gave an emotional reading from *Leaves of Grass* to some of her guests, he covered his embarrassment by tumbling the party into laughter with the remark, "Oh, yes, a great genius, undoubtedly a very great genius! Only one cannot help deploring his too extensive acquaintance with the foreign languages." Thoreau was "imperfect, unfinished, inartistic; he was worse than provincial, he was parochial." Nonetheless —or is it therefore?—he is to be included with those Americans who have written "originally—Emerson, Hawthorne, Longfellow, Motley."

These assessments, which now seem outrageous and sporting, were well within the range of prevailing opinion up to about 1920. And that is the crucial consideration—not that there is anything "wrong" about James or the *Cambridge History*, but that there was no consensus about American literature which could have educated or disciplined their views of it. American literature had so confusedly, so timidly patched itself together out of all kinds of local interests and was so devoid of any critical sense of its proportions that anyone could get away with saying almost anything about it. Admittedly we could gather some similarly outrageous things, at least as we now see them, from commentaries on English literature of the nineteenth century, and there are always differences about where the lines of strength are located in any national literature. This does not mean, however, that the national literature is itself repressed or fails to take shape, as was the case in the United States. The failure sufficiently to recognize the masterful achievements of the one century in which American literature came substantially into existence was, simply, a failure to recognize that America *had* a literature.

It is generally assumed that in 1916 or 1921 or some such date modernism became a dominant force in Anglo-American culture simply because it was more attuned than were Emerson and his followers—that dispersed and ragged lot—to historical realities: the wastings of World War I, the collapse of faith in social and economic institutions, the rise of Fascist and Communist totalitarianism, the exposure of the structural weaknesses in the capitalist system. In fact, however, Joyce was far more oblivious than Emerson to the political events of his own time. Such historical chartings are mostly factitious anyway. Any century could make a similar list of crises and disasters—depressions, insurrections, civil wars, racial injustice, imperial adventures in Mexico were all part of Emerson's troubled political experience. Besides, as a force to be reckoned with in literature, modernism did not at all wait upon World War I and the post-war era to display its characteristics. "Modernism," even for those who believe in it as a twentieth-century phenomenon, began before the war, and, for those who believe it has always existed, it shows itself in different forms wherever one looks in literature, as indicated in Chapter 2, "Modernism and Its Difficulties."

The cultural triumph of the Anglo-American form of modernism was largely, almost exclusively, Eliot's personal triumph. He had the promotional genius to insist that not personal despairs but unique historical cause and effect relationships explain his kind of poetic practice, notably what we have heard him call "the immense panorama of futility and anarchy which is contemporary history." Not being cognizant enough of their own inheritance, later Emersonian writers like Frost and Stevens never felt able or willing, even with William James recently behind them, to push themselves sufficiently forward as offering an alternative way of reading the world or of reading literature—or of reading Eliot. And they were further rusticated by being made to seem, by a kind of modernist raid on the rest of American literature, like country cousins. By that I mean that in the 1920's Melville, Hawthorne, and Poe were "discovered" only by being interpreted as essentially modernist texts, leaving the Emersonians in a subordinate school, in an already subordinate literature, that was thus made to seem relatively naïve, optimistic, and simple. Thus the first important argument for the powerful subver-

siveness of American literature was not by an American but by an
English renegade genius, D. H. Lawrence, in his *Studies in Classic
American Literature* of 1923, a book begun as early as 1917. Emerson
is barely mentioned in the book, even in the chapter on Whitman; its
principal figures are Melville, Hawthorne, and Poe. The year before,
1922, marked the appearance of both *Ulysses* and *The Waste Land*,
close in time to Eliot's concerted apologia, as in "The Metaphysical
Poets" of 1921, for a "modernist" poetry to meet "modernist" conditions:

We can only say that it appears likely that poets in our civilization, as it exists
at present, must be *difficult*. Our civilization comprehends great variety and
complexity, and this variety and complexity, playing upon a refined sensibility,
must produce various and complex results. The poet must become more and
more comprehensive, more allusive, more indirect, in order to force, to dislocate
if necessary, language into his meaning.

Two years later he was to say in his review of *Ulysses* that writers who
fail to observe the example of Joyce (and clearly of Eliot) will continue
to write while being unaware of their "obsolescence." This was an
opportune moment for the discovery, at last, that *Moby-Dick* was a
modernist classic, by virtue, one may suppose, of "a conscious or probably unconscious dissatisfaction with the form" of the novel, which Eliot
attributes to Joyce and Wyndham Lewis.

Anglo-American modernism, as it emanated from Eliot, was strongly
assisted in its subsequent cultural deployments by the simultaneous
emergence, also in 1922, of a group that founded *Fugitive* magazine.
The prominent figures were John Crowe Ransom, Alan Tate, and Robert Penn Warren. With other so-called Southern Agrarians, centered for
a time at Vanderbilt University, they dominated what was to become
the most academically pervasive new (and highly Christianized) critical
movement in the United States for the next half century, particularly
through the vastly influential textbook by Cleanth Brooks and Warren,
Understanding Poetry. These various factions and individuals would
differ on certain matters, like the relative villainy of science with respect
to poetry, but they were all strongly disaffected with civilization as it had

taken shape after the American Civil War or the First World War or
even the English Civil War. Take your pick. In a sense they were
anti-modernist, as was Eliot, insofar as modernism means industrial
capitalism, secularism, the breakup of old communities, the emergence
of new economic-social classes whose feeling for tradition consisted, if
it existed at all, in the acquisition of its furnishings. In such a world the
old values were hard to get to, so they said, and this meant that their
taste for experimentation, fragmentation, dislocation, and the like was
less avant-garde than conservative in spirit, an effort to discover how, by
techniques like the "mythic method," the modern world could be
"made possible for art." A lot of the joy of *Ulysses* and Faulkner, a lot
of the hilarious revelation in Beckett of how conversation spins out of
mere lassitude and inattention, not out of a questing for God—most of
this was lost to students educated in the belief that if they worked grimly
enough on modernist "difficulty," they could come back with Big Meanings, having touched the nerve centers of modern devaluation and
cultural despair.

Emerson had no place in such a story, and neither, conspicuously, did
Frost and Stevens, who were treated for decades as if they were not quite
"with it." The two poets grumbled a bit, but since each felt secure in
his own centrality, they scarcely thought of joining forces, or of making
Eliot more nearly central still by sounding as if they wanted to be where
they did not belong. As late as 1950 Eliot was surprised that there was
no edition of Stevens's poetry in England—*Harmonium* had been published in America in 1923!—where his own firm, Faber and Faber,
would have been its logical publishers. "Although his name and some
of his poems were very well known to the elite who really know," Eliot
noted in *Trinity Review* for May 1954, he "had no book to himself."
In 1953 Faber finally published a *Selected Poems* to see if a collected
poems might be a good idea later on.

Of the important American poets only William Carlos Williams
chose to complain outright about Eliot's predominance. In his *Autobiog-
raphy* of 1951 he makes a rather turgid admission that *The Waste Land*
of thirty years before had had a paralyzing effect on "us," though what
he is recalling is actually how he admits to having felt even earlier, in
1917, about Eliot's *Prufrock and Other Observations*. "There was heat

in us, a core and a drive that was gathering headway upon the theme of a rediscovery of a primary impetus, the elementary principle of all art, in the local conditions. Our work staggered to a halt for a moment under the blast of Eliot's genius which gave the poet back to the academics. We did not know how to answer him." The "we" here refers not to Stevens, with whom Williams was friendly but never close, or to Frost, who barely acknowledged his existence, or to Hart Crane, who annoyed Williams by adopting some of Eliot's mannerisms, but to Alfred Kreymborg, Maxwell Bodenheim, and Walter Arensberg. And it will be clear already that the "primary impetus," as Emerson, Stevens, or Frost would recognize it, and as Emerson or William James meant it, has only in the most mythological ways to do with something called "local conditions."

The "answer" to Eliot was waiting in an Emersonian tradition that is not to be confused with anyone who wants as superficially to put on the mantle as Williams did, or still more loosely Ginsberg and Kerouac. It is a tradition, as we have already seen, that is extremely fastidious even about defining itself *as* a tradition. It is against the spirit of Emerson to conform to a lineage and even less to hold up certain texts as exemplifications of one. So much so that the figures I am looking at most closely in the Emersonian line actually have very little to say about one another. Though both James and Frost wrote admiringly of Emerson, either of them, given a casual opportunity to refer to him, will as likely refer instead to Henri Bergson; Stevens hardly ever mentions him, directly, even though his poetry is suffused with involuntary echoes and paraphrases of an early and obviously intense reading of the essays. Books on Stevens and on Frost continue to be written that refer extensively to Keats, for example, but seldom or not at all to Emerson or James, Thoreau or Whitman. That this can still happen, even after such connections have been extensively pointed out, and that the omissions can go unnoticed or unchallenged, testifies to an ingrained refusal on the part of the Anglo-American institutions of literary criticism systematically to acknowledge the power of the Emersonian heritage in any form, much less the one I am trying to define here. This is not a matter simply of critical preference, or of some disinclination to do the necessary reading, or the desire to keep American poetry within the history of English poetry, where indeed it to some extent belongs. The neglect of the Emersonian connection, as it might be called, goes beyond all this. It reveals, I suspect, an instinctive recognition that Emerson and his influence, if its nuances and skepticisms were deeply enough explored, would prove disturbing, even disruptive of the critical-interpretive enterprise as most people practice it.

I WANT TO TRY to explain further why a tradition of such enormous potential consequence was itself reticent about becoming powerfully a part of general literary culture and why, among those who propose to speak on behalf of that culture, there is still so much resistance to it, mostly in the form of casualness and neglect. Let me use as an example the report on the humanities I have already mentioned, written by William J. Bennett, former head of the National Endowment for the Humanities and after that Secretary of Education in the second Reagan administration. *To Reclaim a Legacy,* as the report is called, was published in November 1984. It is in large part a diatribe about the deterioration since the sixties of American culture and education and about "a failure of nerve and faith" in higher education; it is also a platitudinous call for "a clear vision" of what constitutes an educated person. Obviously, the person is to be "educated" to a purpose, which is to restore to him/her those values we have lost and which are to be found, so it is imagined, by a close study of the humanities, of which literature is a central part. "The humanities tell us how men and women of our and other civilizations have grappled with life's enduring, fundamental questions: What is justice? What should be loved? Why do civilizations flourish? Why do they decline?"

A tall order, but who would not study, and study hard, if we really could learn to "grapple" with these things? Naturally you want a reading list as soon as possible, and if some of your favorite authors are on it, then you are that much ahead of the game. I, of course, looked for Emerson and his fellows. I did not find them. But for the reasons already suggested, this is not surprising nor, really, a just cause for complaint. Within the tough requirements of cultural power, it cannot be said that Mr. Bennett and his study group of some thirty distinguished scholars and educational administrators were under any particular obligation to "reclaim" a legacy that had not been directly claimed even by the writers responsible for creating it. And yet someone conceivably more patriotic than Mr. Bennett might still have wondered why, in the initial section of the report ("Why study the humanities?"), the first reference to anyone writing in English is not to Emerson, known as a great American patriarch even to those who have not read him, but to the great Victorian English man of letters who is inevitably called out of permanent semi-retirement whenever, which is always, the humanities are in crisis. It is he who tells us, to use his word, what should be "propagated" by criticism. "Expanding on a phrase from Matthew Arnold," Mr. Bennett writes, "I would describe the humanities as the best that has been said, thought, written and otherwise expressed about the human experience." This is the prose equivalent of a life-support system, and no doubt it will keep the humanities alive in ways already familiar to them. Still, I was interested in the predictable citation of Arnold because when I read Mr. Bennett's report, I had just finished writing the first chapter of this book, "The Question of Genius," where I wonder at some length why Arnold, and never Emerson, is always allowed to define the utilitarian relation of literature to culture.

As the reader will discover, I conclude that, comparatively speaking, Emerson would not at all serve purposes like Mr. Bennett's. In citing Arnold at the outset, the report merely confirms how entirely predictable will be its assumptions about literature. Had I been a member of Mr. Bennett's study group, it would have taken this entire book to argue, with little hope of success, that Emerson should be substituted for Arnold. It would have meant that the report, with whose diagnoses— that the humanities are in bad shape—anyone may have good reasons to agree, would have had to find remedies diametrically opposed to any it is prepared even to imagine. Could I have suggested, for example, that for the paraphrase of Arnold should be substituted this passage from Emerson's *Journals* for May 18, 1840: "Criticism must be transcendental, that is, must consider literature ephemeral & easily entertain the supposition of its entire disappearance"? While curricular reform proceeding from that "supposition" is, as will become clear, not impossible, it is also not at all likely. What kind of legacy could be reclaimed if the texts, so to speak, were asked to disappear? Under such an exhortation, could the literary past be looked to for what Mr. Bennett calls "the landscape of human thought," and could we still expect, as he says, that "the highest purpose of reading is to be in the company of great souls"? Surely not. Meanwhile, I would rather ponder the question asked by Stevens in *Adagia:* "How has the human spirit ever survived the terrific literature with which it has had to contend?"

Emerson is never mentioned in Mr. Bennett's thirty-two pages, heavy with citations of writers important to "Western culture," and neither is Stevens—or Thoreau or Whitman or William James or Frost. This was clear evidence to me that my book was on the right track. There is a brief allusion to American historical documents and to "such authors as Hawthorne, Melville, Twain, and Faulkner." The instinct, as I say, was perfectly right. Emerson and his contingent are simply too hard to handle in the customary argument, though, as already evident, they have an alternative argument of their own for a beneficial relationship between the living and the literature of the past. I would suggest, in fact, that literature itself takes a view of its own past much closer to Emerson's than to Arnold's or to Arnoldian "reports" on the state of the humanities. Nothing is more recurrent in the canons of literature—or in Emerson—than the call for originality, until it becomes a sort of oxymoron, a tradition created by its own denial.[2] This is a way of saying that it has the status and power of the great mythologies. Emerson echoes the Bible (often parodistically, it is true), Plato, Bacon, Montaigne; William James and Stevens in turn echo Emerson, even while all are at the same time urging the forfeiture of models and the debilitations of copying. In the opening of *Astrophel and Stella,* to go back some five hundred years for an example, Sidney, "oft turning others' leaves, to see if thence would flow/Some fresh and fruitfull showers upon my sunne-burn'd braine," is faced at the end of the sonnet by a rebellion: " 'Foole,' said my Muse to me, 'looke in thy heart and write.' " But if the "sunne" is the influence of the ancients, the Muse is scarcely less so. Indeed, the Muses were instructed by a God of the Sun, Apollo; and when the poet looks in his heart he will find, by tradition, yet another mythic figure, Cupid. Not resistance to convention, but a convention of resistance—this inspires Sidney, no less than the Stevens who exhorts each of us to "become an ignorant man again." One becomes "ignorant" of culture in order more directly to be in touch with the mythological sources of energy which created it.

When Emerson says that literature is "ephemeral" or that we should look toward its "entire disappearance," he is best understood, then, to be participating in an aspiration that is anciently a part of the literary enterprise itself, the aspiration for "originality." Strictly speaking there is no such thing as originality. A literary text, any text, generates itself, word by word, only by compliance with or resistance to forms of language already available to it. The impulse to resist, or at least to modify, is necessarily stronger than is the impulse to comply, but the two factors coexist in a sort of pleasurable agitation which often evokes the image of sexual intercourse. Emerson refers to the "oestrum of speech," to "spermatic, prophesying man-making words," to thought being "ejaculated as Logos or Word."[3] Not an impulse to deconstruct, not an impulse generated even by anxiety, but, to repeat William James, an impulse to "engender," this is something shared by both literature and life. "The World," he writes in *Pragmatism*, "suffers human violence willingly. Man *engenders* truths upon it."

In saying this he of course concedes that "man" and "the world" were themselves "engendered" beforehand. This fact complicates any ambition for "originality" and any desire for the "disappearance" of literature or of the idea of the human, an idea which identifies each of us at birth. I want here to anticipate something discussed at length in Chapter 5, "Writing Off the Self": namely, that any proposal for the disappearance of literature or of the self depends for its language on the existence and perpetuation of the very things scheduled for erasure. The proposal can only be understood, that is, within the system of signs, the community of words and sounds, by which human beings have identified themselves as human.

THE ISSUE GETS down inevitably to language, or, more exactly, to the urgency with which literature so often proposes that it uses language only so that we may be taken beyond it. There is nothing arcane or theoretical about this proposition; people commonly express it in such phrases as "she didn't really mean what she said," or "I can't quite put it into words, but . . ." or "come on, you know what I mean." Language is a way of making things clear but also of insisting that things are not and should not be so clear as to seriously constrain us. At an extreme, it is sometimes supposed that language itself has an origin outside of culture, outside of any social purpose; that its true origin is in nature. This is a very old argument, and Emerson's first book, *Nature*, in 1836, is in part a rehearsal of it. The special value and poignancy of the book comes less from this or any of its related ideas than from the exhilarated sense that in the New World an ancient dream—of recovering lost origins—might actually be fulfilled.

Because he wanted to believe in the "immediate dependence of language upon nature," and that nature in America was as yet relatively unsullied, Emerson admitted only by fits and starts to a nearly contrary view which he felt just as strongly: that language was a cultural inheritance no one could escape, which not even the wilderness could escape, except by and during specific visionary acts of liberation and rescue, and even these were limited, for a writer, by the duration of phrases, sentences, and paragraphs. As in "Circles," written in 1840, and showing a side of Emerson that most strongly influenced Nietzsche, liberation from one enclosing cultural discourse is to be achieved only by drawing another "circle" around it, all the while knowing that eventually it, too, will become an inhibition. Language not as a transparency but as an obstruction, language not as inherently mobile but as static and resistant, unless made momentarily otherwise—these perceptions belong to the most appealing and energetic side of Emerson. The necessity that one must *struggle* with language in the effort to appropriate its otherwise hidden powers is evident everywhere in his writing, and it comes from his recognition of a problem about language which he could no more resolve than could Plato. Plato, however, had not set a national agenda designed to claim, as "Self-Reliance" blasphemously does, "that man is the word made flesh, born to shed healings to the nation," a proposal that makes it hard to envision this same man caught in the toils of his own words. Emerson is interesting and important not for any solutions proposed by his aphorisms, but for the trouble and contradictions into which his aspirations put him. The very phrase "self-reliance," for example, presupposes that there is a "self" already there to be relied upon, already defined by language, and, as we shall see, Emerson only perilously escapes from this linguistic trap of conformity set for him by the title of perhaps his most famous essay.

Controversies about the origin of language—whether it be in nature or in social convention or in arbitrary associations made by the mind—these are important to my argument because they are versions of an idea we have seen conspicuously at work in cultural-literary criticism: that there is something "back there" which we would be well advised to recover. Debates about the beginnings of language customarily evoke some earlier, better time when human beings were closer to reality, could more appropriately name things, and felt less alienated from them. It is further alleged that this human power has been weakened by an increase of estrangement due to the subsequent accumulations of words and languages and the devious social uses to which these are put. Emerson does not attribute this development to cultural or historical causes of any specific kind; unlike modernist or present-day culture worriers, he never blames the "age" for some decline of values or loss of nerve. For him, as later for Frost, there is little difference between this and any other historical period. The human sense of "loss" began when human self-awareness itself began, with "the fall," as he describes it in "Experience":

It is very unhappy, but too late to be helped, the discovery we have made, that we exist. That discovery is called the Fall of Man. Ever afterwards, we suspect our instruments. We have learned that we do not see directly, but mediately, and that we have no means of correcting these colored and distorting lenses which we are, or of computing the amount of their errors. Perhaps these subject-lenses have a creative power; perhaps there are no objects. Once we lived in what we saw; now, the rapaciousness of this new power, which threatens to absorb all things, engages us. Nature, art, persons, letters, religions,—objects, successively tumble in, and God is but one of its ideas.

The exuberances of *Nature* and "The American Scholar" should not persuade us, as it has most interpreters, that "Experience" marks a radical change in Emerson, a subject I take up again in Chapter 4. He had been inured to potentially devastating experiences long before that. They began early and included the death of his first wife, Ellen, in 1831, and of his brother Charles in 1836, along with the severe economic depression of 1837, when, as he said in the *Journals* for May 22, "the land stinks with suicide." All this was before the death by scarlet fever

of his adored five-year-old son Waldo in 1842. It is not that he transcended these experiences. He seems barely to have felt them. Such
occasions for mourning and remorse confirmed something perhaps more
perplexing than the devastating events themselves: his inability to re-
spond in a manner even he would have liked. From the first entries in
his *Journals* he had had the strength unblinkingly to recognize, even in
1822, at age nineteen, that "ungenerous & selfish, cautious & cold, I yet
wish to be romantic. Have not sufficient feeling to speak a natural hearty
welcome to a friend or stranger and yet send abroad wishes and fancies
of a friendship with a man I never knew." He is referring to a fellow
student at Harvard named Martin Gay with whom, though they never
spoke, he had become infatuated. "What is called a warm heart, I have
not," he says two years later. Even after his second marriage, he had to
admit to the justice of Margaret Fuller's remark that she had come to
realize, in 1839, that the best intercourse with him was to be found in
listening to his lectures. He responds to her in the *Journals* for November 14, 1839:

Most of the persons whom I see in my own house I see across a gulf. I cannot
go to them nor they come to me. Nothing can exceed the frigidity & labor of
my speech with such. You might turn a yoke of oxen between every pair of
words; and the behavior is as awkward & proud. I see the ludicrousness of the
plight as well as they. But having never found any remedy I am very patient with
this folly or shame, patient of my churl's mask, in the belief that this privation
has certain rich compensations inasmuch as it makes my solitude dearer & the
impersonal God is shed abroad in my heart more richly & more lowly welcome
for this porcupine impossibility of contact with men.

All of these self-chastisements precede by many years the famous
declaration in "Experience" of 1844 that "the only thing grief has
taught me, is to know how shallow it is. That, like all the rest, plays about
the surface, and never introduces me into the reality, for contact with
which, we would even pay the costly price of sons and lovers." For this
and, presently, for other reasons, I do not subscribe to the usual readings
which, despite persuasive arguments to the contrary made more than a
decade ago, still locate a sharp change of attitude between *Nature* and

Essays: First Series on the one hand, and, on the other, *Essays: Second Series*, where "Experience" first appeared, and later works like *The Conduct of Life*.[4] He is supposed to have moved from undeflected optimism to doubt and to a skepticism whereby man becomes, in Stephen Whicher's phrase, a sort of winner-loser in the game of life. This interpretation has helped perpetuate the view that when he is not naively wide-eyed he is only reluctantly sensible.

His skepticism, in my view, was always implicit in his vision of life, along with his explicit recognition that much of his susceptibility to some "impersonal God" was the result of his incapacity for personal intimacy. Instead of "changes" or "discoveries" of attitude, there are only modulations and shifts of emphasis. Throughout, he was chastened by the intuition that the imposition of language was something which human power could only sporadically resist. Even in *Nature* and in *First Series*, especially the essays "Self-Reliance" and "Circles," language is a hindrance to the infinitude of the private man. The only remedy was to be found *in* language itself, by continuous acts of troping, syntactical shiftings, rhetorical fracturings of the direction set down by the grammar of a sentence. Even these, however, can turn into habits of conformity. It can only be said, in concession to those who insist on an author's "development," that, as time went on, he became less sure that acts of turning, troping, overturning, and the like could accomplish anything beyond their own literary exemplifications of human will and desire: one could do at least that much for want of anything more efficacious to do. Scarcely a truly national undertaking.

Both in his efforts and in his significance, Emerson, I mean to suggest, is essentially a philosopher of language and literature. He is at once totally obsessed with language and totally convinced that literature is the place where the obsession is apt to occur most consequentially. This will please no one who wants writers to be more politically engaged than Emerson managed to be, and I leave the possible reprimands to them. One reason for his emphasis on language as the instrumentality of culture has already been suggested: that there was not much else, institutionally, to be concerned about, not so far as he could see. Slavery, "the woman question," American imperialism in Mexico, all these excited a degree of spirited outrage. But he never imagined that any of them resulted from essential defects in the American system, and in fact could not recognize the presence of a "system," even when he turned on his hero Daniel Webster for joining in the Compromise of 1850 by which the northern states pledged to observe the Fugitive Slave Law in return for the admission of California as a free state. As John Jay Chapman observes in his famous essay of 1898 on Emerson, the attack on Webster was "savage, destructive, personal." Personal all the more because Emerson did not recognize the structural inevitability of the Compromise. He continued to share a nation's view of itself expressed in the *Journals* for April 8, 1823, when at age twenty he wrote that "separated from the contamination which infects all other civilized lands this country has always boasted a great comparative purity. At the same time, from obvious causes, it has leaped at once from infancy to manhood." This "comparative purity" could, he realized, be debased in its movement westward by greed, ignorance, and the fact that "pioneers" are "led to embark in these enterprizes by the consciousness of ruined fortunes or ruined character or perchance a desire for that greater license which belongs to a new & unsettled community," remote from the control of civilized centers.

Aside from that, Emerson's conception of America as "separated from the contamination which infects all other civilized lands" is not a historical but a literary vision. It is little different from those recurrent mythologies of literature which have always tried to imagine a life freed from artificialities and the debasements of secondary desires. Such mythologies commonly want to rediscover the "uncontaminated" sources of language, and Emerson was especially emboldened to do so, as I have already suggested, because of the relative absence on the American scene of those mediating forces *other* than language that were so conspicuous in Europe. "One might enumerate," Henry James famously remarks in *Hawthorne*, "the items of high civilisation, as it exists in other countries, which are absent from the texture of American life, until it should become a wonder to know what was left." And he goes on, as Cooper had done in *Home as Found*, to offer the enumeration. Acting upon a man who worried that he could not in any case get close to whomever or whatever was near him, the very condition of bareness emboldened Emerson to suppose that he might rediscover language closer to its imagined source in nature. There would then be nothing at all between him and the infinite. It was not to be. In the way was the density of language itself; even more in the way was literature, wherein language displays its own immense cultural power, specifically the imperial cultural power of England.

Emerson's obsession with language is not, again, in any sense an American discovery, and I am interested in it because it vividly exposes the nervous system, so to speak, that passes through the corpus of all literature. The roots of it go back at least to the fifth-century Greek sophists. The origins of language are the subject of debate in Plato's dialogue of Cratylus, where Sophocles is the moderator between two positions neither of which finally prevails. One position, argued by Hermogenes, is that the right name for a thing is whatever we agree to call it. That is, language is arbitrary. Emerson found this position expressed also in Locke and in Bacon, who was one of his favorites, and it is sporadically, if rather murkily, favored in Shelley's *Defense of Poesy*, where it is congenial to Shelley's compelling desire to affirm the predominant power of the human mind to change things as it wants to change them. The opposite position is argued by Cratylus: that the meaning of a word is derived from the actual nature, shape, color, texture, mode of the thing it names. Thus, if some particular combination of sounds is shown to be manifestly appropriate to a thing, then it should be possible, by a species of etymological digging, to discover its providential origins.

Emerson, in *Nature*, seems to have been influenced not directly by Plato's Cratylus but by an obscure Swedenborgian French philosopher named Guillaume Oegger in a translation prepared in 1835 by Emerson's friend Elizabeth Peabody of *La Vraie Messie, ou l'Ancien et le Nouveau Testaments Examinés d'après les principes de la langue de la nature*, a work known also to Balzac.[5] Oegger argues that "the passage from the language of nature to the languages of convention was made by such insensible degrees that they who made it never thought of tracing the latter back to their source," and this is what he hopes to do in his interpretation of the Bible. With the same possibilities in mind, Emerson in *Nature* also engages in some quaint etymological excursions:

Every word which is used to express a moral or intellectual fact, if traced to its root, is found to be borrowed from some material appearance. *Right* means *straight; wrong* means *twisted. Spirit* primarily means *wind; transgression,* the crossing of a *line; supercilious* the *raising of an eyebrow.*

But Socrates, in Plato's dialogue, had already shown that either position —that language is from nature, that language is from convention—can be equally well demonstrated by such exercises. More importantly, a position that wants to tie language to nature is thwarted by the Lockean recognition that different words and sounds are appropriate to the same thing in different languages, that signs, as Locke puts it, are not the result of "the steady workmanship of nature" but of the more devious work of particular cultures. A version of the debate still goes on between those who stress innateness theories when discussing the origins of human language and those who stress social and cultural conditioning.

Cultural nostalgia, as I have been pointing out, is forever bringing its problems to the reading of literature, as if they could thereby find compensations for some present degeneracy. What, in fact, *is* to be found? Usually, that the work of literature is itself manifesting the same sort of nostalgia, and that it often expresses this, as in Sidney's sonnet, by a sort of witty impatience with inheritances of language. Along with this goes a determination, which seldom gets beyond the expression of the determination, to make use of another, more "suitable" or "natural" language. Literature is always dramatizing its efforts to find the right way to express itself. Shakespeare had the genius to make that dramatization into the history of England, in ways discussed in Chapter 3. Through his royal personages, he shows the glory and the tragedy of the effort to find language that sounds simultaneously proper both to an ordinary human being and to an extraordinary one, a ruler by divine right, the anointed one. Shakespeare's kings are Emerson's men, at once ordinary and nagged by infinitude. One might call this a difficulty for literature, when it is more like its very substance. Literature finds itself, as it finds language, committed to conventions, usages, grammars, structures, rhetorics, and all of these are the products of inherited systems which often seem artificial or inappropriate to the conditions at hand. Indeed, it is the job of the "original" artist to *make* them seem artificial. He must both use and get rid of them, and in doing so impart a kind of pleasure best described, I think, by Wordsworth.

. . .

IN THE 1800 Preface to *Lyrical Ballads*, Wordsworth calls "pleasure" "the grand elementary principle . . . by which [man] knows, and feels, and lives, and moves." It is "elementary" in that it appears to have nothing whatever to do with nurtured, acculturated, or acquired tastes. In the immediately preceding paragraph, he says that he writes under "one restriction only, namely, the necessity of giving immediate pleasure." By "immediate" he means pleasure that is without mediation (as if his words were not in themselves a mediation). For that reason the person most susceptible to this pleasure is said to be "a human being possessed of that information which may be expected from him, not as a lawyer, a physician, a mariner, an astronomer, or a natural philosopher, but as a Man." Wordsworth has recourse here to what Emerson, in "The American Scholar," calls "one of those fables . . . out of unknown antiquity" which conveys the idea that in the beginning the gods "divided Man into men," but that "Man is not a farmer, or a professor, or an engineer, but he is all." Emerson claims that in the "*divided* or social state," "functions are parcelled out," and it is therefore difficult for a person to rediscover his identity as a Man. This is of a piece with what Wordsworth means, in the 1798 "Advertisement to *Lyrical Ballads*," when he says that the "most dreadful enemy of our pleasures" is "our own pre-established codes of decision." To impart "pleasure" is to restore man to a "native and naked dignity," as he calls it, a condition he has lost to civilization. The only difference here between Wordsworth and Emerson is that Emerson wanted, again, to believe that the condition could more readily be recovered in the culturally barren landscapes of a New World.

Emerson, I mean to suggest, is writing within a mythology common to literature, and it is just as strongly felt by his close English predecessor, Wordsworth. Indeed, there scarcely is a work of literature in English written anywhere at any time which can be said to favor "pre-established codes of decision," whether in a character or a style or the progress of a narrative. That is one reason why much of literature is taken up in satires and parodies, in adverse characterizations of artificiality or mechanical forms of speech, in comic portrayals of predictable behavior or scenery or furnishing. The implication is that if these things can be set aside or modified, then it will be possible to make room for something more natural than, say, Spenser's Bower of Bliss or Jane Austen's Mr. Elton. And yet much of what we enjoy in literature is the portrayal of precisely the people and manners we are not supposed to admire, the meretricious, the predictable, the "pre-established." As I argue in Chapter 3, "Venerable Complications," we seldom get closely acquainted in literature with what is called "the native and naked dignity of man," and when we do, the examples do not prove particularly interesting.

Which brings me to the observation that even for partisans of the "language of nature" it is not simplicity or nakedness that is valued but rather invention and figurativeness. There may be a "language of nature" but there is no such thing as natural language, any more than there is a natural literature. It is all *made up*. Mythologies as to the origin of language have in common the suggestion that at its inception language could never be anything except figurative. The first words are themselves tropes, as Rousseau observes in *Essay on the Origin of Languages*. ("As man's first motives for speaking were of the passions, his first expressions were tropes.") Or note Wordsworth, in the 1802 "Appendix to the Preface": "the earliest poets of all nations generally wrote from passions excited by real events; they wrote naturally and as men." By "naturally" he means "creatively," as when he goes on to observe that "feeling powerfully as they did, their language was daring and figurative." Or recall Emerson in *Nature:* "As we go back in history, language becomes more picturesque, until its infancy, when it is all poetry." This "immediate dependence of language upon nature" necessitates not duplication but troping, or what he goes on to call "this conversion of an outward phenomenon into a type of somewhat in human life. . . . It is this which gives that piquancy to the conversation of a strong-natured farmer or back-woodsman, which all men relish."

In most such examples there lurks an extremely uneasy equation: between, on the one hand, "tropes" or "poetry," "daring and figurative" language, and, on the other, untutored men, real events, "first motives," and "infancy." Somehow, it is implied, the persons or occasions which produced "poetry" were not themselves subjected as yet to language, to definition; they themselves had not, as it were, been troped. We are to suppose that they named things but did not name themselves or one another. The implication is that such language as they used belonged to the unadulterated infancy of the race, and that the men or events who were responsible for this language are now unavailable, except in marginal figures like "back-woodsmen." This is hard to credit except, again, as a merely convenient mythology which allows literature to proceed as if it were perpetually cleansing itself of artificialities, even while enjoying them. "The corruption of man" says Emerson in *Nature*, "is followed by the corruption of language." This has become a truism, but it cannot be entirely or even substantially the case. As Emerson admits in "Experience," the corruption of man coincides with the Fall into self-consciousness, at the moment when man began to know himself in words and therefore mediately. It is impossible to imagine that language was ever anything but a corruption of Man as Emerson conceives of that figure.

Wordsworth tends to be more historically specific than Emerson in accounting for "all the corruptions, which have followed" what he calls "the genuine language of Poetry" ("Appendix," 1802). "Corrupt" language emerged not in opposition to "genuine Poetry," however, but, as he argues, peculiarly in deference to it. People of later times, in Wordsworth's chronology, were so moved by the "genuine Poetry" of earlier times that they were obliged to admit that the feelings thus generated found nothing corresponding to them in the real life around them. Feeling no anxiety about this discrepancy, they took it instead as license to make still wider the separation between the language of poetry and the language of daily life. The result is that poets then resorted to "modes of expression which they themselves had invented, and which were uttered only by themselves . . . to hieroglyphics and enigmas," to "the exaltation of the Poet's character," and to "flattering the Reader's self-love by bringing him nearer to a sympathy with that character; an effect which is accomplished by unsettling ordinary habits of thinking."

This is an astoundingly prescient passage. Wordsworth has other things in mind, but his words seem to predict unerringly what sometimes happened to poetry in the modernist movement of some hundred years later, conspicuously in the case of Pound, as Edward Thomas noted quite early on, in 1909.[6] The passage is astounding for other reasons, too. For one thing, Wordsworth has had to concede that "the language of genuine poetry" was powerfully attractive because "the language of the earliest Poets was felt to differ materially from ordinary language" ("Appendix," 1802), and that it worked effectively on later readers because it was separated from common life as they knew it, even as the earliest poets knew it—their language was "daring and figurative," it was "the language of extraordinary occasions." Again and again in the prefaces and appendices of 1798, 1800, and 1802, Wordsworth refers to the "real language of men" or "language really used by men" or "the very language of men" as if in fact he was not quite sure what the phrase would mean. Ultimately, by 1815, he moved away from it in order to make a necessary revision: that if in fact he is ever to "bring my language near to the language of men," then he will have to show how that language, while *sounding* common and ordinary, is in fact very special, possibly unprecedented in its only apparent simplicity. Most readers, he admits, are going to have to "struggle with feelings of strangeness" in the language he uses.

This adds up to saying that Wordsworth wants to write a kind of poetry that, though quite different from the poetry of Whitman or the prose of Emerson and Thoreau, has the same ambition. He wants nothing less than to *create,* in the reader, the representatives of "Man" to whom he alludes as if they might historically have existed. Their reality exists nowhere outside their evocations. Such "men" must be elaborately forged, and the stylistic effort is the more determined because Wordsworth is convinced, like his American counterparts, that salvation consists in our being allowed to experience the reality of being a "Man" at least in the writing and for the duration of the reading. Thus not only is the situation he posits, with respect to common life and ordinary language, remarkably "American," but so is the idea of reading and of writing that the situation seems to compel. Namely, that the writer and the reader must work very hard to overcome their customary, indoctrinated expectations about language, and then work harder still so as to discover in other, stranger uses of language a hint of realities denied in and by the historical world.

Wordsworth asks questions of himself as a poet, especially questions about originality, that Emerson will later ask, and that Whitman learned to ask from Emerson (and also from French writers in translation, like George Sand in *The Countess of Rudolstadt* or Jules Michelet in *The*

People). He does so in a vocabulary filled with the Emersonian tropes of breakage, displacement, and disappearance: "And where," he asks in "Essay, Supplementary to the Preface" of 1815, "lies the real difficulty of creating that taste by which a truly original poet is to be relished?" And he continues with a series of questions that, as it transpires, are not nearly as rhetorical as they sound:

Is it in breaking the bonds of custom, in overcoming the prejudices of false refinement, and displacing the aversions of inexperience? Or, if he labour for an object which here and elsewhere I have proposed to myself, does it consist in divesting the reader of the pride that induces him to dwell upon those points wherein men differ from each other, to the exclusion of those in which all men are alike, or the same; and in making him ashamed of the vanity that renders him insensible of the appropriate excellence which civil arrangements, less unjust than might appear, and Nature illimitable in her bounty, have conferred on men who may stand below him in the scale of society? Finally, does it lie in establishing that dominion over the spirit of readers by which they are to be humbled and humanised, in order that they may be purified and exalted?

The answer to all these would seem to be an immediate, resounding "yes." It turns out, however, to be only "yes, maybe," "yes" only on condition that certain necessary difficulties in writing and reading are willingly contended with. I will go into the reasons for this caution later on, but here I want to note again that it distinguishes writers like Wordsworth or Blake, and writers in the Emersonian contingent I have specified, from lesser ones who pretend to the same lineage, like Sandburg or, again, Ginsberg, Kerouac, and, more accomplished than these, William Carlos Williams. Such writers are simply not difficult enough to persuade anyone not already given over to their ideologies. I mean "difficult" in the sense adduced by Blake in a letter of August 23, 1799, to Dr. Tusler: "That which can be made Explicit to the Idiot is not worth my care. The wisest of the Ancients consider'd what is not too Explicit as the fittest for Instruction, because it rouzes the faculties to act." In answer to his own questions Wordsworth says that the "real difficulty of creating that taste by which a truly original poet is to be relished" does not lie in the propagation of ideas but only in certain acts of writing and reading by which any idea finds or does not find its "validation," a term that looks ahead to William James.

When it comes to a sense of literature's responsibility and value, the Emersonian position is, then, neither eccentric nor even exclusively American. It is radically fundamental. It represents what literature is most often trying to tell us about itself and how it wants to be read. Wordsworth is useful here because while he is obviously neither American nor chronologically in a position to be called Emersonian, he is the important figure, before William James, who makes the Emersonian *literary* position clearer and more emphatic than Emerson himself was able to do, given his simultaneous promotions of a New World mythology. Wordsworth's attributions of value to the writing and reading of literature is essentially pragmatist. Thus, when he says it is "difficult" to be original or to take pleasure in originality, he is not at all referring to ideas, to affirmations or refutations or truths. He is referring only to literary acts by which truths might be discovered. Heidegger and Hans-Georg Gadamer have since made this sort of argument more familiar. "We have no knowledge," he says in the 1800 Preface, "that is, no general principles drawn from the contemplation of particular facts, but what has been *built up* [my italics] by pleasure, and exists in us by pleasure alone." Later, in 1815, in response to the questions we have just heard him lay down, he remarks that "if these ends are to be attained," then it will not be "by the mere communication of *knowledge.*" The problem is not one of substituting some values or beliefs for others or of affirming the stability of this or that "truth" or even bringing about a change of "taste." "Taste," he points out, is a metaphor taken from the passive sense of the body and then made paramount by "that inversion in the order of things" that is characteristic of "modern Europe." No. The necessary changes must take place in what he calls, with emphasis, "intellectual *acts* and *operations.*" These occur in the writing, by measurable uses of words; but they also must occur in the reading. He insists on "the exertion of a co-operating *power* in the mind of the Reader." "Therefore," he summarizes, "to create taste is to call forth and bestow power, of which knowledge is the effect; and *there* lies the true difficulty."

As we have already seen, this vocabulary of "action" and "power" and "knowledge" is everywhere in Emerson and James. The recognition that "knowledge" is to be the "effect," and is not therefore the source of "power," is crucial. It is a way of admitting that we do not act out of subservience to something we already know; we act so as to discover something presumably worth knowing. "Power" is not obedient to established meanings but opposed to them; it wants to decreate them within the process of some larger creative urge. "Urge and urge and urge,/Always the procreant urge of the world," as Whitman puts it near the beginning of *Leaves of Grass* in 1855. "Power" in large part defines itself by challenges to the already authorized use of words, including those the poet or philosopher will himself make use of. In the 1800 Preface Wordsworth admits to apprehensions that "my language may frequently have suffered from those arbitrary connections of feelings and ideas with particular words and phrases, from which no man can altogether protect himself." And in 1815, he asks us to "remember, also, that the medium through which, in poetry, the heart is to be affected, is language; a thing subject to endless fluctuations and arbitrary associations." It is here that he most significantly predicts Emerson's call for the "disappearance" of literature, or rather his call that we should "look forward" to it. "The genius of the poet," Wordsworth remarks, "melts down" these "arbitrary associations." He "melts" them down "for his purpose," but the process cannot end there. "They retain their shape and quality," he admits, "to him who is not capable of exerting, within his own mind, a corresponding energy." Hence the never to be completed task of literary genius, its acts and operations; the pathos, never to be relieved, of a great writer's ambition for immortality. Even after his death he remains at work and induces us to work within the energies generated by his language.

To recall James's exhortation in *Pragmatism*, "bring out of each word its practical cash-value, set it at work within the stream of your experience," but expect to discover thereby only "a program for more work." Emerson will maintain in "The American Scholar" that "one must be an inventor to read well. As the proverb says, 'He that would bring home the wealth of the Indies, must carry out the wealth of the Indies.' There is then creative reading as well as creative writing." This is an echo of Wordsworth, who says in 1815 that the poet "will be in the condition of Hannibal among the Alps," forced "to clear and often to shape his own road." It cannot therefore be supposed, he adds, "that the reader can make progress of this kind, like an Indian prince or general—stretched on his palanquin, and borne by slaves." The effort of reading, like the effort of writing, is entirely its own reward. To ask for more, to seek security in meaning, is a cheat upon literature and upon life. It is like a surrender to Fate. "The truth of an idea is not a stagnant property inherent in it," James instructs us in *Pragmatism*, "truth *happens* to an idea. It *becomes* true, is *made* true by events"—including the acts and operations of writing and reading. "Its verity," he continues, "*is* in fact an event, a process: the process namely of its verifying itself, its veri-*fication*. Its validity is the process of its valid-*ation.*"

Literature is supremely the place where this process goes on, a process in which, ideally, the reader and writer become indistinguishable as partners in the enterprise of "genius." Emerson, in the *Journals* for August–September 1845, says that we are "here to know the awful secret of genius, here to become not readers of poetry but Dante, Milton, Shakespeare, Homer, Swedenborg, in the fountain through that: here to foresee India & Persia & Judea & Europe in the old paternal mind." We do not go to literature to become better citizens or even wiser persons, but to discover how to move, to act, to work in ways that are still and forever mysteriously creative. Obviously, we are required to read, but in a more self-surrendering and at the same time self-discovering way than is implied by the phrase "readers of poetry." We are to get behind the writing and to find its source "in the fountain" that flows through writing from what he calls "the awful secret of genius." The fountain or source is not situated in any particular time or place. It therefore allows us to foresee what, in effect, has already occurred, to create our own inheritance. "A good scholar," as he remarks later in the 1847 *Journals* for March–April, "will find Aristophanes & Hafiz & Rabelais full of American history."

The implications of this attitude for literature, for language, and for the self as in part a construct of both are not occult. It is close to what I think most people normally feel about themselves and the reading they do; it accurately describes the experience of literature. Only some theoretical professors want their "art without mystery," as suggested in a recent book with that title by Denis Donoghue. When used in the intensely self-reflecting ways that literature uses them, words not only continuously modify but actually tend to dissolve one another, and this tendency, while it may produce in some readers the desire always to be on the scent and never in sight of the prey, is for most of us an occasion for another kind of amazement: that any one person, any author (or reader), can be responsible for what we see and hear going on. At that point it becomes necessary to use a word like "genius," and, in doing so, to re-imagine what can be meant by the word "human" when it is conjoined with "genius."

"Genius," as I will show in the next chapter, describes those moments when language and the person using it reach a point of incandescence. It marks the disappearance of individuality on the occasion of its triumph. And that includes the disappearance of the readers in all the ordinary senses we have of ourselves. But the triumphs, even as we locate them outside ourselves in a word like "genius" or in an artist like Shakespeare, are really also *in* ourselves; we cannot and do not want to know who is specifically responsible for the language of *King Lear* or the sounds of Beethoven or the movements of a great athlete at certain moments when he or she goes beyond the most exacting limits of a discipline. And, as I have elsewhere suggested, in an essay called "Frost, Winnicott, Burke," it is not only persons and the margins of texts that disappear but also what we commonly call "things."[7] Frost was my illustration in that instance, mostly because he seemed such an unlikely one, with his reputedly firm grasp on "reality." I meant to show how it is possible for "things" to become the signs of words, and not, as is usually supposed, the other way around. "Things," that is, have more or less disappeared into the human meanings already implanted in them not by God but, collectively, by all of us.

Emerson's belief that Aristophanes is "full of American history," that we are here not to read but to "become" Dante, that we can foresee ourselves while being part of the "old paternal mind"—the implication is that the New World offers an opportunity less to disown the Old than to rediscover its true origins otherwise obscured within the encrustations of acquired culture. To be worthy of the New World, any "new world," it is necessary to imagine what it was like when the old world was also new. Get rid of culture, get rid of literature, but only after they have taught us how to reach again the sources of both, which are within us. Even the Bible must somehow be gotten rid of so that it might be invented again. Not merely late in the *Journals*, as in 1865, with the complaint that the Bible "comes with a certain official claim against which the mind revolts," but as early as 1838, while *Nature* was being revised and some essays for *First Series* were in preparation, the Bible represents for him (no less than any other written work) what he calls "this problem of a Vocabulary which like some treacherous wide shoal waylays the tall bark, the goodly soul & there it founders & suffers shipwreck."[8] Emerson would have us, like Whitman's singer, freely break out, empty ourselves into the world. "Whenever therefore a soul is true, is simple, & expelling all willfulness consents to God, & receives the Soul of the Soul into itself," he continues "then means, teachers, texts, temples, fall. . . ."

As a minister, however, he had already learned that the more likely situation was the one he must warn against:

If a man claims to know & speak of God & carries you backward to the phraseology of some old mouldered nation in another country in another world, believe him not: he does not speak for God: God does not speak to him. If he interposes betwixt you & your Maker, himself or some other person or persons, believe him not: God has better things for you. This should be plain enough; —yet see how great & vivacious souls, with grand truths in their keeping, do fail in faith to see God face to face, to see Time pass away & be no more, & to utter directly from him that which he would give them to say, but rather imprison it in the old Hebrew language, mimick David, Jeremiah, & Paul & disbelieve that God maketh the stars & stones sing, can speak our English tongue in Massachusetts & give as deep and glad a melody to it as shall make the whole world & all coming ages ring with the sound.

"All coming ages"? The expectation raises an important question. Why should "coming ages" want to hear God in a New England voice any more than the present age wants to hear him in "old Hebrew"? The issue will be clarified somewhat by William James, but questions persist. Why, under the Emersonian dispensation, should anything at all be preserved as an example to the future? Why not erase every sentence just as soon as it is written and read? Wouldn't that be the purest form of action as Emerson imagines it?

WE ARE INVITED to find a solution to this problem in a metaphor indispensable both to Emerson and to James, the metaphor of "transition." Emerson says unabashedly in "Self-Reliance" that "power ceases in the instant of repose; it resides in the moment of transition from a past to a new state, in the shooting of the gulf, in the darting to an aim." Handsomely phrased, but how do we take it? How do we experience a "transition"? I suggest, tentatively, that it is like catching a glimpse of a thing before it is possible to recognize or name it, the moment just before it can be classified by language and thus become composed or reposed in a human corpus or text. But this is too crucial a part of the whole argument I am making to be left up in the air. James nowhere more abundantly reveals his enormous, and largely unadmitted, debt to Emerson than in his use of this term, and we can look to him for assistance. In effect he offers us Emerson clarified and enforced when he shows that "transition" is essential to our understanding of how we are able at the same time to use words and to escape their gravitational pull, their tendency to reduce us to "repose."

In *Pragmatism* he writes about what he calls "parts of reality," the first being sensations, the second, the relations among sensations or among the copies of them in our minds. The third part of reality is what he then calls "the *previous truths* of which every new inquiry takes account." These three parts of reality are, as James imagines them, quite constricting, and, like Emerson, he is far less optimistic, far less confident than he is almost ever thought to be, when it comes to possibilities for newness or for originality or for freedom. "Every hour," he says, "brings its new percepts, its own facts of sensation and relation, to be truly taken account of," and he continues,

but the whole of our *past* dealings with such facts is already funded in the previous truths. It is therefore only the smallest and recentest fraction of the first two parts of reality that comes to us without the human touch, and that fraction has immediately to become humanized in the sense of being squared, assimilated, or in some way adapted, to the humanized mass already there. As a matter of fact we can hardly take in an impression at all, in the absence of a preconception of what impressions there may possibly be.

When we talk of reality "independent" of human thinking, then, it seems a thing very hard to find. It reduces to the notion of what is just entering into experience, and yet to be named, or else to some imagined aboriginal presence in experience, before any belief about the presence had arisen, before any human conception had been applied. It is what is absolutely dumb and evanescent, the merely ideal limit of our minds. We may glimpse it, but we never grasp it; what we grasp is always some substitute for it which previous human thinking has peptonized and cooked for our consumption. If so vulgar an expression were allowed us, we might say that wherever we find it, it has been already *faked*.

Presumably, all we can do is "talk" about doing away with what is "already faked"; with Stevens, we can say that "the solar chariot is junk." So long, Apollo. But neither Emerson nor James nor Stevens cares to persuade us that rhetoric will ever permanently change the situation. The Emersonian insistence on the necessity for "action" presupposes that there are no verbal solutions. Literature is not in itself an effective political form of action, except under the rather limited conditions described later in this book. At best, it can help us to deal more critically and effectively than we otherwise might with rhetorics outside literature, as a regular game of neighborhood softball might have the unintended effect of preparing someone to cope a little better with the rigors of the workplace. This is, so far as I read it, about all Emerson means when, in "Compensation," he advises that "the law of nature is, Do the thing, and you shall have the power: but they who do not the thing have not the power." By "the thing" he means any kind of work that falls to your lot and that interests you, and the "power" is best understood as an intimation, one that can come from "work," of some mysterious identification with the things of this world. So that while you change them, as in farming or cooking, they change you.

One kind of "doing" that particularly occupies Emerson is, of course, writing, and the possibilities in it of modifying our language and thereby ourselves. "Words," he tells us in "The Poet," "are also actions, and actions are a kind of words." At the same time, however, he knows, with

James, that words are "funded in previous truth" and can therefore be a deterrence to "action." Hence, his peculiar admiration for silence or verbal reticence. When, in "Self-Reliance," he speaks admiringly of "the nonchalance of boys, who are sure of a dinner," he has reference especially to their paucity of talk, their instinctive indifference to the language of social accommodation, their "disdain," as he puts it, "to do or say aught to conciliate" anyone. By contrast, "the man is, as it were, clapped into jail by his consciousness," and he goes on, with a pun on the word "committed," to suggest that speech and acts, especially assertive ones—this, from the great American preacher!—are in themselves a jail: "As soon as he has once acted or spoken with éclat, he is a committed person. . . . Who can thus avoid all pledges . . . must always be formidable." Is not this, peculiarly, a recommendation that you do nothing at all? Especially since to act or to speak is not only to imprison yourself in what you do and say but, as "éclat" suggests, to splinter yourself, to divide yourself up among already "committed" parties? Under these circumstances, what can constitute any kind of public action that will empower instead of weaken you?

Here we can perceive a crisis in the Emersonian conception of language, literature, and action. It is a crisis that cannot be alleviated to the satisfaction, obviously, of those who think any such crisis is unnecessary to begin with, people for whom language does not pose a problem, and who, confident of their ability to recognize when language is already "peptonized," are equally sure that cultural discourse easily and benignly allows for effective changes and substitutions. By contrast, the human situation in language, as Emerson imagines it, is barely negotiable; it is precarious, limiting, tense, belabored. To admit that this situation exists is not an admission of weakness, however, but of some degree of confidence, strength, and freedom. Suspicious that any word or act constitutes a commitment and is therefore immediately conformist, Emerson tries to define "action"—as he tries to define literature—as something prior to publication. Action is to be located in the movement toward but never *in* a result. The crucial passage has mostly been ignored in the interpretive effort to make Emerson clear at the expense of his radical complications, and also because what he is saying sounds so threatening to the educated classes. Properly conceived, "action is," he says, "the preamble of thought." It is the movement of mind before thought emerges, especially since, to recall the essay "Intellect," "every thought is a prison also." "The preamble of thought," he writes in "The American Scholar," "the transition through which it passes from the unconscious to the conscious, is action." If this is true, then it is hard to see how "words are also actions, and actions are a kind of words," except in simple cases, as when the umpire says, "Three strikes, you're out!" As a writer Emerson wants to shy away from the logical inference of his own position, the inference, which seems to me wholly impractical, that "action" precedes the use of words and may follow them, but cannot ever be lodged within them.

The important reason why this aspect of Emerson has been missed or ignored by his interpreters is not, however, that it is at odds with daily and essential verbal practices, but because it demeans the kind of discourse to which interpretation and the interpreters themselves are professionally committed. It lays the foundation for the anti-intellectualist direction later to be taken by American pragmatism, especially as enunciated by James.[9] It is antagonistic to any kind of institutionalized discourse about literature or about ideas generally; it is antagonistic to "thinking" as a profession and, finally, to any Godhead of the sort enjoying a revival these days in literary theory as well as in the nation. The Emersonian idealization of action implicitly disparages the power of words, regardless of how explicitly it wishes to insist that words and actions are compatible. James faces the matter more directly and sociably than Emerson does; he treats it as a problem we must all learn to live with. Thus, in *A Pluralistic Universe*, he "talks" to his audience even while he attacks "talking." Talking is the primary weapon of the "intellectualism" which he, like Emerson, wants to discredit:

I am tiring myself and you, I know, by vainly seeking to describe by concepts and words what I say at the same time exceeds either conceptualization or verbalization. As long as one continues *talking*, intellectualism remains in undisturbed possession of the field. The return to life can't come about by talking. It is an *act*; to make you return to life, I must set an example for your imitation, I must deafen you to talk, or to the importance of talk, by showing you, as Bergson does, that the concepts we talk with are made for purposes of *practice* and not for purposes of insight. Or I must *point*, point to the mere *that* of life, and you by inner sympathy must fill out the *what* for yourselves. The minds of some of you, I know, will absolutely refuse to do so, refuse to think in non-conceptualized terms. I myself absolutely refused to do so for years together, even after I knew that the denial of manyness-in-oneness by intellectualism must be false, for the same reality does perform the most various functions at once. But I hoped ever for a revised intellectualist way round the difficulty, and it was only after reading Bergson that I saw that to continue using the intellectualist method was itself the fault. I saw that philosophy had been on a false scent ever since the days of Socrates and Plato, that an *intellectual* answer to the intellectualist's difficulties will never come, and that the real way out of them, far from consisting in the discovery of such an answer, consists in simply closing one's ears to the question. When conceptualism summons life to justify itself in conceptual terms, it is like a challenge addressed in a foreign language to someone who is absorbed in his own business; it is irrelevant to him altogether —he may let it lie unnoticed. I went thus through the "inner catastrophe" of which I spoke in the last lecture; I had literally come to the end of my conceptual stock-in-trade, I was bankrupt intellectualistically, and had to change my base. No words of mine will probably convert you, for words can be the names only of concepts. But if any of you try sincerely and pertinaciously on your own separate accounts to intellectualize reality, you may be similarly driven to a change of front. I say no more: I must leave life to teach the lesson.

James is far less indebted to Bergson than he claims. His argument against "intellectualism" was already well advanced in his first book, *The Principles of Psychology*, published in 1890, before he and Bergson discovered their similarities and their friendship. He had, of course, read and re-read Emerson, who anticipates him, as in the essay of 1850 on "Plato" in *Representative Men:* "If speculation tends thus to a terrific unity, in which all things are absorbed, action tends directly backwards to diversity. The first is the course or gravitation of mind; the second is the power of nature. Nature is the manifold. The unity absorbs, and melts or reduces. Nature opens and creates." This passage is obviously troubled, however. It attributes to nature those acts of resistance and therefore of diversification which he most often attributes to the human mind in opposition to its animal or natural destiny, which is ultimately death. This is a problem which I bring into critical focus in Chapter 4,

"Resistance in Itself," and it is enough to point out here that it suggests Emerson's difficulties in reconciling the results of the "gravitation of mind," which is culture, with the power of mind, if it is derived, as he claims, from "the power of nature."

James is pertinent to our present circumstance and vocabulary because more than Emerson (though less than his friend Charles Peirce) he felt obliged to face the problem that if "action" is somehow hobbled by "talk" and by language, then it might also be disastrously at odds with culture itself, even in the minimal forms necessary to civilized life. Additionally, there is in James something engagingly personal which is hard to find in Emerson. He is willing to acknowledge that his distaste for "concepts and words" is a way of objecting to the past as represented by family, family responsibilities, griefs, traces of infirmity, paralyzing bequests. On this score Emerson is not so much shy as constrained; he simply admits from the outset that he is a cold fish, incapable of feeling very long or very deeply about anything that touches on his close human attachments. It is nonetheless possible with Emerson, as even more with James, to guess that this obsession with "action" expresses a terror of blankness and lassitude. This is a fear that gets carried into the poetry of Frost, as in "Stopping By Woods on a Snowy Evening," and into Stevens, as we shall see, in a number of poems. I want now to turn to James more or less exclusively, for a further but relatively brief explication of the problem of how, if language, concepts, intellectualism, literature are all variously suspect, a writer proposes nonetheless to endow his own arguments, concepts, words, and actions with exemplary value. How, for instance, does a man like James set out to instruct his own children about "life," especially the life of "action"? On what grounds can he ask his son to "copy" him or to "copy" anything?

IN THE SUMMER of 1898, James, at age fifty-six, went to Berkeley, California, to deliver a series of lectures on pragmatism. By then he could have used his own life to illustrate the successful application of one of its tenets: that truth is best seen not as "an accurate representation of reality," but as "what it is better for us to believe." He means that even things we may know to be true do not necessarily have a claim upon us, especially if they entangle us in frustration. When a truth has no relation to a specific situation, or has a relation so inconvenient and inessential that we do not want to deal with it, it is often no more useful to us than a falsehood. In a passage in *Pragmatism* that gradually fills with what appear to be unintended self-admissions, he asks:

When shall I acknowledge this truth and when that? Shall the acknowledgment be loud?—or silent? If sometimes loud, sometimes silent, which *now*? When may a truth go into cold-storage in the encyclopedia? and when shall it come out for battle? Must I constantly be repeating the truth "twice two are four" because of its eternal claim on recognition? or is it sometimes irrelevant? Must my thoughts dwell night and day on my personal sins and blemishes, because I truly have them?—or may I sink and ignore them in order to be a decent social unit, and not a mass of morbid melancholy and apology?

One is put in mind by this last sentence that until his late thirties James, like his father, the theologian Henry James, Sr., had experienced breakdowns in which invalidism was compounded by the threat of insanity; like his brother Henry, fifteen months his junior, he had had acute problems with his back and with constipation; like his sister Alice and another brother, Robertson, he had suffered nervous collapses, then called neurasthenia, which were augmented by recurrent eye troubles. Thanks to the further example of his father, who was famously leisured and vague ("I am determined," he wrote a friend, "to take holiday for the rest of my life and to make all my work sabbatical"), and to his mother's benevolent inducements of hypochondria in all five of her children, William had been in danger of devoting himself, in Alice's phrase, to the "life-long occupation of improving," even as he tried now one, now another occupation. His crises over idleness, illness, and vocation occurred within the context of intense parental and sibling entanglements, which led back to his father's own conflicts with *his* father, the fearsome William James of Albany. There was a high incidence in three generations of the James family, and in many other privileged families in nineteenth-century New England, of affective disorders, alcoholism, and psychopathology.

William nonetheless managed to use his illnesses to effect changes from one form of activity or one place to another, especially if it meant getting away from Cambridge on frequent trips to Europe. He worked for a time in the studio of John La Farge and might have become a talented painter; he went with Louis Agassiz on a scientific expedition to the Amazon; he received a degree in medicine from Harvard, where, despite his abhorrence of laboratory work and mostly to please his father, he instructed in anatomy and physiology, until at last in 1885, and after some quite shrewd academic maneuvering on his part, he became Professor of Philosophy, a subject that had long been his primary interest though not his professional focus. It was not until age fifty that he published his first and possibly greatest work—one should come to it, Jacques Barzun has argued, in "a mood suited to a *Moby-Dick* or *War and Peace*"—the massive *Principles of Psychology.* Just before the trip to California he had brought out *The Will to Believe and Other Essays.* Meanwhile, at age thirty-six he had married a woman selected by his parents. As it turned out, it was an exceedingly happy marriage, and they had had five children, one of whom had died in his first year.

To his youngest child, Alexander, James wrote a remarkable and overlooked letter during this trip to California, enclosing with it a photograph of a girl and boy standing on a rock dangerously perched over a deep ravine in Yosemite Valley. James had visited there the week before on one of the strenuous camping expeditions that had already injured his heart. "Darling old Cherubini," he wrote,

See how brave this girl and boy are in the Yosemite Valley! I saw a moving sight the other morning before breakfast in a little hotel where I slept in the dusty fields. The young man of the house had shot a little wolf called a coyote in the early morning. The heroic little animal lay on the ground, with his big furry ears, and his clean white teeth, and his jolly cheerful little body, but his brave little life was gone. It made me think how brave all these living things are. Here little coyote was, without any clothes or house or books or anything, with nothing but his own naked self to pay his way with, and risking his life so cheerfully—and losing it—just to see if he could pick up a meal near the hotel. He was doing his coyote-business like a hero, and you must do your boy-business, and I my man-business bravely too, or else we won't be worth as much as that little coyote. Your mother can find a picture of him in those green books of animals, and I want you to copy it. Your loving Dad.

James's correspondence is filled with passages equally appealing in their intimacy and openness to life. In writing to his son he does not sound significantly different from the James of the lectures and essays. Toward his audiences and his readers he is often equally solicitous, conversational, even affectionate, and this was but one of his ways of dissociating himself from the "intellectualism" for which he expressed such frequent distaste. Most of his books first existed as lectures or talks and, as he says in the Preface to *Pragmatism,* these were "printed as delivered, without developments or notes"; they are "essays in popular philosophy," to recall the subtitle of *The Will to Believe.*

So as you come upon them, the writings are not difficult in the way modernist literature would in a few years choose to be, bristling with allusions and jagged with discontinuities presumably because God is at last dead. James thought he was dead, too, but as even this brief letter to Alexander shows, he welcomed bareness, the clean heavens. He is committed to fairly casual forms of sense-making because he does not see why language needs to be cluttered with discredited implications and associations. But he was not at all naïve, as we have seen, about the inescapability of cultural inheritance or cultural burden. The letter to Alexander is quite beautifully about what it ostensibly seems to be about, the lonely virtues and necessities of individual action. At the same time, it is also about models for action. Dad sleeps in the fields and he is up and at it before breakfast. More directly still, it is the couple on the rock and especially the coyote who are held up for emulation. Though they are meant to illustrate a willingness to take risks without outside help, they are recommended by father to son as precisely a source of outside help. Which prompts the inevitable question—just how naked can a learned nakedness be? James is never without density, and the letter becomes very complicated about bravery. It is bravery of a kind that involves what Faulkner will call "dispossession," as when another boy, in *The Bear,* earns his chance to envision the mythical beast only after he lays to one side his stick, his compass, and his watch. You must, these writers seem to be saying, take your chances, if you want to be saved, and the only way to do so is without an arsenal. For James as a writer this means that you do not lean, except critically, on traditional philosophic terms like Truth and Knowledge.

This association of heroic action with denudation ("without any clothes or house or books or anything") is part of an ancient dream to which American writers have no exclusive claim, but it vividly recurs from Cooper and Emerson to Stevens, Hemingway, and the Mailer of *Why Are We in Vietnam?* James is telling his son what he tells us in *Pragmatism*, that "truth is *made*, just as health, wealth, and strength are made, in the course of experience." Popularizers of James have often been satisfied with observing that at such moments he is merely saying "do your thing." That indeed, for starters, is what he is saying; it is, remember, the very words we hear from Emerson in "Compensation" and in the *Journals*: "Do your thing and I shall know you" (July 7, 1839). But both were aware that if to "do" something is to look forward to a result of some sort, it is also to look backward at earlier examples so as to guess what the results might be. In any case, there is no escape from the prior human presence in the very words we use, as James maintains in *Pragmatism:*

Our nouns and adjectives are all humanized heirlooms, and in the theories we build them into, the inner order and arrangement is wholly dictated by human considerations, intellectual consistency being one of them. Mathematics and logic themselves are fermenting with human rearrangements; physics, astronomy and biology follow massive cues of preference. We plunge forward into the field of fresh experience with the beliefs our ancestors and we have made already; these determine what we notice; what we notice determines what we do; what we do again determines what we experience; so from one thing to another, altho the stubborn fact remains that there *is* a sensible flux, what is *true of it* seems from first to last to be largely a matter of our own creation.

There is no way, that is, to divorce yourself from cultural inheritance, and surely no father writing to his son would want to suggest that there is, especially a father who in the same context says that "man *engenders* truth" upon the world. The letter concerns itself with reproductions, and not merely in a generational sense. It refers at the outset to a photograph in which the boy is asked to "see" how "brave" two young people are and it ends with instructions for the mother to find a sketch of the "brave" coyote and for the boy to copy it. "Copying" and "correspondences" were vexed questions for James, in his life no less than in his writing, especially given his intricate relations to father and siblings. If "truth" is indeed something "made" in "the course of experience" rather than something already existent, grounded in philosophical concepts, then "experience" must nonetheless include an appreciation of what already has been done, those actions which have created the world so far and which invite us to additional acts of creation.

This ought to raise certain questions for any advocate of cultural freedom, and some of them might well be asked by the child of such an advocate. You deny, he or she might say, that truth is something already *there,* waiting to be discovered in what has been said and done. And yet at the same time you go right ahead and discover incidents wherein truth was "made," and you then recommend that I "copy" them. What are we doing with these "makings" if not discovering them, finding them *there* waiting for us? What is to prevent them from being institutionalized, classified, made into a burden no different from the ones you want to save me from? James's answer to these questions is also, again, essentially Emerson's. (When Emerson visited the James home in New York's Washington Square in 1842, six weeks after the death of his son Waldo, he was taken upstairs by Henry James, Sr., to bless his three-month-old son, William. It was, as Gay Wilson Allen remarks in his biography of James, "a prophetic event for the future philosopher of Pragmatism.") Echoing what we have already heard him say in the *Journals* about Dante, Emerson tells us in "The American Scholar" that "out of unhandselled savage nature, out of terrible Druids and Berserkirs, come at last Alfred and Shakespeare," and cautions that "meek young men grow up in libraries, believing it their duty to accept the views, which Cicero, which Locke, which Bacon, have given, forgetful that Cicero, Locke, and Bacon were only young men in libraries, when they wrote these books." He means that what we should look for in works of art, or works of any kind, is not some static or inert relation to truth—"we have to live to-day by what truth we can get to-day," James remarks, "and be ready to-morrow to call it falsehood"—but rather those creative acts by which the works were produced, the performative movements, the "executive faculty" which Emerson praised in Shakespeare above all others. What we, no less than Alexander, should "see" and "copy" are acts and motions of acts. These will not reproduce the past; they will add to or "engender" truths upon it, all acts being in any case no more than acts of interpretation which help create the objects that are to be interpreted. Thus James can say in *The Meaning of Truth* that "theoretic truth, truth of passive copying, sought in the sole interests of copying as such, not because copying is *good for something,* but because copying ought *schlechthin* [absolutely] to be, seems, if you look at it coldly, to be an almost preposterous ideal." His admonitory alternative here, and again at the end of *A Pluralistic Universe,* is that "the essence in any case would not be the copying, but the enrichment of the previous world." It is he, and not the coyote, who gives us the coyote.

In the essay in *Pragmatism* called "Pragmatism's Conception of Truth," James addresses the problem of copying and of its relation to the "making" of truth in a figure that might easily have found its way, as did so much of James, into the poetry of Frost. I am thinking especially of what I have already called the poems of work, apple picking, wood cutting, and the like, poems where he discovers as in "Mowing" that "the fact is the sweetest dream that labor knows." "Truths," James writes, "emerge from facts; but they dip forward into facts again and add to them; which facts again create or reveal new truth (the word is indifferent) and so on indefinitely. The 'facts' themselves, meanwhile, are not *true.* They simply *are.* Truth is the function of the beliefs that start and terminate among them. The case is like a snowball's growth, due as it is to the distribution of the snow on the one hand, and to the successive pushes of the boys on the other, with these factors co-determining each other incessantly."

If the making of truth is like the making of a snowball, then truth is more a product of the imaginings that accompany the commonest acts of work or play than of intellectualist pondering. Truth cannot be abstracted from an action so that its validity may be tested by other actions in the form of logic or science. His notion that "truth *happens* to an idea. It *becomes* true, is *made* true by events," bears little resemblance, therefore, to a scientific method—James was weak in mathematics and impatient of the laboratory—nor does it even concede that the testing of truth depends on the coordinated or confirming investigation of colleagues. It is here that James differs markedly from his prickly life-long friend Charles Peirce, who can be said to have bestowed the name "pragmatism" on American philosophy in a paper James heard in 1872. Both James and Peirce were indebted in their pragmatisms to a definition of belief given by the Scottish philosopher-psychologist Alexander Bain: "An attitude or disposition of preparedness to act." But they diverged on the crucial matter of "verification," and Peirce energetically pointed this out in letters and in his quite tough review of *The Principles of Psychology.* As John Dewey put it, "Everything ultimately turned, for Peirce, upon the trustworthiness of the procedures of inquiry. . . . The appeal in Peirce is essentially to the consensus of those who have investigated, using methods which are capable of employment by all."[10] Though Peirce, along with James and the British philosopher F.C.S. Schiller, took the view that truth consists in a state of achieved satisfaction, Peirce was obliged to point out that while for them "satisfaction" was a matter of individual experience, he himself was concerned with "the satisfaction which *would* ultimately be found if the inquiry were pushed to its ultimate and indefeasible issue." This, he wrote in 1908, "is a very different position from that of Mr. Schiller and the pragmatists of today."[11] And he had earlier said, in the same vein, that "the very origin of the conception of reality shows that this conception essentially involves the notion of a COMMUNITY, without definite limits, and capable of a definite increase of knowledge."[12]

These differences with Peirce help reveal something disturbing about James, despite the vibrant optimism with which, in most instances, he specifies that individual experience is the primary source of truth and also its confirming agent. Other instances tend to be curiously frightening, and lead to the conjecture that a nightmare of solipsism lurked within his individualistic dream of salvation by action. Thus in the crucial chapter "The Stream of Thought" in the *Principles,* he claims that "absolute insulation, irreducible pluralism is the law. It seems as if the elementary psychic fact were not *thought* or *this thought* or *that thought,* but *my thought,* every thought being *owned.* Neither contemporaneity, nor proximity in space, nor similarity of quality and content are able to fuse thoughts together which are sundered by this barrier of belonging to different personal minds. The breaches between such thoughts are the most absolute breaches in nature."

It is not, then, that the discovery of truth should or should not involve Peirce's "notion of a COMMUNITY," but that for James it is impossible that it do so, except in a merely procedural sense or as part of an individual's discovery that he shares a common lot with others. In the passage just noted from *Principles* there is evidence, I think, that his insistence on the necessity of individual actions is inseparable from a fear of the "absolute insulation" of his own mental processes. One can understand why he preferred, in *Varieties of Religious Experience*, to attribute to an unnamed Frenchman an experience his son Henry later attributed to him, which will be discussed further in the last chapter. It was a sight that made him forever "sympathetic with the morbid feelings of others," the recollected image, in a state of depression, of an epileptic patient who "sat there like a sort of sculptured Egyptian cat or Peruvian mummy, moving nothing but his black eyes and looking absolutely non-human. This image and my fear entered into a species of combination with each other. *That shape am I,* I felt, potentially. Nothing that I possess can defend me against that fate, if the hour for it should strike for me as it struck for him."

James's boundless energy and enthusiasm were both an antidote to and a likely consequence of his fear of "absolute insulation." All his life he was hospitable to a wide range of people, not only students and colleagues, to whom he was unstintingly generous, but outcasts and eccentrics whom he welcomed into his home. His avidity for travel and movement comes close to hysteria on his walking-climbing expeditions, like the one to the Adirondacks in 1898, where he injured his heart by climbing up and down four mountains in one day with a group of people less than half his age. He courted physical hardship, especially when it involved groups or when it induced people to work together, and he was delighted to be on the scene of the San Francisco earthquake of 1906 and its aftermath. In a letter to his brother Henry (addressed also to his son, William James, Jr.) he exults, with amazingly competitive gusto, in his capacity to be one of the active survivors, to share the "common lot," to discover that the disaster produced not lethargy but, as he would have expected, hope and *activity*. "*I* play with boys who curse and swear," said

William at age eight to Henry at age six, when refusing his brother's company on an excursion onto lower Broadway, and at the ages respectively of sixty-four and sixty-two the relationship, even the tone, has not changed:

Cambridge, May 9, 1906

Dearest Brother and Son,

Your cablegram of response was duly received, and we have been also "joyous" in the thought of your being together. I knew, of course, Henry, that you would be solicitous about us in the earthquake, but didn't reckon at all on the extremity of your anguish as evinced by your frequent cablegrams home, and finally by the letter to Harry which arrived a couple of days ago and told how you were unable to settle down to any other occupation, the thought of our mangled forms, hollow eyes, starving bodies, minds insane with fear, haunting you so. We never reckoned on this extremity of anxiety on your part, I say, and so never thought of cabling you direct, as we might well have done from Oakland on the day we left, namely April 27th. I much regret this callousness on our part. For *all* the anguish was yours; and in general this experience only rubs in what I have always known, that in battles, sieges and other great calamities, the pathos and agony is in general solely felt by those at a distance; and although physical pain is suffered most by its immediate victims, those at the *scene of action* have no *sentimental* suffering whatever. Everyone at San Francisco seemed in a good hearty frame of mind; there was work for every moment of the day and a kind of uplift in the sense of a "common lot" that took away the sense of loneliness that (I imagine) gives the sharpest edge to the more usual kind of misfortune that may befall a man. But it was a queer sight, on our journey through the City on the 26th (eight days after the disaster), to see the inmates of the houses of the quarter left standing, all cooking their dinners at little brick campfires in the middle of the streets, the chimneys being condemned. If such a disaster had to happen, somehow it couldn't have chosen a better place than San Francisco (where everyone knew about camping, and was familiar with the creation of civilizations out of the bare ground), and at five-thirty in the morning, when few fires were lighted and everyone, after a good sleep, was in bed. Later, there would have been great loss of life in the streets, and the more numerous foci of conflagration would have burned the city in one day instead of four, and made things vastly worse.

In general you may be sure that when any disaster befalls our country it will be *you* only who are wringing of hands, and we who are smiling with "interest or laughing with gleeful excitement." I didn't hear one pathetic word uttered at the scene of disaster, though of course the crop of "nervous wrecks" is very likely to come in a month or so. . . .

I have just read your paper on Boston in the "North American Review." I am glad you threw away the scabbard and made your critical remarks so straight. What you say about "pay" here being the easily won "salve" for privations, in view of which we cease to "mind" them, is as true as it is strikingly pat. *Les intellectuels*, wedged between the millionaires and the handworkers, are the really pinched class here. They feel the frustrations and they can't get the salve. *My* attainment of so much pay in the past few years brings home to me what an all-benumbing salve it is. That whole article is of your best. We long to hear from W., Jr. No word yet. Your ever loving,

W.J.

The evidence of sibling rivalry here is relatively less interesting than are the terms which express it. They resound with Emersonian preoccupations: the expectant sense of "the common lot"; the enthusiasm for the "scene of action"; the pride in the learned capacity to create "civilizations out of the bare ground." The evident creative inducement is "the bare ground itself," as in Stevens's poem "The Rock," or the "bleak rocks" of Emerson's "Experience," where he says that we "must hold hard to this poverty, however scandalous."

James's insistent recommendation that one must "act" has a likely source, as does his fear of passive literary appreciation, in anxieties about inaction that resulted from years of illness, depressing irresolution, and a fear of insanity further increased by the fact that his father also had had visions which made him doubt his existence as a person. Like many of his generation James, at least till 1873, was convinced that mental disorders required a physical basis, and that the tendencies were transmittable to offspring by progressive degeneration. This had much to do with his reluctance to marry earlier than he did. It is possible, too, that his decision not to pursue a career in painting and his often agitated impatience with the more elaborated of Henry's novels are to be understood only in part as a reaction against his father's claim that "our highest mode of action is aesthetic." He did not want to be excited by art to feelings, beliefs, or awarenesses that would then only sicken him for want of the ability or opportunity to act upon them. Just what the "act" should be was sometimes a problem, as witness his merely charming remonstrances in the chapter called "Habit" in *Principles:*

There is no more contemptible type of human character than that of the nerveless sentimentalist and dreamer, who spends his life in a weltering sea of sensibility and emotion, but who never does a manly concrete deed. . . . The habit of excessive novel-reading and theater-going will produce true monsters in this line. The weeping of a Russian lady over the fictitious personages in the play, while her coachman is freezing to death on his seat outside, is the sort of thing that everywhere happens on a less glaring scale. Even the habit of excessive indulgence in music, for those who are neither performers themselves nor musically gifted enough to take it in a purely intellectual way, has probably a relaxing effect upon character. One becomes filled with emotions which habitually pass without prompting to any deed, and so the inertly sentimental condition is kept up. The remedy would be, never to suffer one's self to have an emotion at a concert, without expressing it afterwards in *some* active way. Let the expression be the least thing in the world—speaking genially to one's aunt, or giving up one's seat in a horse-car, if nothing more heroic offers—but let it not fail to take place.

James is not, then, a figure, and I doubt that there are any, who is best understood within the so-called history of ideas. In assessing the severe, suicidal depressions of 1869–70, for example, to which the death of his beloved cousin Minny Temple greatly contributed, all commentators so far, except Howard Feinstein in his *Becoming William James,* [13] follow James himself and Ralph Barton Perry's great two-volume *The Thought and Character of William James* (1935) in saying that his recovery was due in large part to his reading of the French philosopher Charles Renouvier. Always quoted in evidence is James's diary for April 30, 1870:

I think that yesterday was a crisis in my life. I finished the first part of Renouvier's second Essay and see no reason why his definition of Free Will— "the sustaining of a thought *because I choose to* when I might have other thoughts"—need be the definition of an illusion. At any rate, I will assume for the present—until next year—that it is no illusion. My first act of free will shall be to believe in free will. For the remainder of the year, I will abstain from the mere speculation & contemplative *Grublei* [grubbing among subtleties] in which my nature takes most delight, and voluntarily cultivate the feeling of moral freedom, by reading books favorable to it, as well as by acting. After the first of January, my callow skin being somewhat fledged, I may perhaps return to metaphysical study & skepticism without danger to my powers of action. For the present then remember: care little for speculation; much for the *form* of my action . . .[14]

This passage is supposed to demonstrate that James's "will to believe" required a prior leap of faith in the will itself, and that his decision is evidence therefore of a most consequential change in his life. But the entry can be read quite otherwise, as marking the perpetuation of his problems and in terms by which he deludes even himself. What sounds like an affirmation of free will is really a denial of it, a determination to thwart it. Can a man be said to believe in free will when, ambitious to be a philosopher and to get out of the scientific activities which please his father more than himself, he must forbid himself philosophy, at least in the form in which he defensively chooses to think of it? Further evidence of the problem is in a sentence deleted by Perry from the diary entry with which commentators have contented themselves. James goes on to say that "today has furnished the exceptionally passionate initiative which Bain posits for the acquisition of habits." Bain, in his role of associationist psychologist, tended to be a moralistic disciplinarian; he was especially partial, for example, to the therapy of getting up early in the morning. Renouvier and Bain were both used by James actually to prevent himself from recognizing that what he needed to learn was freedom *from* the will. In line with this, the terrifying vision of the epileptic should be located not in 1870 but, as Feinstein argues, in 1872, two years after his diary entry on Renouvier and Bain. The affirmation of belief in the will was followed, that is, by an intensification of the symptoms it was meant to cure.

I go into such detail because it lends support to the argument I have been leading into, which is that James's fear of stagnation and of inaction extended into his fear of speculation itself, especially when this led, as he felt it often had done in philosophy, to the system building of "intellectualists," to entrapment within concepts, to the danger of fixation even within one's own formulations. In that regard we can better understand what James meant in *Principles* when he remarked that "to explain our phenomenally given thoughts as products of deeper lying entities is metaphysics," and therefore not within his intentions.

With Nietzsche and Emerson, and in anticipation of Foucault and Deleuze, James was essentially trying to release himself and the rest of us from any settled, coherent idea of the human, from the conceptual systems and arrangements of knowledge by which man has so far defined himself. In his work and in his life, he was drawn to the marginal, the transgressive, the misfits. That is the tender urgency behind his proposal that his son should "copy" a coyote, or his devastating imagination of himself as an epileptic—like an Egyptian cat—or his worry in *Pragmatism* about the "grub" within the Darwinian design ("To the grub under the bark, the exquisite fitness of the woodpecker's organism to extract him would certainly argue a diabolical designer"), or his supposition, in the same book, that "were we lobsters, or bees, it might be that our organization would have led to our using quite different modes from these of apprehending our experiences. It *might* be too (we cannot dogmatically deny this) that such categories, unimaginable by us to-day, would have proved on the whole as serviceable for handling our experiences mentally as those which we actually use." He welcomed all manifestations of life, even the tremors of that San Francisco earthquake. In an essay called "On Some Mental Effects of the Earthquake," he reports that when it threw him out of bed, his "emotion consisted wholly of glee and admiration, glee at the vividness which such an abstract idea or verbal term as 'earthquake' could put on when translated into sensible reality and verified concretely; and admiration at the way in which the frail little wooden house could hold itself together in spite of such a shaking. I felt no trace whatever of fear; it was pure delight and welcome. 'Go it,' I almost cried aloud, 'and go it *stronger!*'" Perhaps James's greatest achievement, as Dewey said, is "the fundamental idea of an open universe in which uncertainty, choice, hypotheses, novelties and possibilities are naturalized."

Human genius, the subject of the next chapter, is a manifestation of some such impatience with the codifications of life, but how far the impatience can remain itself and at the same time be "naturalized" is a question too lightly passed over in Dewey's appreciation of James. Genius involves itself in processes which, when they arrive at practical expression, especially in any mode of writing, become immediately filled with the apprehension of dissipation and loss of energy. To overcome this apprehension we need to convince ourselves, as Emerson says in the essay "Art," that "the real value of the Iliad, or the Transfiguration, is as signs of power."

Chapter 1

THE QUESTION OF GENIUS

THE CHALLENGE OF EMERSON

"THE ONLY OBJECTION to *Hamlet*," according to Emerson's *Journals* for 1841, "is that it exists." What is the best way to take this? Is it merely feisty or provocative? is it nationalistic? is it Oedipally anxious? It could be all of these and as easily none of them. Any such characterization of a remark like Emerson's would be culturally rigid and defensive, as if— the value of *Hamlet* being beyond debate—inquiry should direct itself only at motives for devaluing it. But what if such a remark is taken as seriously as I think it ought to be taken? What happens to literature if you can imagine doing without it? What happens to the reputed transactions between life and art if, apparently for the sake of life, "great" works are wished out of existence?

Such questions, which have to do with the status and, finally, the usefulness to life of literary culture, belong to the larger question of "genius," its possible nature and location. From what Emerson says about that subject, it is obvious that his position on *Hamlet* is a passionately held one: for him, monumental works of art become inimical not merely to other artists but to the human vitalities that go into them. He objects to any text which purports to incorporate "genius"; and, needless to say, he is still more opposed to efforts which imbue it with moral or ethical purposes that have any kind of social or ecclesiastical derivation. The more esteemed the work or the artist has become, the greater the possibility of its also becoming dead and deadening. "For it is the inert effort of each thought, having formed itself into a circular wave of circumstance,—as, for instance, an empire, rules of an art, a local usage, a religious rite—to heap itself on that ridge, and to solidify and hem in, the life," as he remarks in "Circles."

Emerson's essential objection to *works* of genius is that they cannot in themselves ever adequately convey the *workings* of it. As he sees it, one complication in the transmission of culture is that genius is thwarted by the very shapes in which it is alleged to re-present itself. This may sound obtusely theoretical or intransigent or radical or simply weird on Emerson's part, but I think it is none of these things. He felt as if he were coping with a problem shared gregariously with the rest of us, as if, in some way or other, all of us get around to raising the question of "genius." "Genius" is a necessary idea because like the idea of God it is an abstraction a great many people want and need to believe in. And the belief depends on the fact that without it people would find it more difficult if not impossible to talk to one another about the extraordinary effects upon them of the created world. The term is useful in direct proportion to its vagueness; it conjures up something that cannot be specifically traced out; it describes things we suspect about an artist or a work but cannot know for sure. To use the word "genius" is to express a desire that human attributes should exist that are beyond human understanding.

Where is genius and whose is it? How do we find it even when we know it is there, as in Mozart's Fortieth Symphony or Balanchine's *Concerto Barocco,* or Caravaggio's *The Conversion of Saint Paul,* or *Don Quixote?* Part of the difficulty is that as we attend to such works all of us want, in a very real sense, to attribute the "genius" to ourselves, to an always imminent part of ourselves that has waited only upon the capacity for expression: in most cases a long wait. "The great poet," Emerson writes in "The Over-Soul,"

makes us feel our own wealth, and then we think less of his compositions. His best communication to our mind is to teach us to despise all he has done.

Shakespeare carries us to such a lofty strain of intelligent activity, as to suggest a wealth which beggars his own; and we then feel that the splendid works which he has created, and which in other hours we extol as a sort of self-existent poetry, take no stronger hold of real nature than the shadow of a passing traveller on the rock.

Emerson is an appropriate guide to the question of genius for several reasons. First, because, of those who address the subject, he seems to me to have the best, which is to say the most uncompromised and troubled, sense of its elusiveness. Second, because his idea of "the over-soul" persuades him that what attracts us to genius has less to do with particular works and authors than with something we want to discover in ourselves, something that resides not in the sentiments and pieties and moral values abstracted from texts, but in corporate human power. And third, because the strongest evidence for me of Emerson's own genius is that his way of writing simultaneously affirms and calls into doubt his, or anyone else's, individual authority over language, the language he himself chooses to use. He calls into doubt the very existence in language of the individual self, even while he famously affirms it.

Indeed, when he talks about the self, there is something peculiarly unsettling about his aphoristic bravado, as if the aphorisms are meant to transcend the occasion of their utterance and of our reading. "All that Adam had, all that Caesar could, you have and can do," he says at the end of *Nature*. Is anyone supposed to believe this? Should we act upon the conviction that it is true? He does not really expect us to, and his careless combination of references ought to indicate as much. Anyone who has "all that Adam had" would be utterly indifferent to all that Caesar did. And neither figure is being proposed as a model. He is dismissing both of them in favor of whatever version of their "genius" may exist in each of us, now. "Why, then," he asks a bit later in "The Over-Soul," "should I make account of Hamlet and Lear, as if we had not the soul from which they fell as syllables from the tongue?"

Classic figures and texts of the past, as Emerson invokes them, are very often objected to, rebuked, lumped together indiscriminately or, as in *Representative Men*, offered as exempla of efforts rather than of specific achievements. He wants to suggest that on behalf of all of us he is clearing the way for some forever postponed and unparalleled human performance. This, too, is how he deploys the sentences of his own writing, as if he feared being trapped by them. Within a given paragraph, he tends not to develop an argument in the direction already laid down by a previous remark but to veer away from it, as from some constraining influence. He wants always to be several steps ahead of himself. "It avails not, time nor place—distance avails not,/I am with you, you men and women of a generation, or ever so many generations hence." Whitman was to write these lines in "Crossing Brooklyn Ferry." It is an Emersonian gesture meant to transport the poet beyond any compositional occasion into some future where the poem finds itself being read, where Whitman would be the effluvium of his own writing.

It is frequently said of this Emersonian tendency—this apparent obliviousness to the present circumstance, this living into the future— that it conveys a dangerous indifference to historical and political realities, offering in their stead an illusory notion that individual freedom will someday actualize itself in a New World, a place, unlike any other in history, where there are no contrived impediments to the expression of desire. Here was a chance to give practical realizations to liberal Enlightenment hopes for individual autonomy. Superficially, therefore, it might seem as if the gaps Emerson likes to create between "genius" and the texts it is supposed to inhabit, between "genius" and the artists who are supposed to have it, or between one sentence he has written and the one that will follow it—that all this expresses his confident hope of effecting a break from inherited culture, even from the more immediate historical or cultural commitments implicit in his own uses of language. The prologue to this book, as well as my earlier *A World Elsewhere*, is meant to refute the illusion that any effort of style can radically transform history or language or effectively break the coherencies they impose upon consciousness. It seems to me apparent that Emerson himself recognized the limits of his own enterprise.

He had a tragic view of the disparity between desire and possibility, all the more so because the physical continent of America did sometimes seem like a bridge between the two. The disparity, the chasm, was enforced by the fact of language. Wherever you are, you live within its necessities, within the cultural inheritances carried in its syntax. "Build, therefore, your own world," he exhorts us at the end of *Nature* when, for a brief time, he imagined that we could learn language from "nature." But in only a very few years he would find it obvious that language had already "learned" us, so to speak; it had already taught us the words by which we can communicate to ourselves any knowledge of ourselves.

Even while the country's bareness might be an invitation to "build, therefore, your own world," it could as easily be construed as a threat. In the *Journals* for October 27, 1851, he offers a particularly affecting example:

It would be hard to recall the rambles of last night's talk with H. T. But we started over again, to sadness, almost, the Eternal loneliness . . . how insular & pathetically solitary, are all the people we know! Nor dare we tell what we think of each other, when we bow in the street. 'Tis mighty fine for us to taunt men of the world with superficial & treacherous courtesies. I saw yesterday, Sunday, whilst at dinner my neighbor Hosmer creeping into my barn. At once it occurred, "Well, men are lonely, to be sure, & here is this able, social, intellectual farmer under this grim day, as grimly sidling into my barn, in the hope of some talk with me, showing me how to husband my cornstalks. Forlorn enough!" It is hard to believe that all times are alike & that the present is also rich. When this annual project of a Journal returns, & I cast about to think who are to be contributors, I am struck with a feeling of great poverty; my bareness! my bareness! seems America to say.

More than Cooper in *Home as Found,* more even than Henry James in the book on Hawthorne, Emerson saw that America's bareness did not make it innocent of inherited culture. It actually made it more complicit, as if the country's "enormous disproportion of unquickened earth" (*Journals,* October 1842) totally exposed it to foreign radiations. It was without any protective cultural cloud layers of its own. "We are not the first born," he admits at one point, "but the latest born . . . we have no wings . . . the sins of our predecessors are on us like a mountain of obstruction" (*Journals,* April–May 1846). Neither in America nor anywhere else is there any way to resist the overwhelming cultural inheritance which is language and, especially, literature. "Literature,"

we may recall him saying, "has been before us, wherever we go," and
he continues, in the *Journals* of June–August 1845:

When I come in the secretest recess of a swamp, to some obscure, and rare, &
to me unknown plant, I know that its name & the number of its stamens, every
bract & awn, is carefully described & registered in a book in my shelf. So is it
with this young soul wandering lonely, wistful, reserved, unfriended up & down
in nature. These mysteries which he ponders, which astonish & entrance him,
this riddle of liberty, this dream of immortality, this drawing to love, this
trembling balance of motive, and the centrality whereof these are rays, have all
been explored to the recesses of consciousness, to the verge of Chaos & the
Neant, by men with grander steadfastness & subtler organs of search than any
now alive; so that when this tender philosopher comes from his reverie to
literature, he is alarmed (like one whose secret has been betrayed) by the terrible
fidelity, with which, men long before his day, have described all & much more
than all he has just seen as new Continent in the West.

If Emerson's America is bare of native culture, then wherever you
look, European art precedes you to perception. America may be, as he
says in "The Poet," "a poem in our eyes," but that is because in our eyes
there are already so many poems. The invisible and therefore the most
potent and unavoidable instrument of inherited culture was language
itself. That, I think, is what Emerson means by the taut phrase "this
riddle of liberty." He was ready to teach us, long before Foucault, that
if we intend ever to resist our social and cultural fate, then we must first
see it for what it is, and that its form, ultimately, is the language we use
in learning to know ourselves. Language is also, however, the place
wherein we can most effectively register our dissent from our fate by
means of troping, punning, parodistic echoings, and by letting vernacular idioms play against revered terminologies. Through such resistances,
more than through directly political ones, sporadic evidences might
emerge of some truer self or "genius." Language is the only way to get
around the obstruction of language, and in his management of this
paradox Emerson shows why he is now and always essential.

I want to explore these matters further by considering the antagonism
in his writing between what he calls "genius" and the institutions
represented for him by the word "culture." How could "genius" propose

to survive in language? How could what he considered the true Emerson not get lost in his own writing, when, as he saw it, the language he must use to express himself already belongs to a cultural and a literary inheritance in which "genius" is presumably misshapen? How, with respect to culture or to literary textuality, does "genius" find itself, and, indeed, can it find itself in language at all?

Consider what he has to say, for instance, about cultural change, especially in an essay like "Circles," where he often means to *sound* as if changes can fairly easily occur. "The things which are dear to men at this hour," he writes, "are so on account of the ideas which have emerged on their mental horizon, and which cause the present order of things. . . . A new degree of culture would instantly revolutionize the entire system of human pursuits." Such a proposition could be expected from Nietzsche or from Foucault, but not in a tone at once so gingerly and confident—and so confused by its own geniality. The passage has a characteristically Emersonian blur or density. The tempo is polite and yet a little on edge, as it passes rapidly through quite subversive proposals, proposals which are hurried along against a number of inferable blockages. In a quite characteristic manner, Emerson's enthusiastic utterances come into being from the foreknowledge of their implausibility. Thus the excitement at the prospect of "a new degree of culture," with its instantaneous revolutionary results, has as a prior condition what he calls "the present order of things." But this "present order" has already been described in a phrase ("dear to men at this hour") which ought to preclude the emergence of any such "new degree," especially one which would immediately change "the entire system of human pursuits."

When a writer heads into perplexities of this kind, the reader should, I think, simply follow him there. Any paraphrasing effort at clarification, any tidying up in the interest of making more available what he is supposedly trying to say, only falsifies the experience we are being offered. Let the experience be perplexing. After all, if you follow a writer into the maze, you can at any time decide simply to leave him there, particularly if your confusions and impasses turn out to be caused by his incompetence or laziness or by his limp dependence on someone else's terminology.

But why, so often, do we decide to stay in the thick of it? For the reason, I suspect, that we discover that for the writer, too, language has at a crucial moment become an antagonist, and that this has happened by virtue, oddly enough, of the writer's keenest attentions to it. Thanks to his placations and seductions, language has finally had to reveal that it is devoted to someone or something else. At such moments the writer probably touches upon some nerve center in his culture; he discovers that his culture, as embodied in language, has all the while been *de-*forming him and what he is trying to say. Emerson frequently discovers this, and is then at his most attractive. The movements of his style let us know that, despite any difficulty, he intends to keep at it, to court the rebuffs of language in the hope of turning it, troping it, no matter how slightly, to his purposes. The infidelities of language—Santayana called them "the kindly infidelities"—in no way make him resentful or resigned. He pushes ahead into the next sentence—a detour, likely as not, from the one he has just written—confident that he is leaving behind a sign that will mark for the future yet another stroke, though it can never be a victory, against that fate embodied in the institutional force of words.

No wonder it is sometimes so extraordinarily hard to know how to take him. The uncertainty has only partly to do with his tendency to indulge in profuse illustrations or in shifts and substitutions of terms. Such vagaries are the very substance of his writing. Any greatly ambitious writer risks the same sort of slippage, and the only difference between Emerson and quasi-scientific writers like Darwin and Freud is that he more actively instigates the process. He wants to evade formulas even while indulging in them; he wants to say things, as Frost once remarked of his own writing, "that suggest formulae that won't formulate—that almost but don't quite formulate."

Emerson has a predilection for what he calls "abandonment."[1] "The way of life is wonderful," he says in "Circles." "It is by abandonment." In "The Poet" he speaks of "abandonment to the nature of things." The word helps explain his tendency to move out of any rhetorical position he has just occupied into another one, as if in hot pursuit of a truth elusive of more orderly verbal and syntactic inquiry. He sometimes gets almost audibly exasperated with any reader who might be satisfied only with what he has just said; he seems uncomfortable even with such concessions as he makes to the propriety of sentences and paragraphs, with their implicit commitment to ideas of duration, sequence, and logical progression. Obviously I am not describing what dreary criticism likes to call "verbal strategies," as if language were passively available to an author's already premeditated intentions. His, rather, is a design *upon* language and syntax—he is, in this, very like Shelley—an exploratory and never completed effort in which the reader is asked to join. He struggles, and he knows he struggles, within the mediations which consciousness creates for itself through language. "The Emersonian self . . . is voice and not text," Harold Bloom remarks, "which is why it must splinter and destroy its own texts."[2] By "voice" I take Bloom to mean the many voices that can be heard in the essays, each purporting to be Emerson. These, too, are splintered and blurred. The language that issues from these voices refers us not to a consistently structured moral or psychological self; the voices exist, rather, on the periphery of such a self, wondering what it might be like, playing with its possibilities, joking with and about it. In a nice little witticism that unites this way of writing with the idioms of everyday life, Thoreau proposes in *Walden* to be "beside" himself "in a sane way," or, as Whitman phrases it, "both in and out of the game and watching and wondering at it."

These reflections on the destiny of writing and reading point directly toward that aspect of individualism called "genius." "Genius" is commonly assumed to involve a mastery of the codes and signs by which a culture structures itself. It therefore also offers a clue to any latently subversive content that these codes and signs might have accumulated during their long passage through many histories. Marvell's punning is an example of this, as is Thoreau's; so, too, is Shakespeare's troping of words within different contexts. Shakespeare manages, for example, to establish discreetly hidden linkages between characters otherwise wholly different, like Falstaff and Bolingbroke in *Henry IV, Part 1*. Both are called "portly," one for a fat gut, the other for a swelled head; one is a glutton for sack, the other for power and expropriated inheritance. Both of them are thieves, one on the king's highway, the other of his crown. Taken together they constitute a surreptitious indictment of an insatiable appetite let loose at all levels of society as England passed from the medieval into the Elizabethan-capitalist period.

By such examples I want to suggest that when "genius" finds itself in language, the result can be a productive multiplication, a thickening of possibilities. These are by way of a challenge to those clarifications of purpose and design which are essential to public and institutional life —and which those institutions insist on discovering in literature. For "genius" to find itself in a thicket does not, however, sufficiently complete its task. If it creates densities, it also, and as a consequence, creates something nearly the reverse: an idealization of simplicity, as in Wordsworth, or of transparency, as in Emerson. Remember that Wordsworth and Emerson associate "genius" not with writing merely, but with what we have heard them call the "power" available to all human beings, many of whom do not write or read. The discovery that even literary "genius" must negotiate and connive with language, no matter how productively, that even "genius" cannot clarify itself—this discovery brings with it an acknowledgment that there may be a need for cultural changes of great magnitude, changes, for example, that would bring about an end to man as that figure is now represented to us. Such acknowledgments will most profoundly occur to someone who, in the act of writing and reading, experiences the sloth and intractability of the languages which the culture makes most readily available to him but which he must, in the effort to mean what he wants to mean, continually reshape.

On the issue of cultural reformation, Emerson has already confronted problems whose exposure is nowadays credited to his admirer Nietzsche and, after him, to Foucault. Nietzsche speaks to these problems, for instance, when he wants both to affirm and to deny the burdens of historical consciousness, as does Foucault when he concludes that man came into being, came to knowledge of himself, by virtue of previous discursive formations whose source is not determinable and whose power is therefore to be resisted only indirectly. Can this power be resisted at all? That is an inevitable and probably unanswerable question. If it is assumed that life is wholly subordinated to language systems, then they can be resisted only through manipulations *within* the discourse already believed to be utterly ubiquitous and, in its effects, claustrophobic. So much so that it must wholly determine the self-knowledge, the self-representation, and the affiliations even of those who propose to elude these things. Arguing in the first volume of *The History of Sexuality* that "it is in discourse that power and knowledge are joined together," Foucault, for instance, proposes, apropos homosexuality, that:

There is no question that the appearance in nineteenth-century psychiatry, jurisprudence, and literature of a whole series of discourses on the species and subspecies of homosexuality, inversion, pederasty, and "psychic hermaphrodism" made possible a strong advance of social controls into this area of "perversity"; but it also made possible the formation of a "reverse" discourse: homosexuality began to speak in its own behalf, to demand that its legitimacy or "naturality" be acknowledged, often in the same vocabulary, using the same categories by which it was medically disqualified.

Resistance and the possibility of reform find a voice, in this view, only after, and by virtue of, submissive compliance. A similarly dispiriting conclusion can be inferred from Emerson, but it never becomes for him, as it does for Foucault, the incentive for proposals to do away altogether with the idea of the human. Emerson's might be called an American form of alienation in which, as George Kateb puts it in his study of Hannah Arendt, "the moral unit . . . is the individual, not humanity or masses of people heaped together traumatically. The individual is the democratic individual, not some unconditioned and unsituated ghost." Thus imagined, the self is "loose fitting," indifferent to social identification, and capable of that "doubleness" which makes it possible to be inside and outside society all at once, inside and outside the self. The self becomes a form of the Other. Thus, Emerson will often use words evocative of the enterprise of American capitalism, like "work" or "build," in describing enterprises of the human spirit for which the business ethic has little patience. It is sometimes mistakenly assumed that he is promoting not the soul but the idea of property, when he is instead conducting a raid on the opposition party of Property, stealing its language for purposes it finds ulterior. His own position, within this complex operation, is candidly explained in "New England Reformers":

It is handsomer to remain in the establishment better than the establishment, and conduct that in the best manner, than to make a sally against evil by some single improvement, without supporting it by a total regeneration. Do not be so vain of your one objection. Do you think there is only one? . . . Do you complain of the laws of Property? It is a pedantry to give such importance to them. Can we not play the game of life with these counters, as well as with those; in the institution of property as well as out of it. . . . No one gives the impression of superiority to the institution, which he must give who will reform it. It makes no difference what you say: you must make me feel that you are aloof from it; by your natural and super-natural advantages, do easily see to the end of it,— do see how man can do without it.

To put Foucault next to Emerson is a provocative way of reiterating that Emerson's writing makes claims upon us to which we have not yet sufficiently responded. Particularly as it explores the question of genius, the writing discovers the necessity and the enormous difficulty of cultural reformation. It continually struggles with its own resources. Emerson refuses to separate the problem of language from the problem of culture or either of these from the troubled relation of "genius" to culture, especially as it embodies itself in written texts. Instead, he willingly submits to the contradictions and questions that follow when all of these are put into active conjunction. For example, in the passage I have quoted from "Circles" about "the present order of things," what is the inferable source for any "new degree of culture"? And how, if that source is located in individual "genius," does it make its way to the center of any "mental horizon"? Who or what authorizes its centrality? Even if the promulgation of some "new degree of culture" is assumed, how could it dislodge or encircle the present one, especially when, as Emerson admits, it is the present "order of things" that allows man to make sense of the world, to find a home in it? And, if, as he further claims in "Circles," "history and the state of the world at any one time [are] directly dependent on the intellectual classification then existing in the minds of men," it is hard to see how any individual, except vaguely or intermittently, could manage even to recognize those facts which necessitate or accompany "a new order of things," a new "circle" or discursive formation.

Any proposal for cultural reformation creates such imponderables as these. Emerson's efforts to negotiate among them depend heavily on his use of the term "genius," and help account, too, for those effusions, fractures, and mobilities in his writing which are for me testimony to his own "genius." Instead of being a solution to the problem of language, "genius" is itself confounded by language. What he calls the "influx of divinity into the world" does not and cannot reach us except by words, with their associated histories, their ties to "things" already in place from whose influence "genius" might commonly be supposed to free us. "Genius," that is, is itself interrogated by "the present order of things"; it cannot simply or on its own move to the "center" of the horizon; indeed it can go unrecognized, be put to one side, made to disappear. "When the great God lets loose a thinker on this planet," Emerson says, "then all things are at risk"—including, it should be added, the "thinker." When "genius" enters history, when it articulates itself in the effort to expand or embrace existing "circles," it thereby submits to the distortions that are a precondition, apparently, of its being seen or heard at all. Any "circle" produced by an act of "genius" soon begins, like the ones that precede it, "to solidify and hem in the life."

Carrying on against these odds, it is not surprising that when Emerson praises specific examples of "genius," especially historically credited ones, his remarks are frequently edged with a flickering and disconcerting sarcasm. A telling instance occurs in "Experience," when he refers to that great example of "an influx of divinity" or "genius," namely Jesus, a figure who was great, according to Keats, partly because he did *not* write. As it is read and re-read, the passage becomes increasingly slithery; you begin to hear in the voice the pressure of something wanting to be articulated but at odds with what is being more directly said. One can sense Emerson's exasperation with any cultural *placement* of genius, even in Jesus:

People forget that it is the eye which makes the horizon, and the rounding mind's eye which makes this or that man a type or representative of humanity with the name of hero or saint. Jesus the "providential man," is a good man on whom many people are agreed that these optical laws shall take effect. By love on one part, and by forbearance to press objection on the other part, it is for a time settled, that we will look at him in the centre of the horizon, and ascribe to him the properties that will attach to any man so seen. But the longest love or aversion has a speedy term. The great and crescive self, rooted in absolute nature, supplants all relative existence, and ruins the kingdom of mortal friendship and love.

Time and again his approbations of figures like Jesus are preyed upon by critical aloofness about the process by which "genius" gets recognized within (and appropriated by) cultural hierarchies. Though Jesus is not put into a list with several others, which is Emerson's usual way of modifying enthusiasm for anyone in particular, the claim that he is the "providential man" is accompanied by the curious suggestion that "the type of humanity" who is hero or saint is actually only the beneficiary of "the name hero or saint," and that even Jesus was perceived as "the providential man" not because of indisputable merit, but because "many people [were] agreed that these optical laws shall take effect." It is as if while being in earnest with us and himself, Emerson is plagued by afterthoughts and misgivings generated by his own language as it takes shape. Since he has so often insisted that any man may aspire to be Jesus, it is perhaps incumbent on him to say that this "type" of humanity may be seen in "this or that man." But why and how? The workings of such "optical laws" may, for example, be conditioned by special interests, so that not all but only "many men agreed" on Jesus. If everyone is called, how are the very few chosen, unless the choice proceeds from local historical necessity? And if to be chosen means that you are convenient to necessity, then what is the relative importance, if any, of the personal attributes of "genius"? How is "genius" kept from being sullied by its need to shape itself (if it is to be recognized at all) into particular "circles"? At issue, then, is not Emerson's idea of "genius," or any of his ideas in the abstract, but rather the career, the status, the plight of the term as it twists itself into time and history. What happens to "genius" as it tries—this is the central question—to transmit itself to later times through the medium of language?

It is this—the necessary textuality of "genius"—which puts immense strain on Emerson's discourse. There is, for instance, something like surly, even competitive resentment in his going on to say of Jesus that "by love on one part and by forbearance to press objection on the other part, it is for a time settled, that we look at him in the centre of the horizon, and ascribe to him the properties that will attach to any man so seen." This kind of talk is familiar enough if translated into formulaic Emerson: do not, he keeps telling us, be overawed by cultural tradition. What is apt to be less familiar is the derisive undertone—"it is for a time settled," "forbearance to press objections," "we will look at him" (as if someone else had already placed him there), and we will "ascribe" virtues, which implies that the same virtues might accrue to "any man so seen" or emplaced.

And yet, Emerson's implicit disenchantment, his near contempt for the forms of cultural and historical ascription, is never allowed fully to assert itself, and is immediately deflected in a characteristic maneuver by which he reaffirms the value of that same human power whose practices have just provoked his skepticism. His rather disdainful undertone gives way to an ecstatic evocation of "the great and crescive self" which ruins the kingdoms of mortal friendship and love." The transition is accomplished, however, by the innocuous linking remark that "the longest love or aversion has a speedy term." Jesus does not stay forever at "the centre of the horizon," but neither, he suggests, do our affectionate attachments, which he cleverly gives a statutory or institutional weight by calling them "kingdoms." Lest the reader be flattered by such glamorous excuses for his own affiliations, he should notice that "the order of things" is being manipulated here merely in Emerson's tactical interests. He wishes to evade, or at least not to push further into, the remarkable suggestion that all cultural artifacts which achieve historical celebrity, all persons who attain the title of "genius," all works which can be called "classic," are products not so much of the influx of God or Intellect or Omniscience or Soul as of the prior needs of what Hawthorne calls "artificial system."

Precisely at the point when "genius" enters history, when it offers itself as a text, it becomes for Emerson blurred or ensnared. He finds this even truer of writers than of those he calls providential people who do not write at all, like Jesus or Socrates, and this helps account for the crankiness of some of his literary judgments. "When we adhere to the ideal of the poet," he says in "The Poet," "we have our difficulties even with Milton and Homer. Milton is too literary, and Homer too literal and historical." Shakespeare and Dante are, he grants, "geniuses," and while he knows this by virtue of their work as it has been written, transcribed, and read, the implication of his larger position is that their "genius" is in fact made less accessible by their writing and by any reading of it. In appreciating a writer of "genius," a reader of "genius" is not required. Nor, for that matter, is any sustained act of reading. "The genius is a genius by the first look he casts on any objects," as he says in his essay "Montaigne." "His thought has dissolved the works of art and nature into their causes, so that the works appear heavy and faulty."

Apparently we are to imagine a criticism which finds genius only after the demolition of texts, the disappearance of writing, the collapse into itself of the historicity of composition. This idea, to most people, seems absurd, and Emerson's interpreters tend to deal with it by explaining that he really does not mean what he is saying. They often try to release his terminology from any of the binds into which it puts itself, so that "man," "reader," and "poet" are allowed at difficult junctures to stand duty for one another, as would the "work of art" for "natural objects." But while this is loyal to Emerson's theory of tropes, it is also a way of not facing up to those radical challenges and contradictions which are evident in his work, not just in the later essays, but wherever we choose to look. In his essay "Art," for example, he means both to approximate a position Eliot will take in "Tradition and the Individual Talent" and to dismiss all works of art as "hypocritical rubbish" unless they "open your eyes to the masteries of eternal art." Similarly, when he grants that the artist functions within "the thought amidst which he grew" and which "he cannot avoid or wipe out of his work," he wants still to maintain that "the reference of all production [is] at last"—he likes his "at lasts"—"to aboriginal Power." It is this "Power," in turn, which explains "the traits common to all works of the highest art—that they are universally intelligible; that they restore to us the simplest states of mind." How any work of "genius," especially in language, can possibly be "universally intelligible," leaving aside the issue of literacy, is a question to which there is no satisfactory answer, and it is not surprising that he offers so few examples of literary "art" in the essay. The problem is not resolved by his saying in "The Poet" that "the man is only half himself, the other half is his expression," or that "every man should be so much an artist that he could report in conversation what had befallen him," especially since he says in "The Over-Soul" that "the soul answers never by words," and that "an answer in words is delusive," and, in "Intellect," that "silence is a solvent that destroys personality, and gives us leave to be great and universal."

To make art "universally intelligible" would require the disappearance of the media which give art its existence as a public event. It would yield to a transparency through which reader and writer, viewer and painter would share in the "executant power," as Wordsworth calls it, that still makes its ghostly transits through the work of art. The ideal reader of literature might then be supremely competent or of no competence whatever, a person of "simple tastes and susceptibility to all the great human influences" which "overpower the accidents of local and special culture" ("Art"). We are thus left with the peculiar prospect that works of "genius" may enhance and create human life by the degree to which they make themselves inconspicuous. A particularly engaging example, in the essay "Art," describes, if that is the right word, an experience in Rome:

When I came at last to Rome, and saw with eyes the pictures, I found that genius left to novices the gay and fantastic and ostentatious, and itself pierced directly to the simple and true; that it was familiar and sincere; that it was the old, eternal fact I had met already in so many forms,—unto which I lived, that it was the plain *you and me* I knew so well,—had left at home in so many conversations.

This "plain *you and me*" that shouts at us in italics, what is to be said of it? "Seen with eyes" (is there another way of seeing them?), can they really be the same "plain *you and me*" he had "left at home in so many conversations," especially when "the soul never answers with words"? Is it not more likely that "plain *you and me*" resembles the friends he imagines for himself in the essay "Friendship," "friends" with whom he prefers *not* to have real talk, but rather what he calls "this evanescent conversation"? "I will receive from them, not what they have, but what they are," is how he oddly puts it.

To bring the problem of representation closer to the question of

"genius," the reader needs to know from other sources that "plain *you
and me*" are meant to be joined not on "the thread of talent" ("talent
makes counterfeit ties," he warns us in "Montaigne"), but on "the
thread" of "genius" (which "makes real ones"). "Talent," according to
the 1843 *Journals*, "is applicability. A human body, an animal, is an
applicability," but "the Life, the Soul, is Genius." Not for him, then,
the colorful surface, "the figures of exaggeration." Instead, like the
painters of genius whose work he sees in Rome, he will "pierce directly"
to some kind of pentimento beneath the visible surface of the paint, or
he will let some "aboriginal Power" emerge through the color, dissolving
as it does so the extravagance, the animal figures, the "applicable"
representations of the human. What comes through to him as he stands
there in Rome or sits there writing in Concord is not the image of a
human figure but the images of a "stroke," a "stroke" as of the brush
or of the pen as it makes the figure. We are left to suppose that in the
painting he sees an inscription or a hieroglyph, as John Irwin might put
it,[3] emanating from some "gigantic hand" which guides the hand of the
artist. "The whole extant product of the plastic arts," he writes in "Art,"
"has herein its highest value, *as history;* as a stroke drawn in the portrait
of that fate, perfect and beautiful, according to whose ordinations all
beings advance to their beatitude." The product of art is not the work
you read or look at, much less the animal figures it tries to represent;
instead, it is the inferable "stroke" which, by its own forever unsatisfied
anticipations, at once creates, passes through, and banishes the solidified
aspects of the work.

"The transparent eyeball" is an example of such a "stroke" both as
an occurrence in life and as an occurrence in writing. It has also notoriously resisted interpretive rendering, any translation into "applicability."[4] As a figure it epitomizes Emerson's anatomy of man at the
moment when he is possessed by "genius," when he is in it and it is in
him. It is only one of many related instances, however, where there is
a precipitation in the writing which paradoxically is the sign that "genius" is to emerge as a figure of radiant clarity, much as revelation has
traditionally signaled itself by obscurity. In life, however, such moments
are few, and Emerson is especially sardonic if the promised advent of
"genius" in the Concord area turns into something less, as when in the

Journals he discovers that "Alcott is a tedious archangel" who "can as little as any man separate his drivelling from his divining," or when, in "The Poet," in a possible comment on the "transparent eyeball" passage, he comically describes a local versifier as "this winged man" who instead of "carrying me into the heavens," takes me "like a fowl or a flying fish, a little way from the ground or the water." The day he and the world truly "discover a poet," he adds, "shall be better than my birthday: then I became an animal: now I am invited into the science of the real."

An inquiry could be made, though not here, into some tortured affiliation between Emerson, in the moods I am describing, and some later figures mentioned sympathetically in *A Pluralistic Universe* by William James. Referring first to the Mills, James and John Stuart (presumably for the latter's entry called "Mental Chemistry" in *A System of Logic*), and to Wilhelm Wundt's "psychic synthesis," James goes on to list such writers as "Spencer, Taine, Fiske, Barratt and Clifford [who] had promoted a great evolutionary theory in which, in the absence of souls, selves, and other principles of unity, primordial units of mind-stuff or mind-dust were represented as summing themselves together in successive stages of compounding and re-compounding, and thus engendering our higher and more complex states of mind." These, like the still later "genetic codes," are secularized versions of the oversoul, and Emerson is to me often most intriguing when he proposes a structure for man that reduces his animal and sentimental features to a field of energy wherein, as he puts it in the *Journals* for November 1862, he would speak "in the interest of no man & no party, but simply as a geometer of his forces."

THE PROBLEM FOR CRITICISM

EMERSON'S CONSTANT TROPING of himself, from poet to farmer, from transparent eyeball to "a geometer of forces," is a way of suggesting that any work a man does, any stance he honestly assumes, may offer a momentary, partial glimpse of his potential for "genius." And even this will be denied us if, instead of emulating the *actions* prompted by examples of genius, we merely admire what it has in the past already produced. Recall that in "The Over-Soul" he advises that "the best communication to our mind," by a great poet, "is to teach us to despise all he has done." This reluctance to let "genius" take a permanently measurable form in language or in any sort of text, literary or otherwise, has made Emerson largely incompatible with critical and interpretive practice in and, especially, outside the academy. Why is it that even those who, like me, think of him, in William James's phrase, as "the divine Emerson," and who would endorse what he says about "genius" and about language, find it nearly impossible to conduct a critical argument that fully satisfies his notions of how writing ideally gets written, and how it ideally ought to be read? One obvious reason is that for him writing and reading never occur under ideal circumstances; they are always conditioned by the historical and institutional factors under which they proceed.

There are contradictions in Emerson between his optative, his desiring theories of "genius," and his worldly recognitions of the restrictive circles imposed by any available discourse. These contradictions are not resolved by his rhetorical insistence that the circles can be broken, especially since the result is then only a new circle which will ultimately hem in life. Emerson is quite disconcertingly mistrustful of the value of human culture as it has so far evolved. Why would we read works of reputed "genius," much less anything else that lacks an immediately utilitarian value, if the reason for doing so is only that we may "despise" them? Probably he means to suggest that the work is good only for the exercise it affords our faculties while we read it. But if so, then how are the benefits of works of "genius" ever to be transformed from individual experiences of reading into those values presumably beneficial to the commonwealth, even his own Commonwealth of Massachusetts? These questions are made inevitable by the circle of discourse within which Emerson himself wrote and within which he necessarily is read, and they suggest how close he comes to proposing that literary culture, including the Western idea of man as the object of its concern, gets in the way of true self-realization. Once again he anticipates Nietzsche and Foucault while proposing an alternative to the latter's incipient hopelessness. Through his concept of "genius" he manages to hold onto an idea of the self, even though it is a self far more shadowy than his rhetoric of individualism has led people to suppose. The self in Emerson is not an entity, not even a function; it is an intimation of presence, and it comes upon us out of the very act by which the self tries to elude definition.

Understandably, then, Emerson has not lent himself to any of the institutional forms of criticism in the last, or in this, century. The reasons take on a particular interest, however, if we compare him, more fully than I have so far managed to do, to that other massive figure of the nineteenth century, the source and sustenance of a still prevailing humanistic thrust in Anglo-American criticism, Matthew Arnold. Why, again, did Arnold and not Emerson become the dominant figure in literary-cultural criticism in America up to the present moment? (I mean Arnold as he has been generally understood, not the Arnold made more congenial to contemporary theory by some recent revaluations.) Arnold's predominance probably has something to do with the slow, begrudging acceptance of American literature as a fit subject for study in colleges and universities. But of much greater importance are stubborn convictions that language exists as a servitor to established ideas of the self, and, as a result, that a fairly direct relation can be assumed between some version of that self and any voice located in a literary text. Where language proves nonetheless resistant to clarity, or where narrative appears to disperse or fracture expectations, then criticism has chosen to take these difficulties not as real in themselves, but only as a reluctant and nostalgic deviation from some prior and more authoritative form. The job of criticism under these circumstances thus becomes fairly simple: it is to make these deviations accord with humanistic assumptions about the self, and with the self's presumed desire to exist and to be redeemed in ways already paradigmatically familiar. Allowance is made, that is, for fracturings, dislocations, and like manner of literary behavior, but these are taken as a communication of longings for lost continuities; Molly Bloom's soliloquy in *Ulysses* makes perfect sense, a renowned Joycean once assured me, if you put in the punctuation which Joyce left out. Anglo-American criticism has in large part striven to perpetuate the cultural traditions which Emerson chose to write against, and his oppositions extended well beyond that relatively benign version of the anxiety of influence which he proposes in the essay "Intellect." "Take thankfully and heartily all they can give," he remarks of writers of genius. "Exhaust them, wrestle with them, let them not go until their blessing be won, and, after a short season, the dismay will be overpast, the excess of influence withdrawn, and they will be no longer an alarming meteor, but one more bright star shining serenely in your heaven, and blending its light with all your day."

This sort of advice can be followed, though even here, established academic criticism has until quite recently been mostly hostile to its effective practice. But it is advice from a writer who, as we have seen, more frequently recommends practices that cannot be performed at all. If, for example, you set out with Emerson's help to discover the evidence of "genius" in a text, you would quickly find that the text had to surrender its wording and become in some way volatile. "Criticism," to recall a remarkable passage in the *Journals* for May 18, 1840, "must be transcendental, that is, must consider literature ephemeral & easily entertain the supposition of its entire disappearance." Here, as everywhere, Emerson means to detextualize, to dehistoricize, to un-authorize "genius," leaving in place only an activity, and a barely traceable one at that.

It is this phenomenon—"genius" as an activity, an influx, a movement, "genius" as energy—that has always, with or without Emerson, posed problems for humanistic criticism and for the culture it looks to for support. As a phenomenon of energy, "genius" in Emerson lays waste to generally perceived humanistic images of authorial and therefore of individual human purpose and intent. "Genius" is antithetical to the proposition that "all human values, all human emotions, are of social growth if not of social origin . . . [and that] much of what man does for himself depends upon what society allows him to do." This is a remark by Lionel Trilling in his study of Arnold, though any of Trilling's subsequent works would offer a comparable illustration. Even in its stylistic deportment, it illustrates why Trilling became the most self-consciously urbane of the American successors to Arnold, and why he tried to cultivate "a mind never entirely his own," to recall Blackmur's characterization of it, "a mind always deliberately to some extent what he understands to be the mind of society, and also a mind always deliberately to some extent the mind of the old European society taken as corrective and as prophecy."[5]

The issue is not whether you should "cultivate . . . the mind of the old European society," of which Emerson wrote with ambivalent yearning, but how you set about to do so. Principally, of course, you immerse yourself in the texts it has produced. Humanistic criticism has always been suspicious of "genius" as a possibly disruptive force, a force that brings into question even the idea of authorship. And yet it has all the while found the products of "genius"—the writing, the texts, and what Arnold called "touchstones"—indispensable to its larger cultural purposes, the purposes which the texts are continually being reinterpreted to serve. By contrast, Emerson implies that by its very submission to written form, genius is repressed and deformed even before it is further adulterated by institutions of reading.

To emphasize how antithetical is the Emersonian to any Arnoldian aesthetic, consider the famous preface of 1869 to *Culture and Anarchy:* "The whole scope of the essay is to recommend culture as the great help out of our present difficulties; culture being a pursuit of our total perfection by means of getting to know, on all the matters which most concern us, the best which has been thought and said in the world." Culture may be "the pursuit of our total perfection," but it is being recommended at the same time for reasons more immediately practical ("the great help out of our present difficulties"). And while in "The Function of Criticism at the Present Time" (1864), criticism is defined as "a disinterested endeavour to learn and propagate the best that is known and thought in the world," it gets to sound somewhat less "disinterested" when, four years later, we are asked to know the "best" rather more selectively ("on all matters that most concern us"). A criticism that proposes to find in literature things "to know," "to learn," "to propagate," has already decided that literature is not to "flow," as Emerson would have it, but to "freeze" ("The Poet"), a kind of permanent treasure trove out of which "thoughts" and "sayings" and ideas might be lifted, according to the varying preferences of successive ages and the cultural needs of various groups.

Consider, in contrast, a few comparatively unfamiliar aphorisms of Emerson, all of them filled with a sense of the vehicular, transitive, mobile nature of "something" passing through writing. This, from the *Journals* for 1835, "The truest state of mind rested in becomes false"; or this from the *Journals* for 1830, "Genius . . . finds its end in the means"; or this, from "The Poet," "Art is the path of the creator to his work"; or this, "An imaginative book renders us much more service at first by stimulating us through its tropes, than afterward, when we arrive at the precise sense of the author" (though nowhere does he suggest that this "precise sense" can ever be reached). Or, finally, in the essay on "Plato," this: "The experience of poetic creativeness . . . is not found in staying at home, nor yet in travelling, but in transitions from one to the other, which must therefore be adroitly managed to present as much transitional surface as possible."

In our own "present order of things" it would, I think, be impossible to plan either a literary history or a course of study which would account for the initial "stimulation" offered by tropes or by the movements on a text's "transitional surface." And the difficulty of doing so attests to the chasm which has always separated literary history or pedagogy from the moment by moment experience of reading. "Genius," and not only as it is conceived by Emerson, disrupts the prevalent humanistic design of—and upon—literature.

The quality of debate on these issues is now so coarse, and the chance of being misunderstood so likely, that I want to clarify my position a little more carefully. I think that a truly disinterested effort to trace the workings of "genius" in literature, no less than in the musical structures of Bach, would severely challenge, and in many instances reveal as a mere come-on or flirtation, the humanistic intentions and values commonly ascribed to the arts. At the same time it would be senseless to deny or in any way begrudge the existence in literature, or other artistic forms, of traditional humanisms. Humanism is not, after all, merely a school of criticism; it is, in its many variations, a way of believing in the world, of finding how life might offer some moments of clarification and purpose, and most works of literature, for obvious historical reasons, are compelled to represent it. I would argue, however, that humanistic representation in, say, a novel by Dickens or a play by Shakespeare, a poem by Wordsworth or Frost or Stevens, is not the likely purpose of the work but is instead part of its process, its operation, its method.

Humanism often plays the straight man to performative "genius"; it is the material which genius works in, and not necessarily for. Emerson says repeatedly of "genius" what he says of the soul in "Self-Reliance": "This one fact the world hates, that the soul *becomes;* for that for ever degrades the past, turns all riches to poverty, all reputation to a shame, confounds the saint with the rogue, shoves Jesus and Judas equally aside." To focus on performance or on the exercises of troping will therefore seem a trivialization of literature only to politicians of high culture for whom taking literature seriously consists in finding how it might help us "out of our present difficulties."

Politics cannot be considered extraneous to these matters, since criticism is very often covertly or unconsciously political in its efforts to scramble the power of "genius," to make it conform. Criticism customarily assigns the effects of "genius" to various moral or semiotic, numerological or historical functions. In opposing such assignments, Emerson insists on the utter indifference of "genius" to them, its indifference to standards of good and evil, its refusal to participate even in the assumption absolutely central to humanistic interpretation and its continuities: namely, that some subjects are necessarily of greater magnitude than others. In this regard, it would be instructive, he tells us in "Experience," to watch what might be called a "circle" in action: "a kitten chasing so prettily her own tail."

In elaborating this appealing suggestion he again attacks, to recall the discussion of the paintings at Rome, "the gay and fantastic and ostentatious" and carries forward the implications that when performance is "simple and true," it is by nature also solitary:

Do you see that kitten chasing so prettily her own tail? If you could look with her eyes, you might see her surrounded with hundreds of figures performing complex dramas, with tragic and comic issues, long conversations, many characters, many ups and downs of fate,—and meantime it is only puss and her tail. How long before our masquerade will end its noise of tambourines, laughter and shouting, and we shall find it was a solitary performance?—A subject and an object,—it takes so much to make the galvanic circuit complete, but magnitude adds nothing. What imports it whether it is Kepler and the sphere; Columbus and America; a reader and his book; or puss with her tail?

"Genius" in Emerson is linked to an awesome indifference to preferences which conventional representations are likely to have created in the reader, even while it may be using these very preferences as the materials on which it works its transformations. In this passage, the metaphors combine in a way that reiterates the connections he frequently makes among reading a book, scientific inquiry, geographical explorations into the unknown, and the comfortingly dense familiarity that is the substance, at times, of domestic conversation, including the soliloquies and conversations of our cats. Moral strictures are not much help in reading any of these, nor is any of them usually initiated by moral imperatives. It is this fact which especially disappoints the votaries of talent, who are committed to the already known, the already re-presented.

A particularly arresting instance of Emerson's astringent sense of things occurs just before "puss and her tail," in a brief discussion of murder. "Murder," he remarks, is not a crime to the intellect, "for there is no crime to the intellect." He means "intellect constructive," which, as he says in the essay "Intellect," "we properly designate by the word Genius," and he calls it "constructive" because it produces systems, designs, poems, sentences like his own. To this "intellect," "the world is a problem in mathematics or the science of quantity, and it leaves out praise or blame and all weak emotion." Thus, murder is susceptible less to moral than to some quantitative or geometric measure of always evolving human possibility. It is a factor in what Henry James, while discussing his responsibilities to his characters, calls "compositional resource." For Emerson, the reading of life or of art is not a search for morally stabilizing moments or summary, but for infusions and diffusions of energy, for that constant redistribution of forces called troping, including the troping of the self.

His is a lonely genius, as he acknowledges at a later moment, whose poignancy has already been noted:

And yet is the God the native of these bleak rocks. That need makes in morals the capital virtue of self-trust. We must hold hard to this poverty, however scandalous, and by more vigorous self-recoveries, after the sallies of action, possess our axis more firmly. The life of truth is cold, and so far mournful; but it is not the slave of tears, contritions, and perturbations ("Experience").

All active "genius" is an instance of "self-reliance" but not all self-reliance is an instance of "genius." Indeed, the exercise of "genius" puts self-reliance not just continually but continuously at risk, as it moves within the unrelenting, the constantly disconcerting and distorting pressures of cultural discourses. That is why Emerson endows "genius" with so strong a counter power of effacement, transparency, reduction, all of which dangerously consort with idealizations of silence, of flowers born to blush unseen. That is why, too, it is inadvisable to press him too hard for a working definition of "genius." The term is essential to him, and to all of us, not because it means this or that, or because it puts "talent" in its place. It is an essential word, as I said at the beginning, for the very reason that it is vague and can stand for a dream of human power and mastery that is a challenge to other Gods. People have always been obsessed with "genius" for reasons that are in every sense good ones. No matter what its source, no matter how supremely human or strangely non-human it might be thought, it has had results ascribed to it which truly excite people about the possibilities of human life. Ideally, the ideas of the "human" and of "genius" are tolerant and wary of their mutual incursions, and the task set by Emerson (and no less by Shakespeare or Melville) is to prevent one from usurping the other, in what Emerson derisively calls "manipular efforts to realize the world of thought." The proper destiny of "genius" and of the "human" is to claim the other as a field of resisted and never-to-be completed action. The two words belong to that syntax of possibility which moves with serial grandeur through and beyond the last sentence of "Experience": "The true romance which the world exists to realize, will be the transformation of genius into practical power."

It is impossible to say what this transformation would mean, or how in our present state we would even be able to recognize it. We would have to be there already, in a future that seems to recede as we approach it, thanks to Emerson's accumulated terms of postponement. We cannot project ourselves into this future since in the present we are already fractured into occupations and prejudices; even the language we would use to describe such a future is, as Emerson would have it, flawed and partial. It is therefore appropriate that the sentence makes no mention of human beings at all; it is "the world" that exists to realize this "true romance." We are left, instead, by the immediately preceding sentence, in "the solitude" to which "every man is always returning"; there to have "revelations" which can be carried, it is said, into "new worlds." A "revelation" is, alas, far short of a "transformation"; it is something that might occur for only a moment in our present condition. All we can do to the world or about the world is to get to "work," in the special sense in which he uses that term. "Do your work, and I shall know you," he says in "Self-Reliance"; "Do your thing," was the way he put it earlier in the *Journals* (1835), "and I shall know you." "Work" is a way to confront the essential facts of existence and to discover in doing so the power of human desire which turns facts into mythologies and mythologies into facts. There is a charming instance of this in the section of *Nature* called "Commodity," where he remarks that man "no longer waits for favoring gales, but by means of steam, he realizes the fable of Aeolus's bag, and carries the two and thirty winds in the boiler of his boat." Typically, he chooses an example which combines poetry and industry, an example, too, in which transport is an aspect of transformation and of transition from one state to another. Criticism is enjoined by him not to stop or slow this perpetual process in the hope of some sort of clarity or extractable wisdom. Language must conform not to any God of tradition but to the still emergent "genius" of the race. And yet if Emerson must admit in "The Poet" that "I look in vain for the poet whom I describe," we need not wonder that we look mostly in vain for such a criticism as he proposes.

Chapter 2

MODERNISM AND ITS
DIFFICULTIES

THE CHARACTERISTICS and location of literary modernism, even its claims to existence, are nowadays pretty much up for grabs. What was modernism? what is it? when did it happen? can it be said ever to have happened? is it possibly no more than an aspect of literature that every now and then comes to the surface? It is the privilege of any people at any time in history to claim that they are living in the "modern age," in the sense of the Latin *modo*, just now or lately, and works that by any prevailing standards prove to be unconventional or especially difficult have been called "modernist" since at least the seventeenth century. Features thought to be unique to twentieth-century literary modernism are to be found, often with corresponding evidences of cultural disenchantment, nearly everywhere in English literature. In many respects, Spenser's *The Shepheardes Calender* is a modernist work par excellence; so, in other respects, is Marvell's "Upon Appleton House" or Burton's *Anatomy of Melancholy.* And there are still other arguments against thinking of modernism as something exclusive to this century, especially in view of what is said in this book about Emerson and those who have taken their lead from him. Feelings associated with modernism—a mosaic compounded of nostalgia, belatedness, cultural burden, and a distrust of language—are, from an Emersonian perspective, part of the human condition itself, so that what has gotten arrogated to recent times can be said to belong to any period. Emerson evokes some still earlier condition when, as mythology would have it, "we lived in what we saw," but history has no record of it, and if things seem since then to have gotten worse, that is only because they have always been worse.

Such nostalgia as can be credited to Emerson derives from his larger, unrelenting obsession with language, an obsession that shaped his opinions about nearly everything else. He implies that language is both the gift of consciousness and its exacting price, and that because of it we live not in a natural but in a conventional, and therefore artificial, relation to the world and to ourselves. This could be a highly pessimistic diagnosis were it not transformed by him—not merely in theory but by virtue of his own rapid shifts and transitions and tropings of language —into an expectant one. "Our American literature and spiritual history," he writes in "The Transcendentalist," "are, we confess, in the optative mood." Skepticism becomes the source of his optimistic postponements into the future. If, since the Fall, we suspect our instruments of perception and expression, then it is absurd to trust in the past more than in ourselves as we move out of the present. We are as well or as ill equipped to discover reality, he suggests, as any ancestors were, and to live forever on the edge of doubt is to live also, in Stevens's words, "unsponsored," "free," on the edge of expectation, troping burden into hope. Emerson refused to be a modernist for many reasons, and one of them is that he never suggests that his intuition of loss also marks its historic or recorded beginning. By his calculations, the starting date for modernism would be the Garden of Eden.

Nonetheless, even if one is persuaded of Emerson's position, it still makes sense, I think, to agree with those who argue that modernism is a literary phenomenon of fairly recent date. At issue is not the validity of the claim so much as the enormous cultural influence acquired and exercised by it. If enough people believe in an idea, then it exists. More than anyone else, T. S. Eliot secured a place for literary modernism in Anglo-American culture, to the point where Saul Bellow later referred, rather querulously, to "the waste-land ethos." So that while it seems to be the case that certain feelings of loss, anxiety, burden, and doubt are inherent to the human condition, this is less important, and by any odds less interesting, than the evidence that for over a century the exacerbations of these feelings in literature have been widely attributed by writers of acknowledged power and intelligence to an unprecedented break in cultural continuity and to a remission of some of the authorizing principles behind language. More or less simultaneously, and often quite independently of one another, a strong contingent of novelists, poets, critics, artists of all sorts seem to have discovered that they must confront the reader with stylistic and structural evidences of dislocation. It is of course also true that Melville of *Pierre*, Mark Twain of *Pudd'nhead Wilson*, Poe in some of the tales, Mallarmé, Eliot, Joyce, Proust, and Virginia Woolf all wrote out of inferable personal disturbances that might (but also might not) tell us something about modern culture. But they preferred to suggest, and literary criticism has abetted them in doing so, that they were representing something about that culture, something that is so far from being merely personal, much less regional, that it is not even a respecter of national boundaries.

To offer a quite provisional definition, literary modernism is the systematic pressing of a claim—made in writing and therefore in a requisite discipline of reading—that many of the anxieties which Western culture has often associated with the human condition have been immensely intensified by contemporary life. These anxieties, it is implied, were once manageable within habitual discourse; they could, as it were, be "talked over" without anyone's having to change the terms or tones by which ordinary social exchanges made sense. But under modern conditions, the argument runs, such talk has become increasingly meaningless, even to a point, as in a play like Beckett's *Happy Days*, where the audience finds in dialogue, at once plaintive and comic, evidences that human communication consists merely of the constantly induced desire to communicate *something*, anything. Chatter becomes the sign of life. Again, it is not necessary to assent to this modernist view, but only to allow for it as a possible and possibly convincing one, and to agree, further, that it provided legitimate provocation for writings and readings produced in compliance with it.

Modernism "happened" when reading got to be intimidated or at
least threatened to become so for those who decided to bother with it
at all. (Sometimes they decided not to, a phenomenon discussed in the
next chapter.) I am suggesting that a good way to identify modernism
is as a special kind of reading habit or reading necessity. Modernist texts
—and it will be remembered that in the annals of twentieth-century
writing these are by no means the majority—mostly prevent spontane-
ous acts of reading, even for people with a high degree of learned
competence. Who does not feel like gullible company in the presence
of authors who inform you that they are not at all satisfied with what,
with some effort, you have just managed to appreciate? "That was a way
of putting it—not very satisfactory." Understandably, there have been
far fewer persuasively critical than doggedly interpretive readers of twentieth-century or modernist classics. Speaking only of English and American literature, while having in mind a corresponding argument about
Mallarmé advanced by Leo Bersani and Malcolm Bowie, I would say
that modernism is to be located not only as it commonly is—in *ideas*
about cultural institutions or the structures of life—but also in two
related and verifiable developments discussed at several other points in
this book: first, in the effort by a particular faction of writers to promote
the idea that in twentieth-century literature, difficulty is particularly
necessary and virtuous, and, second, in the complicit agreement, by a
faction of readers, that the act of reading ought to entail an analogous
degree of difficulty attributable, again, to cultural dislocations peculiar
to this century.

Modernism is an attempt to perpetuate the power of literature as a
privileged and exclusive form of discourse. By its difficulty it tries,
paradoxically, to reinvoke the connections, more or less severed by the
growth of mass culture, between the artist and the audience. Since this
special connection can no longer be based on inherited class, as it was
up to the Restoration, and since it is impossible that we should have a
Spenser, a Milton, a Marvell—great writers who were also members of
a governing class for whom they wrote—a corresponding select community of writer and reader had to be created. This may sound as if
modernism were a snob's game. And that is pretty much what it is,
despite the middle-class keys and guides to the club. It was and is,

needless to say, much more than that. As it appears in the English language, modernism is, significantly, scarcely English at all. Even allowing for the modernist aspects of Ford Madox Ford and Virginia Woolf, it is nearly exclusively the work of American and Irish writers and a Polish one: Pound, Eliot, Joyce, Yeats, Conrad; while Melville and Hawthorne, in what they often require of the reader, are modernist in theory and practice. As we have seen, it took the inculcation of difficulty-as-a-virtue before either of these began to be read as they are now.

There is involved here something like a colonial protest against the shapes that language had assumed as it came forth from England, still the seat of imperial cultural and political authority during much of the period in question. More important, the protest occurred when English literature had itself begun, in the novel and in the great popular poets of the nineteenth century, to cater to the ethos of the so-called common man or common reader, though we have seen in Wordsworth how very uncommon was even his "common" man. Indeed, it was to escape incorporation into the ethos of the common that modernist writers turned to the City (with its sharpened social and cultural discriminations), to ancient myth (as a way of capturing contemporary experience for literary tradition), and to the coteries of French literature. And in its expressed admiration throughout the second quarter of this century for the literature of the seventeenth century, literary modernism in England and America further showed its taste for a literature of privilege by demoting Spenser, Milton, Bunyan, and Defoe in favor of Anglican poets, save for Marvell. It is consistent with all this that the two great twentieth-century writers who often seem comparatively easy, Lawrence and Frost, were regarded by all but a few of their modernist contemporaries as somehow lacking in the sophistications of culture embodied in the University, the modern City, and the Church. Some sense of the oddity of these developments is caught by Northrop Frye's witty observation that the notion that the best English poetry was orthodox, hierarchical, non-democratic, and neo-classical came from two men, Eliot and Pound, one from St. Louis, Missouri, and the other from Hailey, Idaho.

Modernism can be thought of as a period when, more than in any other, readers were induced to think of literary texts as necessarily and rewardingly complicated. It represents a demand made upon readers not by anything called twentieth-century literature, but rather by a few peculiarly resistant texts which during this century were also promoted as central ones. The authors in most cases were remarkably persuasive as literary critics, both in their poems and novels, and in critical writing itself. They rewrote literary history as if it were a prelude to their own grandeur, expected or achieved, and so successful were they in doing this, that only in about the past two decades has it become possible to bring to vividness on the map of English literature those areas left rather dingy since the advent of modernism as a critical fashion. If through the preeminence of Eliot early in the century it became necessary to give prominence to Donne and Marvell, it is also in part because of the later eminence of Stevens that Wordsworth has been seen as an ever more strange and wonderful poet, just as it is thanks in part to Frost, Stevens, and Crane that the extraordinary and demanding importance of Emerson is receiving its due acknowledgment. Indeed, it became necessary for Eliot to suppress the recognition given to Donne, Marvell, and Dryden by Emerson and Thoreau as part of his larger repression of Emersonian elements in his own background.

Literary history is to a great extent the product of such tactical moves and thrusts for power, which is why Robert Adams, in his essay "What Was Modernism," can aptly remark that "one odd if forceful proof of [the term's] reality is that we've so far been unable to write a coherent history of modern English literature." This seems to me a cause for celebration and not an occasion for holding one's breath. A major achievement of recent criticism, as in Frank Kermode's *Forms of Attention*, has been the effort to break down exclusionary coherencies that have often passed for literary history, and to question the principles on which they depend. It is possible now to see that the cult of modernism is in itself a demonstration of the self-interests and special pleadings by which literary history gets made and remade. Fortunately there is no longer a "coherent history" of English poetry to replace the one in which Leavis read Shelley out of the line of succession and tried to dislodge Milton, or in which Pater and Wilde are treated as "sports." There is no coherent history of American literature, nor, in my view, should there even be an attempt at one. The kind of coherencies we should start looking for ought to have less to do with chronology or periods than with habits of reading (including fashions in classroom pedagogy) and with the way poets "read" one another in the poetry they write.

Modernism is only incidentally an idea or a social condition and more particularly an experience of reading, an experience of *how* certain ideas, which are not in themselves peculiar to any historical period, have recently been apprehended. Thus, some of the ideas ascribed to Eliot or Joyce or Faulkner belong just as much to Matthew Arnold or to Diderot; they can be extrapolated from the late plays of Shakespeare or from the tragedies of Seneca. But none of these earlier writers initiated a modernist literature. None of them has written a book which ostentatiously asks to be read with a kind of attention required by Eliot or Joyce, or the Faulkner of *The Sound and the Fury* and *Absalom, Absalom!* It is through Joyce and Eliot especially, and the works published roughly between 1914 and 1925, that most English and American readers have learned about modernism, have learned to think of it as a phenomenon of the first half of this century, and have learned also that it is supposed to entail great difficulties, both for the writer and for the reader.

The peculiar and contradictory nature of that difficulty has been alluded to in the Prologue, and I return to it now, and to the passage in Eliot's 1921 essay "The Metaphysical Poets," where the necessity for a modernist "difficulty" was put in an unabashedly intimidating way: "We can only say that it appears likely that poets in our civilization, as it exists at present, must be *difficult.* Our civilization comprehends great variety and complexity, and this variety and complexity, playing upon a refined sensibility, must produce various and complex results. The poet must become more and more comprehensive, more allusive, more indirect, in order to force, to dislocate if necessary, language into his meaning." (As if Virgil, Dante, Spenser, Milton, Keats, Whitman, Tennyson were not all inveterately allusive!) Eliot's prose on occasions like this has a Brahmin indirection, as of a fastidious gentility reluctantly, but no less imperiously, turning its attention to "the mind of Europe" or to the whole of the twentieth century: "We can only say that it appears likely that poets in our civilization as it exists today . . ."

The pomposity of such formulations, coming from a great poet, raises other questions. His explanation of why modern poetry is of necessity "difficult" is a self-protective and defensive one. The passage wants to ascribe difficulty to social and historical causes merely, even though these are not at all peculiar to "our civilization." It is an attempt actually to vulgarize the necessity for "difficulty," offering yet another reason to wonder, especially after Peter Ackroyd's biography of Eliot, how much of his own "difficulty" derived from causes more intimately personal. No matter how self-serving, however, the representative importance of this insistence on the necessary difficulty of poetry and prose in the twentieth century—Eliot makes similar remarks in several of his essays—achieved the status of doctrine. It became the bedrock of literary criticism and of the study of literature from about 1930 onward. No one can object to difficulty, and anyone who refuses to cope with it had better forget about reading literature altogether. The issue, rather, is two-fold: first, the implication that the difficulty was something only the poet could confront on our behalf, and second, that the reader should be selfless and humble and thankful for the poet's having done so. At its core, the problem posed by the modernist view of difficulty has to do with the *kind* of relationship to difficulty that literature asks for and the kind of pleasure given or denied by that relationship.

It has been argued on a number of occasions, for example, that, out of ill-advised deference to the common or ordinary reader, academic interpreters have set out to make modernist texts more understandable, more rationally organized, more socially and historically referential than they truly are. The proper job of criticism, it is then proposed, is to preserve the inherent mystery of these works, their irreducible power to baffle. These arguments have been made most effectively by Denis Donoghue, and there can be no objection to them, it seems to me, especially if it is kept in mind that one explanation for some of the reductive misreadings and interpretations that modernist texts have received lies in the works and writers themselves. Modernist texts make grim readers of us all, and in part by offering so many convenient handles for analysis as constantly to remind us that we are in dire need of them. We are met, as some examples will presently show, with inducements to tidy things up, to locate principles of order and structure beneath a fragmentary surface. We work very hard to deserve the help, if help it is, only to have it then suggested by other elements in the text that we have been acting in a rather fussy and heavy-handed fashion, embarrassingly without aristocratic ease. Apparently we should have left things as they were, problematic, with the meanings in abeyance.

I do not want to suggest that it is therefore better to be casual with modernist texts than to be grim. There is, in fact, not much of a choice. At best the reader must make do *within* unsatisfactory alternatives, and the virtue of this is that he may find in the process that the reader's situation is analogous to the writer's own and that there really is, after all, a human agency or presence, however elusive, within the workings, the industry of modernist writing. This is not an inconsiderable discovery. From the writing, or more precisely from the way it is composed or executed, emerges something not usually thought to be there, given the much-touted impersonality of modernist literature. There emerges at least a functional self, a human initiative. Against Eliot's dictum, it should be obvious that the man who writes may also be the man who suffers. In this view, the modernist writer is working within the same contradictions as the reader. The text becomes a drama wherein the culturally or biologically determined human taste for structure or for structuring is continually being excited into activity and just as continually frustrated. Each thrust toward order proves no more than another example of the urgency to achieve it.

Modernist literature is tough going, and there is no point in deluding ourselves, and especially students, with talk, out of Roland Barthes, about "an erotics of reading," an escapade of reading, claims for the sheer fun that awaits us in the pages of Pound or Pynchon. In his useful and engaging *Ezra Pound,* for example, Donald Davie proposes that the best way to read the *Cantos* is to read them "many at a time and fast":

This indeed is what irritates so many readers, and fascinates an elect few—that the *Cantos,* erudite though they are, consistently frustrate the sort of reading that is synonymous with "study," reading such as goes on in the seminar room or the discussion group. It is hopeless to go at them cannily, not moving on to line 3 until one is sure of line 2. They must be taken in big gulps or not at all. This means reading without comprehension? Yes, if by comprehension we mean a set of propositions that can be laid end to end. . . . Which is not to deny that some teasing out of quite short excerpts, even some hunting up of sources and allusions, is profitable *at some stage.* For the *Cantos* are a poem to be lived with,

over years. Yet after many years each new reading—if it is reading of many pages
at a time, as it should be—is a new bewilderment. So it should be, for so it was
meant to be. After all, some kinds of bewilderment are fruitful. To one such kind
we give the name "awe"—not awe at the poet's accomplishment, his energy or
erudition, but awe at the energies, some human and some non-human, which
interact, climb, spiral, reverse themselves and disperse, in the forming and
reforming spectacles which the poet's art presents to us or reminds us of.

As might be evident by now I find Davie's account congenial in many
respects, especially his reference to non-human energies, and his praise
of "bewilderment." But in the case of Joyce, Eliot, and Pound, Lowell's
poetry up to *For the Union Dead,* the poetry of Hollander and Merrill,
and much of Pynchon—to refer only to examples of a kind of "difficulty" that often seems to me laudable—Davie's recommendations are
impossible to live up to until *after* what he calls, in the quarantine of
punctuation marks, "study." He sounds as if, in Pound, we are dealing
directly with what in the next chapter I define as "density," when, in
fact, we can seldom get to that aspect of his poetry at all except through
some initial resolution of its difficulty.

I am saying that modernist writers lend themselves to and encourage
a programmed and widespread misreading of a kind that calls attention
mostly to structural complications and designs of allusiveness. This results in interpretations that are demonstrably less synchronized with the
vital energies at work in these texts than are misreadings that result from
at least trying to play fast and loose on the advice, even before Davie's,
of Emerson and Pater. The fact that most readers have been led astray
by the intimidations of structural and stylistic difficulties can only be in
part explained by the presumption that such difficulties were made
incumbent by unique historical conditions. There has also been, on the
part of the writers themselves, a curious determination to reduce and
impoverish what the texts have to offer. The kinds of clues supplied by
Eliot's famous notes, Joyce's handouts, Yeats's system, the leads offered
by Faulkner's loud Christian symbolisms and Pound's cryptograms—all
tend to nullify a reading experience which in itself is ideally meant to
mock the efficacy of such schematizations. As a result, there have been
for many readers at least two texts of works like *The Waste Land* or

Ulysses. One is full of marginalia by which the work is translated into something orderly, fit for class discussion, lectures, and articles, while the other is remembered with fondness for all kinds of fragmentary pleasure, like Leopold Bloom's endearing little ways, or Eliot's "bats with baby faces," or Faulkner's Quentin and his sister Caddy fumblingly making love in the branch water.

There has been only infrequent critical acknowledgment that these works are a sort of battleground: the flow of material wars against a technology which, however determined, is inadequate to the task of controlling it. The imbalance is of course a contrived one, meant to demonstrate the breakdown of any technique or technology in the face of contemporary life, and it received one of its most articulate expressions not only from Henry Adams but from Henry James, when he remarked in *The American Scene* in 1905 that "the reflecting surfaces, of the ironic, of the epic order, suspended in the New York atmosphere, have yet to show symptoms of shining out, and the monstrous phenomena themselves, meanwhile, strike me as having, with their immense momentum, got the start, got ahead of . . . any possibility of poetic, of dramatic capture."

Thomas Pynchon is a remarkable instance of a writer who uses literary techniques as an analogue to other more obvious kinds of technology and does so in order to show that where technique or technology works it is very often at the expense of the material it proposes to take care of. He seems to call for a labor of exegesis and to encourage the illusion that he will be best understood by those who bone up on entropy or quantum theory or theories of paranoiac closure. In fact, his works can best be appreciated by those who can take his arcane knowledge for granted and are in no way confused by the elaborateness of his "plotting," who can treat it not as a puzzle to be solved but as a formal, often parodistic, literary representation of modernist cultural myths about social, historical, and economic "plots" against "us." His structures are an image of the so-called network. Again, no such perfectly tuned and accomplished reader exists, and it is of no practical use to badger anyone into thinking that he might become wholly adequate to a text like *Gravity's Rainbow.* It is not absurd to posit an ideal reader, but only to insist in cases like these that there can in fact be one. Meanwhile, reverential concessions to modernist difficulty lead the hapless to suppose that all they need do is to keep trying harder. No one *can* be the right kind of reader for books of this sort—open, excited, titillated, knowing, taking all the curves without a map—and theoretical proposals that there should be such a reader smack of the high-culturalist fantasy that one can be at the same time casual and encyclopedic.

There is no need to blink at the truth: writers as well as readers of twentieth-century modernist classics—and I mean all readers, including the most learned—have to do more book work than writers and readers have ever had to do before in history. Why is this the case, even for people with good college educations? And why have so many assented to its being necessarily the case? I ask these questions even while assuming that anything can become stranger the more deeply you get into it. Those who really bother can discover the marvelous impediments to clarity that occur whenever a work dares to release the full resources of its own language, as so often happens in the old familiars, Shakespeare or Spenser, Milton or Marvell, Wordsworth, Dickens, Emerson, or Frost. But for all the learning and submerged allusiveness in such writers, they only infrequently exhibit the particular kinds of difficulty encountered in what can be called modernist literature. If Eliot's proposition is granted—that "our civilization at present" requires a "difficult" kind of writing—why need that difficulty register itself as at once compendiously learned and disjointed, at once schematic in its disposal of allusions and blurred in the uses to which it puts them?

There is a clue, curiously enough, in that plainest of twentieth-century novelists, Hemingway. Hemingway is not a difficult writer; to read him requires no special knowledge and a familiarity with only a limited repertoire of vocal tones, of sentence sounds. So the comparison is made with the proviso that only after the bookishness of Joyce and Eliot has been mastered, if it ever can be, may the reader fully appreciate their sensuous and rhythmic pleasures. Ideally, that is, the apparatus of Eliot or Joyce functions the way bullfighting or boxing functions metaphorically in Hemingway—as a primer of connoisseurship for people who are invited at the same time to pretend that they are already connoisseurs. The apparatus therefore probably deserves, though still on the other side of a bookishness that Hemingway does not require, the same kind of pretend-casualness of response.

Ironically enough, it is probable that the best way to read most modernist texts is in the manner proposed by Emerson and his anti-modernist successors. The ostentatious learning, the cultural displays, the mechanical structurings would not then be taken as directives to the reader that he or she must look behind these things for heavy significances but as indications instead of extreme procedural hesitancy. They are forms of stamina, persistence, of discipline where there exist no other forms of authority. This making of form is effective only because it is temporary, satisfying only when, as on the recommendation of William James, it is allowed to remain local and finite. Eliot was in no sense an adherent of James but an admirer, quite critical at times, of James's antagonist, F. H. Bradley, on whom he finished a doctoral dissertation (without taking the degree) in 1916. Eliot laments the very conditions of uncertainty which James asks us to celebrate, even while he recognizes their necessity. Nonetheless, his combinations of diffidence and dogmatism, of a desire for order that continually dissolves into irresolution, along with the frequent habit in his critical writing of disowning earlier assertions, all this makes his work susceptible to a reading in which achievements of form are, in Frost's sense, only "momentary stays against confusion." What to Eliot is a problem of belief is to Frost a solution. Hence the plaintiveness of Eliot's "Notes" to *The Waste Land*, where he is not giving the reader much of anything except examples of how he can cheer himself up with bits and pieces: "The interior of St. Magnus Martyr is to my mind one of the finest among Wren's interiors. See *The Proposed Demolition of Nineteen City Churches* (P. S. King and Son, Ltd.)." Thus also the relish of Joyce in lists, parodies, schemes. The best way to take such things is as evidence of what a writer is *doing* in a posited situation. It is not the substance but rather the act of allusiveness or of schematization which should occupy the reader. Generally speaking, middle-class anxieties about culture and about the need therefore to imagine the possibility of some terminal form of interpretation—needs and anxieties fostered by the mythologies of general education—were only further increased by the often thin or boned-up erudition of the middle-class "great" writers of the twentieth century, with their religious and cultural nostalgias.

Eliot and Joyce are not romantic writers; they are not classical writers either. In Eliot's telling phrase about Joyce, they were "classical in tendency." "Tendency"—they are what they are in an action, and by virtue of a kind of self-monitoring in which a writer interprets the forms he has just offered up to the reader for interpretation. A particularly accomplished reader helps in his reading to create the text; Eliot and Joyce may be classified as among the readers of the texts they are also writing. Critical reading, that is, is simultaneously a part of the performance of writing, and to some extent it always has been. At the outset of "Tradition and the Individual Talent," Eliot remarks, apparently innocent of his debt to Emerson, that "criticism is as inevitable as breathing, and that we should be none the worse for articulating what passes in our minds when we read a book and feel an emotion about it, for criticizing our own minds in their work of criticism." And this is what he does, continually, in his poems.

In thus suggesting the kinetic, the volatile nature of both reading and writing, Eliot himself calls our attention to an active authorial presence even while forswearing it. According to him, that presence is supposed to be notoriously hard to find; it does not have a "voice" even in the great varieties of style displayed in modernist writing. I propose that it can be found, if not in any of the styles, then in the transitions, the modes of variation among them. It is to be found not in any place, despite all the formal placements made available, but in the acts of *dis*-placement by which one form is relinquished for another.

Eliot is so much a poet of probing additions, additions seeking a destination, that he could easily accept the sort of deletions and abridgments made by Pound in *The Waste Land*. The penultimate admission in "Preludes" that "I am moved by fancies that are curled/Around these images, and cling:/The notion of some infinitely gentle/Infinitely suffering thing" comes from a poet who, for reasons that have nothing necessarily to do with the twentieth century, could not commit himself to narrative destinations of a kind imagined if not experienced daily in a life more determinedly sexual than his was. He can never take anything in stride; he moves, falteringly, toward the formation of images and concepts which dissolve as soon as he has reached them. The indecisiveness was as pronounced after as it was before his religious conversion. In the later poetry of *Four Quartets*, as Leavis shows, the reader is not invited to translate abstract concepts about "time present and time past" but rather to witness and participate in the intensity of Eliot's personal engagement as he tries to arrive at some security, never actually achieved, about them and about the feelings they engender. Eliot became a poet precisely because he embraced those conditions which prevent others from becoming one, of being "moved" by something even while not knowing what to make of it. Writing was for him more or less indistinguishable from a critical reading that was all but crippling.

For Eliot's use of images that remain at once evocative and random, there are well-documented poetic precedents in Laforgue and others. But the images do not refer only to other images; they refer us also to a man named T. S. Eliot and to a feeling in him—he allows only an intermittent sense of it—that is close to a yearning for a nature more masculine, at least more traditionally masculine, than he could find in himself. It is as if he imagines that for some other man the images in a poem like "La Figlia che Piange" would not remain merely transient and painful. They would instead initiate and sustain a plot. Eliot is someone, man as well as poet, incapable of initiating a plot within which the image could be secured and thus released from desire.

Joyce exhibits, flamboyantly, altogether more psychological, sexual assurance. The Joycean hero is customarily on the fringe of activities— a game, a dance, a family dinner, a boisterous conversation. Other people can take pleasure in these activities unconscious or careless of what the hero knows about them. And what he knows about them is mostly derogatory: that they are bound by sometimes deadening rules and clichés, that the activities are programmed and encoded without any prior consultation with the participants. Privileged consciousness, as the French would have it, is not at the center but on the circumference of the area of inhabited space and it is ready to move still further out into abstractions, as at the end of "The Dead." But Stephen is not Joyce's hero any more than Gabriel is, and to read him properly one has to have a taste more for displays of authorial power than for sentiment. Joyce took a sadomasochistic pleasure in the fact that figures like Stephen and Gabriel could be forced by him to confront and to be intimidated by the energy, the exuberance, the virtuosity (however prefabricated) that is implanted in the suffocatingly programmed or encoded life which he himself has mastered. His repeated condescensions about failed or stunted sensibility are a reminder that only he is the calculating master of the codes, only he can break them and release them onto the page. Joyce exulted in the evidence that he, and not Yeats, was really "king of the cats," king of techniques, of the revelry of forms. Writers at work are of necessity cold and calculating, but no one more brazenly celebrates his own sheer capacity for what James called "doing." Unlike Eliot he delights in *not* feeling put upon or anguished by what he has just written. Joyce is the quintessential celebrant of literary technology.

Literature's indicated awareness of itself as a form of technology is scarcely confined to works written in the modern period. Examples, as I indicate in the next chapter, "Venerable Complications," are scattered in English and American literature from their beginnings. As a movement, however, literary modernism is constituted by a clamorous gathering of such works in the last century and a half. Techniques are brought so directly to the fore as to constitute an effort for the reader and, evidently, a problem for the writer. Both writer and reader are trying to determine if any kind of place can be found for an active human presence, one which can exert itself with some measurable effect within the technological order of things. Any such effect is never more than inferable, however; it is never sustained; it is sporadic, disruptive, and ultimately frustrated. One evidence that a text is "modernist" is the degree to which it continually *exposes* the factitiousness of its own local procedures and does so as a prelude to substitutions that prove no more satisfactory. Modernist texts reveal the corrosive effect of reading, by author and reader, upon what the writing has just accomplished. A modernist writer keeps going, one might say, because in reading what he has just written he finds provocations only for alternatives. The human presence, as a creative force, resides less in characters, who are in any case part of some larger expressive intention, than in the performance of writing and reading, in transitions or shifts that occur in reactive movements away from what has already been structured, even down to the placements of a word. Modernists could as well be called Emersonians with a vengeance, if there were such a thing.

This may sound like a rather reductive account, as if the experience of modernism consists in a dry provision of formal strategies, technical ingenuities, and the monitored movements of language. This, it seems to me, is indeed what modernism most distinctly offers, but not necessarily to the diminution of other more conventional pleasures. Each of us has all kinds of preferences as, for example, among Proust, Kafka, or Joyce, Virginia Woolf, Faulkner, or Pynchon. In my own case I may think one writer "better" than another because the particular forms of life which he characteristically represents seem important to me, because he shows how they are important also to some world larger than my own, and, above all, because he reveals an unusual capacity not to be intimidated by them. Having been born into a half-Irish, would-be pious Roman Catholic family in an anglophilic New England town, I was quite naturally disposed to admire *A Portrait of the Artist as a Young Man.* Joyce could recreate cultural forces that had offended my boyhood and adolescence. What is more, he could "take them on." He exposed their weaknesses and strengths as matters of great cultural and historic resonance, in ways traced out by Eliot in his essay "Arnold and Pater." A writer can seem "great" because he or she confronts the bullies in one's life, and Joyce helped me imagine a history for myself, not merely because of the materials he chose but because of his great tactical prowess, his knowing what to make of them, how to use them.

There were of course other, simpler reasons for admiring him. One can recollect Leopold Bloom's relish for "liver slices fried with crust-crumbs" as affectionately as the gustatory appetite of Tom Jones, while Gretta's memories in "The Dead" of the young boy from the gas works who loved her are as unforgettable as anything in *La Bohème.* But such moments in Fielding or in Italian opera come to us in vastly different ways from those allowed by Joyce, and the differences are finally what matter. Criticism based on recollection, no matter how affectionately detailed, is not in my view criticism at all. Criticism should engage itself not with rendered experience but with the experience of rendering; it must always go back to acts of rendition, to language, which is one reason why there are so many quotations in this book and so much verbal analysis of them. Probably there are readers who can with great fondness talk intimately about technical accomplishments, but most of us, when we are away from the text, tend to maunder on in a clubbable way about inexactly remembered scenes or characters or bits of phrasing. In that sense when we remember good ol' Proust he becomes not in any important way different from good ol' Tolstoy, even though the two could never have been mistaken for each other when we first met them in their writings. Represented life in a modernist text, I am suggesting, gets to us by routes quite different from any we are likely to encounter in a novelist even so sophisticated about the cultural implications of literary form as was William Dean Howells. It is, then, not merely that in modernist texts the formal and technical efforts are, as I have said, pushed to the fore; it is, even more, that this very process can, as with Joyce, endow itself with an appearance of bravery.

The idea that innovation in the arts is a form of cultural heroism— this is perhaps the central mythology behind the modernist cult of difficulty. In *Ulysses*, no less than in *Women in Love*, whose preface announces that the "struggle for verbal consciousness should not be left out in art," intended eccentricities of design, as against those considered at the time more conventional, are meant to imply that life calls upon the writer to rescue it from its entrapments in cultural systems, secular, ecclesiastical, and literary. Literary technique in modernist writing is, as it were, put on high alert in response to what other techniques or technologies have already done to life and language. In this way modernist texts make conspicuous a function which literature has always assumed, and they ask to be especially admired for doing so at a time which they project as culturally degenerate. They induce in the reader a corresponding bewilderment and concern that perhaps all experience, including the most private, arrives mediated and arranged by cultural institutions or practices which meanwhile are exhibiting their own decay. The reader is to infer that literary technique must be arbitrary because other ways of arranging experience which, in the past, were able to support literary representations of life, no longer make sense. Modernism managed to implement, within the self-analytical mode of its texts, a form of cultural skepticism whose uniqueness was not supposed to be put into question by the fact that, sporadically, something similar is to be found earlier on, as in, say, Spenser's transformations of the allegorical tradition, or Shakespeare's distrust of the hyperbolic language on which depend the structures of his own imagination, or Sterne's efforts to open the plotting of fiction to the vagaries of human distraction, or Byron's self-parodies in *Don Juan*. Indeed, it is fair to say that these early evidences of modernism became fully appreciated, as did Melville's, only because later evidences, in Pound, Eliot, and Joyce, were made unavoidably visible.

Modernism proposes to enter history, that is, not with a mirror, not even with a lamp, but with an x-ray, a lamp and mirror combined. It hopes to expose what George Eliot, with her premonitory genius, called the "stupendous fragmentariness" left behind by institutions—she was referring in *Middlemarch* to Rome and the Vatican—that once gave the impression of order to public and private existence. The effort itself is meant to exemplify the human capacity to recognize this fragmentariness and, in the act of so doing, to evade it for at least the duration of the act of recognition. The reading of modernist works is, similarly, an activity by which with great difficulty we can become conscious that any structure, technique, code, or system of signs is likely to prove no more than extemporized and transient. Even as we face the page, modernist texts teach us something about the limitations of technology, especially as embodied in literary technique—its failure significantly to account for all that it pretends to account for. In that sense, readers who neither shun this difficulty nor pretend wholly to master it are open to discoveries of spiritual as well as cultural importance.

Chapter 3

VENERABLE COMPLICATIONS:
LITERATURE,
TECHNOLOGY, PEOPLE

THIS IS TO BE A PARABLE about Literature and Technology, their problematic relations to each other and to a third party named People. I begin with an observation which while quite obvious is generally ignored by pietistic devotees of Literature: for nearly all of human history practically no People could read. Literature included them as subjects, compliant to the comic and idealizing tendencies of Literature, but People seldom knew that they were being "used" unless they happened in on a masque or a play or the oral transmission of, say, the *Iliad*. Except for an extremely small number, People did not have to be thought of as an audience for Literature and even when some rare lower-class person did acquire a reading capacity—like the sixteenth-century miller named Menocchio described in Carlo Ginzburg's *The Cheese and the Worms*, a study of the Inquisition—he was provided with reduced, fragmented, and aphoristic versions that bore little resemblance to the original works read by his betters. Literature was a minority enterprise, read and supported by the economically and politically privileged classes. But even though it was written by them, for them, and under their patronage, it was and still is the best exhibition of a kind of human power within language which is not at all confined to writers, readers, or the literate, a power to shape and trope language in obedience to human desire that is everyone's inheritance and opportunity.

Meanwhile, the relative historical positions of Literature and People have undergone an extraordinary change. Literature in recent times has found itself worried about and worried by People. There are, for one thing, so many of us. Sanitation, agricultural methods, transportation, medicine, and manufacturing—all these forms of Technology have allowed a fantastic growth in the production of People and in the prolongation of lives. There are now five billion People, and the current increase among illiterates and semi-literates is approximately twice what it is among the largely literate ones. But in respect to Literature, People are different from what they were not simply because they are more numerous. They are different because nearly all of them, at least in England, the United States, and Western Europe, can now read.* This is a wholly unprecedented development, and it follows that People are at last able, if they choose, to assert a new authority over a Literature which heretofore was not obliged even to speak to them.

People have acquired enormous cultural power. But they do not exercise it by reading; they choose instead, as they could never have done before, not to read, at least not to read Literature. Indifference to Literature is consistent with the aims of mass education as it began to be formulated only about a hundred years ago. It was created and motivated by a desire less to make Literature more available, except in token doses, than to make goods and services more abundant, and as an instrument for civic regulation. The same Technology that produced billions of People also created an economy that required a mass of skilled and relatively docile labor. The literacy given them had and has little to do with Literature, nor should it. Literature is scarcely for everyone now, any more than it ever was; I mean, of course, Literature in the sense

---

*However, there are reports in the mid-eighties of alarming increases in the number of functionally illiterate English-speaking Americans: twenty-six million, or one out of five adults. Twenty-five percent of recruits into the armed services cannot read teaching manuals leveled at the seventh grade.

in which I am trying to describe it. But in being exclusive (and ultimately partisan) about Literature, I am not being condescending to People. In fact I would hope to see People rid of the idea that unless they have a productive relationship to Literature, they are necessarily denied the moral or ethical benefits reputedly accruing to those who do. Literature is a particularly disciplined form of language and, therefore, of life. But there are other forms of life whose disciplines and vocabularies can be equally beneficial to human beings, like sports or gardening, like the achievements of domestic intimacy, like any kind of creative work. As Emerson tells us in "Self-Reliance," there can be "prayer in all action. The prayer of the farmer kneeling in his field to weed it, the prayer of the rower kneeling with the stroke of his oar." Would anyone argue for long that those who read and write Literature, especially as a profession, are therefore in any way morally or ethically superior to those who cannot read or write at all? It seems sometimes as if the reverse were true. In my view Literature is preeminently an activity, an example of what I have called elsewhere, with respect to poetry, "the work of knowing."

Such "work" can go on in many places, and one such place is in Literature. It is most successful when it creates still more work, when it leads, that is, not only from density into clarification but out of clarification into still other densities. That there are ways of knowing that have nothing to do with the writing or reading of Literature is clear from Literature itself. That is why it is forever finding analogues to its own compositional acts. It proposes metaphors for literary composition in the act of love (Herbert or Donne), in farming (Thoreau), in apple picking (Frost), in sports (Hemingway), in exploration, scholarship, or the cultivation of roses (Parkman), in money-making (Dreiser), in social manipulation (Henry James), and in raids upon nature for images and tropes (Wordsworth). "Is it only poets and men of leisure and cultivation, who live with nature?" Emerson asks in "The Poet." "No; but also hunters, farmers, grooms, and butchers, though they express their affection in their choice of life, and not in their choice of words." Literature allows these analogies between itself and other activities, however, only on condition: the lover, the explorer, the athlete must be committed to his or her task with a dedication, a genius, a discipline worthy of a great writer. It is not to be supposed that Literature is more available than Thoreau's harvest of beans in *Walden*. "I was determined," he tells us, "to know beans."

Literature is necessarily a less available harvest, since we cannot ever merely watch it grow or reap it. The performance of Literature is complete neither in the writing nor in the reading. Reading is writing in that it produces language; writing is reading in that it interprets the possibilities in what has already been written for what subsequently can be written. The "work" required by Literature is in that sense never finished and cannot be. I would therefore summarily define Literature, for the time being, as any written text whose points of clarification, whether these occur by local or by larger design, bring you only to densities different from but flexibly related to those from which you have previously emerged. Literature is that writing whose clarities bring on precipitations of density.

This can be said, I think, of the Literature of any period. But for the last hundred years or so, as I have already proposed in the previous chapter, Literature has become, to an unprecedented degree, self-conscious and defensive about its own complications. It has developed a sort of bunker mentality and has begun to insist not only on its necessary density but on its necessary difficulty. *Moby-Dick* is an obvious instance of difficulty, *Bleak House*, in the peculiarity of its narrative organization, only a somewhat less obvious one, and by the beginning of the century Henry James directly attributes the causes of difficulty to what he calls "monstrous masses." Literature, he says, cannot catch the life of the modern city or touch its inhabitants, a deduction expressed both in *The American Scene*, with respect to New York, and, with respect to London, in the Prefaces, especially the Preface to *The Altar of the Dead*. "The general black truth," he remarks, is "that London was a terrible place to die in":

It takes space to feel, it takes time to know, and great organisms as well as small have to pause, more or less, to possess themselves and to be aware. Monstrous masses are, by this truth, so impervious to vibration that the sharpest forces of feeling, locally applied, no more penetrate than a pin or a paper-cutter penetrates an elephant's hide. Thus the very tradition of sensibility would perish if left only to their care. It has here and there to be rescued, to be saved by independent, intelligent zeal; which type of effort, however, to avail, has to fly in the face of the conditions.

What is imagined here is not a mere stand-off between "monstrous masses" and "the tradition of sensibility." James proposes a more drastic alienation. If the "tradition" is to be saved by "independent" effort, then both the effort and the independence call for the abdication by Literature of a kind of public power it once enjoyed. Instead of applying its forces "locally," instead, that is, of creating "vibrations" within a civilization known to be susceptible, Literature must now "fly in the face of the conditions," and these are nothing less than the civilization's "imperviousness." James's image, with its suggestion of movement prompted by an encounter with something hostile, well enough describes how he and other late Edwardian writers, specifically including the line from Pater to Joyce, were to confront the common reader. If the "tradition of sensibility" is to be rescued, it is implied, then it will be by embedding it within stylistic fortifications made intentionally and necessarily intricate. James perceived this well before World War I and its aftermaths. Let it be remembered that Literature by its very nature would already have excluded even a solicitous semi-literate People. But even a literate People are in James's account grown elephantine in size and thickness, and his own later novels are an instance of the stylistic release from any determining obligation to them.

All this suggests some reasons why in England, from about 1900 to 1914, modernist characteristics began to manifest themselves in some central examples of Literature. This had happened earlier in America during the decade before the Civil War, with Poe, Hawthorne, and Melville. In each country these were times when demographic and educational developments helped to produce James's "monstrous masses," in America first for a number of reasons, including extraordinary growth in the economy, in compulsory education, and, later on, in land-grant universities. There emerged great numbers of People who could read and write and make unprecedented demands on cultural production. But the "tradition of sensibility," assumed to be the preserve of Literature, was not necessarily a tradition for them.

Literature was forced, as it were, to extemporize an audience *out of itself.* The consequences are measurable not only with respect to modernist difficulty, but in the efforts of literary criticism, as led by T. S. Eliot, F. R. Leavis, and the Southern "new critics," to locate a "tradition of sensibility" in earlier English literature, especially of the seventeenth century. Here, too, the cult of difficulty expressed itself. It was suggested that because of the degenerative effects of life in the twentieth century, its barbarisms, discontinuities, and vulgarizations of taste, even the works of the past had become inaccessible to all but a few trained readers. In England the critical enterprise of Leavis's *Scrutiny* (following in 1932 on the earlier *Calendar of Modern Letters*, 1925–27) and in America the bi-monthly called *The Fugitive* (published at Nashville, Tennessee, from 1922 to 1925, with writings by John Crowe Ransom, Allen Tate, and Robert Penn Warren) were in large part meant to show, as I indicated in the Prologue, that only by a quite strenuous sort of reading was it possible to recover from the past those values that presumably were disappearing everywhere else. The Southern regionalism of the Fugitive group had its corollary in *Scrutiny*'s celebration of Bunyan's and Lawrence's England. It was proposed that Literature offered an experience not of ideas but of sounds and movements in the English language that carried with them traces of a rich and fulfilling community of assumptions. The experience could be had only by those who could enter most fully into Literature's vital and dramatic and exploratory uses of languages. Tradition, Eliot warned, "cannot be inherited, and if you want it you must obtain it by great labor." It was to be largely a labor of close reading.

I have previously argued in *The Performing Self* ("What Is English Studies? And If You Know What That Is, What Is English Literature?") that there are ways in which these notions might be quite sentimental, wrong-headed, even pernicious, and I am trying here only to describe the consequences of believing in them, consequences that have had much to do with the place assigned to Literature within the discourses of modern culture. Working your way into a text by "close reading" was supposed to be a way to get close also to a "tradition of sensibility" otherwise fading from daily life, along with the institutions which had supported it. Reading was in that sense implicitly a critique and rejection of the new civilization of People which Technology had helped create. Thus the reader of the Literature of the past, no less than the modernist writer of Literature, was to find a community only in remnants, redoubts, pockets of resistance within a larger civilization that was indifferent even to their existence, like a whale to some mollusk encysted on its flank.

Lawrence was an especially important and complicating figure in this imagination of the estrangement of Literature from twentieth-century life. For Leavis and others, he suggested that there still might be tenuous connections between contemporary life, if conducted in a certain way, and surviving shreds of a redeeming past. Leavis's gradual disenchantment with Eliot[1] is best understood, I think, as part of his larger conviction that by nationality, religious feeling, and sexual fastidiousness Eliot was rendered incapable of understanding what the barely existing English culture of the mining villages could still have meant to Lawrence. No American like Eliot, so it was suggested, no Irishman like Joyce, for that matter, could really know, as instinctively as did Lawrence (and Leavis himself), the vital resources alive in the English language. There is no need here to rehearse or enter into these arguments except to note that they are a rather touching symptom of how desperate were the efforts to imagine some possible resuscitation of a "tradition of sensibility." Not only Literature but the proper way to read it was fraught with difficulty because, it would seem, the only way the tradition could affirm itself was by being at once radical and reactionary.

Distortions of form, dislocations in language, exclusivity and effortfulness in criticism—these were meant to restore certain kinds of life presumably displaced by the emergence and empowerment of People. That not all Literature or criticism subscribed to these notions is evident enough from the careers of, say, Hardy in the novel, Frost in poetry, and, in criticism, both a figure like Edmund Wilson and a brilliant antagonist of modernist fashions like Edward Thomas, whose reviews of Pound, suitably wary from the first, are among the most subtle diagnoses of literary modernism ever written. The death of Thomas in the first World War probably made an immense difference, as David Bromwich suggests,[2] to the direction of criticism thereafter, as it moved, subserviently in most cases, into the service of modernist apologetics. The point was made and it held: Literature was not even to pretend that it was meant for People. Instead it was to be, as was criticism, an extraordinarily demanding and self-conscious inquiry into its own resources and procedures. Literature was deemed to be necessarily unpopular; it was to be ignored by People; it was to be read and understood by an elite. And yet it wanted at the same time to claim for itself a degree of historical and cultural significance which it had never before so explicitly and under such compulsion been required to claim. Literature assumed an enormous historical mission—to record the demise of the cultural traditions that sustained it—precisely in the act of abdicating its traditional centrality, its place in the community. At the moment of its exile, Literature said to People, "I banish *you,*" and then set about, as Coriolanus never could, to build another empire.

Literature feels, if anything, even more embattled now. It found itself after World War II confronted with People still more indifferent, as if Literature were not there at all. Starting with radio early in the century, then with recording mechanisms, tape machines, television, and the miniaturization of these, Technology, which created vast numbers of People to begin with, went on to provide the equipment which allowed them, to a degree they could never before have expected, to become both visible and articulate *to themselves.* Visibility and articulateness had, until recently, been for the most part exclusively bestowed on the literary minority, who chose to represent the illiterate classes only sporadically and to suit its own aesthetic and political sense of things. It was not intended that People should be given a history. For the first time People who in earlier centuries had no way to register their existence at all, except in church records, no way to tell anyone what it was like to be as they were day by day, could now record, could re-present themselves, could tell their story—or so it seemed—and hope that it would be heard by those who before had suppressed it.

But in what if any sense is this really the case? And who is to say that the relative obscurity of People was not for them a preference and a blessing? It is only literate clerks, after all, who are given to the lamentation "Full many a flower is born to blush unseen,/And waste its sweetness on the desert air." If, nonetheless, writers, readers, and critics need to be reminded that much of the world is excluded from Literature, it does not then follow that more of the world or of its People will in any important sense be accounted for by Literature's rival, the electronic media. Should the development by which these media now promise to give visibility and voice to People prove a hoax, as I suspect it already has done, then that will in itself prove immensely instructive. It will further demonstrate that there is perhaps no way in which expression is ever free from the economic, political, and cultural structures that are implicated in the very nature of any and all media. Third World and displaced minorities are now encouraged to insist, for example, upon a history for themselves that is more than a sub-plot in the Western story of man, but there is little evidence so far of success, as I have argued elsewhere.[3]

Literature, and those who want to care for it, ought to acknowledge, as the other media dare not do, that it does not and cannot reveal much of the history even of those it favors with attention. It is in this regard, too, that the literary modernist notion that the twentieth is the worst of centuries might again be questioned. Worst for whom? One presumption of Anglo-American-Europeans is that their experience, or what it is said to be by certain writers, defines the nature of contemporary life. So that the recorded ravages of the twentieth century, while indeed horrible by any standard, are given unquestioned predominance over what can nonetheless be known about the mute, sporadically recorded, unnarrativized miseries of vast numbers of people in centuries past, as in the greatest genocide in history during the hundred years after Columbus landed in the New World, an episode examined in Tzvetan Todorov's *The Conquest of America: The Question of the Other*. Those who say in common-room banter that really they belong in the eighteenth century imagine that if transported there they would still be in the common room, though differently dressed, when in all likelihood they would be sweeping chimneys, assuming they had survived long enough even to do that.

But who, it must nonetheless be asked, can inquire most effectively into this question of narrativity, of a place for People in the plot of history, if it be not those—like Todorov or Edward Said in *Orientalism* —who have been prepared to do so in large part by their educated knowledge of analogues in the necessarily repressive plottings of Literature? It may be encouraging to suppose that Technology has, for the new mass of People, removed literacy as a prerequisite for securing a place of sustained significance in historical narrative, and in a nicer world that might be the case. In fact, however, the allowance for such a place is now within the domain of corporate institutions far less disposed than is Literature to surrender any of their power to the powerless. Technology, in this parable, seems to grant to the hitherto "invisible man" an opportunity for self-articulation, and this might persuade him that Literature is even less important now than it was in the past. Such technological benefits are utterly illusory, however. And it is not surprising that when it calls attention to this illusion, Literature also likes to exult in itself. Literature as a custodian of language and as a representation of life is now in a position to show the consequences on People of a Technological power which only pretends to rescue them from obscurity. It can show what it is like for People to live under the aegis of media other than Literature. What Henry Adams half suspected in *The Education*, Thomas Pynchon projects as a saturnalia in *Gravity's Rainbow*.

IF AT THIS POINT in the story one is tempted to commiserate with Literature, give thought, however, to a few historical contradictions and peculiarities. Before Technology struck back, it had for centuries been victimized by Literature. There is a haunting instance in Book II of Spenser's *The Faerie Queene*. Book II was given to the printer in 1589, but Spenser describes it as an "antique" mirror of a faery land. The past for which it is an image has always been an imaginary past. Near the end of that book Sir Guyon descends from the open fields and virgin lands of chivalric England into the Cave of Mammon. The Cave has ascribed to it the detailed horrors of what would later be called an industrial-factory system, along with many of the blandishments of finance capitalism. For one thing, it is filled with currency that reproduces its own value without in the process contributing to the growth of anything other than money, filthy lucre. The Cave is a perversion of nature in the interests of financial and industrial progress. Guyon is so appalled—or tempted—that he faints when he reaches the surface.

Milton, whose father was a moneylender, finds Guyon's heroism vali-
dated by the fact that in order to confront Mammon he had to digress
from his main business, which is to discover and bring to governance
those extremes of eroticism which can weaken the zeal for public service
to the Queen. But the encapsulation of the Mammon episode within
this larger purpose is also, I think, a symptom of the difficulty, given
Spenser's historical situation in an England determined on economic
development, of dealing with financial enterprise and its technological
counterparts. Apparently, the misuse of the body for private pleasure
could be more critically and dialectically treated than could the misap-
propriations of the body by economic institutions. Perhaps that is why
the standards and ideals evoked in the episode seem already in the
sixteenth century to be rather wistful.

What I am suggesting is that Literature from some of its earliest and
now classic instances seems *always* to have been nostalgic for something
that has been lost. What can be the origin of a loss that was always there?
It was to meet such a logistical and logical gap that Literature introduced
Technology as a villain. It is obvious, again, that I am using the term
Technology to describe manifestations whose early forms are quite unlike later, more familiar ones. Literature did not wait for Mark Twain
or Lawrence or Pynchon before it ascribed demonic and destructive
powers to what can be called Technology. Nearly from the beginnings
of English literature, images of exploitative control over environment
are, embryonically, images also of Technology. Usury is an aspect of this,
of money that begets only money so that, as in the opening of *Volpone*,
accumulated wealth rivals the sun, the source of natural energy and
generative power. Writing about this in *Religion and the Rise of Capitalism*, R. H. Tawney helps bring me to the point I want to make—that
Literature, paradoxically, depends on and partakes of Technology: "Behind the genii of beauty and wisdom who were its architects"—he is
speaking of the emergence of the modern from the feudal world—
"there moved a murky, but indispensable, figure. It was the demon
whom Dante had met muttering gibberish in the fourth circle of the
Inferno, and whom Sir Guyon was to encounter three centuries later,
tanned with smoke and seared with fire, in a cave adjoining the mouth
of hell. His uncouth labors quarried the stones which Michelangelo was

to raise, and sank deep in the Roman clay the foundations of the walls to be adorned by Raphael."

To read Tawney is to be reminded that electronic media are, for Literature, only the most recent version of what was anciently imagined as a Technological threat to cultural health and continuity. With precedents for which there are forever other precedents, Literature has always asked us to be nostalgic for some aspect of the human and the natural whose essential purity resides in the fact that it begins to perish under Technology's pressure. So much so that it seems as if the ideal forms of the human and the natural do not in fact or in reality ever actually exist; as if when they appear, even in represented life, they can be no more than fleeting and pitiable remnants, like Sir Guyon, or shepherds, like Melville's Starbuck or Wordsworth's Michael, like Lawrence's Mellors or Joyce's Bloom. One might call it the Cordelia syndrome—these creations of a nostalgia for human goodness uncontaminated, a nostalgia so strong that its embodiments emerge from the doom that awaits them.

Again, why has Literature persuaded itself, and us, that this should be so? When a villain is hard to find, there is always, after all, "original sin." But "original sin" is one likely source of Literature itself. "Original sin" was probably invented to explain and relieve some feeling in each of us that something was lost, abandoned, betrayed in the process of our becoming human. We love our cats and dogs with a certain pathos, a sense that we somehow left them behind, along with other creatures, in an inarticulateness that once was also ours. The Fall of Man, to recall a remark in Emerson's "Experience," "is the discovery we have made that we exist." This is the fall from the womb into some terrible consciousness of unitary existence. Literature, one of the great human creations, is in this view a compensation for the Fall. It offers consoling evidence of a community of loss but also (implicit in the shaping of language itself) a promise of corporate creation. Without the Fall there could be, as Milton tells us, no *Paradise Lost.* What then has compelled Literature to invent yet another instrument of loss and call it Technology?

Even to ask this question reveals why Literature has so frequently expressed a suspiciousness of its own enterprise. And why should it not? Because if it locates a cause for human alienation in Technology, what prevents the indictment from reaching back, beyond the Fall to the prelapsarian human attribute of Reason itself and thence to the mental technologies, including Literature, to which Reason gave birth? If the accusing finger points to science, it points also at any act of interpretation, of which Literature is a genre or species. For Literature to deny its collusion with Technology would require it to claim not merely that it re-presents life but that it actually created it. Indeed, Literature does frequently indulge in such exorbitant and heroic self-assertions even while asking to be pardoned for them. This is the beautiful pathos of Joyce/Stephen in *A Portrait,* of Shakespeare in the Sonnets, of Marlowe in the punishments meted out to his over-reachers, of Milton's Satan, and of Coleridge, who worried about his "genius" as something that might cut him off from the supposedly natural bonds between man and nature.

Literature acknowledges in these instances that its own operations are akin to exercises of the technological power which it writes against. Like Technology, Literature appropriates, exploits, recomposes, arranges— within inherited but constantly "modernized" mechanisms of literary form—materials that all the while are also said by Literature to belong to something called "life." This concern for the power of technique in Literature is especially pronounced in the English Romantics, as in such poems of Wordsworth's as "Nutting" and Book I of *The Prelude,* where, as David Ferry and others have shown,[4] human intrusions, acquisitive destructiveness, or theft, all of them visited upon an otherwise silent, awe-ful, and serene nature, are a metaphoric equivalent of the poet's own seizure of objects for use in poetry. Wordsworth includes in his poetry the criticism later made of him by Lawrence, that he was "impertinent."

The dialectic concern for form as against fluidity, for figuration as against fracture, for a protean self—these are not, however, original to the Romantic or modernist concern about the usurpatory-creative nature of writing. They are everywhere in Literature expressions of concern for order that is always also an anxiety about its possibly brutal and deforming rigidities. More recent literature is especially useful for illustration only because it tends to treat earlier writing as if in itself it were a kind of Technology, as if it had created forms and predictable movements that have become reified and potentially deadening.

Literature's distaste for Technology reveals, at last, a squeamishness about its own operations. This is perhaps most evident in the degree to which it idealizes an emphatically non-literary contingent of People. I refer to characters who are themselves almost never interested in Literature. In some central instances—and there are of course many exceptions to this—the most admired and commendable human figures in works of genius, especially since 1800 or so, are either unliterary or positively suspicious of Literature. The worthy rustics of Wordsworth's poetry, no less than Faulkner's enduring Dilsey, could hardly be expected to *read* about themselves. Indeed you might say that the reason they are exemplary is that they do not engage in the exploitative enterprise of reading and writing. Leopold Bloom can, of course, read, but no one would expect him to read *Ulysses*. Literature seldom includes among its implied readers the kind of people it most admires, and when it includes literary people they are often a shady or tortured lot. If Literature is something "we" need, why is it apparently not needed at all by some of the finest types Literature has imagined? This was the case long before such "ordinary" people were presumably corrupted or lost to Literature by the T.V. screen. A little of such literary demography might dampen the bravado of those who take it for granted that since Literature makes such redeeming use of ordinary people, it follows that ordinary people can make redeeming use of Literature.

To put it another way, it is quite generally assumed that because ordinary people are available to Literature as a resource, they are also available to it as an audience, had they not been otherwise seduced. How else explain the voluble and confused disparagement visited, in the name of print culture, on television? But if critical competence in the reading of Literature requires some sort of productive engagement with difficulties made inevitable by the nature of language itself, then it requires some measure of critical incompetence to complain that Literature should or could be in competition with T.V. for the attention of a general public. Many avid readers of Literature spend, as I do, a great deal of time watching television, but it does not follow that the reverse might also be true—that inveterate watchers could care about Literature and language in ways they can most rewardingly be cared about. Leaving aside the masses in the world who cannot read at all, it is evident that reading citizens, wherever they are, would not necessarily read more or read better if they watched television less. And much of what they do read in newspapers, magazines, and what sometimes passes for good fiction and poetry is often lacking in the nuances that can be heard not only in movies but on video tape. Arguments that the emergence of video is largely responsible for the decline of reading or literacy are no more tenable than long-faced suggestions that the so-called art of conversation (never a conspicuous feature in the T.V.-less childhoods of people my age) disappeared from the family circle because of the intrusion of the tube. To judge from the endless conversational murmur in movie houses, which used to be much quieter, people may have been convinced by T.V. that they can and should become more, not less, voluble before any available screen.

A habit of phrasing epitomizes the confusions I am trying to sort out: the tendency to refer to all instruments of expression *except* Literature as "the media," often with the omission of such qualifiers as "electronic" or "mass." The implications are especially glaring in linked phrases like "print and media culture." What is being suggested is that video is one of "the media" and that print is not; that print, and especially Literature, are exonerated from the contaminations associated with media.

The implication, not dispelled by any amount of critical theory however ancient, is that language and Literature are "natural" while all other media, like T.V. or the movies, are not. This is at the heart of the confusions of those who assume that life would somehow be better if Literature could prevail over video for a general audience. What seems to be forgotten is that language is in itself a mediation—another point that cannot be emphasized enough, no matter how embarrassingly obvious. Every word is a form of re-presentation. And Literature, by virtue of its formal conventions and the conscious struggle by which it appropriates language to poetry or the novel, is yet another and still more formidable example of media and re-presentation. Language and Literature are the most indispensable and resilient cultural resources which human beings have invented for themselves. And yet, no matter how "natural" language is judged to be, it is obviously an artifact in large part created and fashioned by all kinds of social, religious, economic, and political pressures.

Language itself is a particular form of Technology. Perhaps the tendency to think otherwise, to think that language partakes of nature—instead of knowing that nature partakes of language—is a result of the quite understandable desire to believe that language and Literature should be identical with the *kinds* of nature and humanity which they idealize and preserve. It is a very costly mistake, however, an unnecessary concession to vulgarians, mediacratic or literary. It implies, ridiculously, that culture, in its literary or high artistic manifestations, can be absorbed pretty much the way T.V. is absorbed, that somehow, in its competition with popular culture, high culture has gotten not less but more readily available than it has ever been in history.

Language, however, is not virgin "nature" available as fully to video or to radio or to movies as it is to Literature. It is a resource which Literature, more effectively than any other media, can productively mine and develop. The detrimental effect of video on the general public has been exaggerated to the extent that some positive effects of Literature on the general public have been idealized. Regis Debray's remark that "the darkest spot in modern society is a small luminous screen" is a sample of the kind of silliness that can pass for thinking on this subject. What has happened, and for a variety of reasons that include but are not exhausted by Technology, is that there have been in the last hundred years or so some accelerated changes in ideas of the natural, the traditional, and, especially, of the human. These ideas, which are in part the invention of Literature, are essential to its prosperity and to the prospect of its being able to maintain some degree of its ancient cultural-social power. But this is not to say, in the mood of the culturally conservative, that Literature ought to preserve any particular image of nature, the human, or the past. Precisely the reverse. Literature exists to challenge the inherited forms of language. It exists in and through the act by which it questions what at the same time it proposes; it challenges in one period—in one phrase—the images predominant in another, and it exposes as a figuration, a shadow, any term, like "human" or "natural," which the culture at large may want to idealize for its own political or historical convenience. So that what is truly threatened by Technology in the form of electronic media is exactly that play of dialectical complication in language that is inseparable from the act of literary creation.

What I have been implying can now be said more directly. A feature of Literature essential to its value is quite simply its refusal to offer, in the parlance of T.V., a clear image. The obvious implication of electronic media is that Literature's kind of opacity is inessential, evasive, and obscurantist. This is also, to expose the full and tortuous ironies of our cultural situation, the charge customarily leveled against Literature itself by those middle- would-be high-brow elements of the literary-critical establishment (as featured in such politically and culturally conservative journals as *Commentary, The American Scholar,* and *The New Criterion*) whenever the canon is disrupted by the appearance of experimental or theoretical work. "Inessential," "evasive," "obscurantist"—this has at some point been said of nearly every innovative writer, specifically including some who have subsequently proved to be the most important critics, in recent history. Those who want Literature to be widely available, on the assumption that it is socially and morally enhancing, generally oppose T.V. on the grounds that it is socially and morally injurious, but their criteria are as simplistic in the one case as in the other.

We are left with the task of finding a way to describe how Literature, unlike T.V., manages to put itself out of focus no matter how hard we try to bring it into focus. I have already said that Literature is a kind of writing whose clarities bring on precipitations of density and have used the word "difficulty" to characterize a particularly self-conscious or modernist aspect of this. I want briefly to discuss these terms and their utility in the larger argument I am making. By "density" I mean to describe a kind of writing which gives, or so it likes to pretend, a fairly direct access to pleasure, but which becomes, on longer acquaintance, rather strange and imponderable. Shakespeare is a good example; so is Herbert or *The Prelude* or Emerson's essays or *Middlemarch* or Frost. Another kind of writing may, on first encounter, seem quite bristly, resistant, "difficult." If somehow, maybe with the help of notes and annotations, you master the "difficulty"—you cannot in the same sense master "density"—you may then find that there is little or no "density" behind it. Stephen Dedalus's tortured prose in the "Proteus" section of *Ulysses* is for me a case in point, as are such episodes as "Oxen of the Sun" and "Ithaca," where formal mechanisms, more than the information carried by them, rather statically communicate the significance. To put it very crudely, the Joyce of "The Dead" is more dense than is the Joyce of *Ulysses,* where he is being both difficult and dense; *Ulysses,* relatively speaking, is difficult while *Nostromo, Women in Love,* and *A la Recherche du temps perdu* are dense; Pound is difficult; Stevens is dense, as are Dickinson and Whitman, who are deceptively easy.

Twentieth-century criticism and theory have tended to prefer "difficulty" to "density." Difficulty gives the critic a chance to strut his stuff, to treat Literature as if it really were a communication of knowledge rather than a search for it. Difficulty also carries with it a lineage of theoretical, historical, and cultural justification. Writers in the sixteenth century had religious theories about the virtues of obscurity in poetry, but in this century "difficulty" has been made to seem the inescapable social and political responsibility of the artist. You are already on notice that when something is hard to read there are Big Reasons for its being so, and that you, reader, had better shape up. Density is another matter. No guide book will help you. It does not announce itself in Literature, any more than it does in some of our most intimate conversations, and it can go unnoticed in either case by those who do not care to encounter it. Density is very often something that strikes the ear rather than the eye; it is often something you hear happening to voices as they modify words and phrases which, at another point, seemed quite clear or casual. Density is usually accompanied not by the extruding allusiveness of modernism but by the covert allusiveness of troping.

Troping gives evidences of the human involvement in the shaping of language, and it prevents language from imposing itself upon us with the force and indifference of a Technology. It frees us from predetermined meanings. Troping is the turning of a word in directions or detours it seemed destined otherwise to avoid. Thus Emerson, admitting in *Nature* that "the charming landscape which I saw this morning, is indubitably made up of some twenty or thirty farms," owned by people he then proceeds to name, goes on to say that "none of them owns the landscape. There is a property in the horizon which no man has but he whose eye can integrate all the parts, that is, the poet." This is a nice example, because even while Emerson is troping on the idea of possession, he is at the same time claiming that the power to trope is greater than any more obviously economic power. Frost is being notably Emersonian, for example, when he remarks in a letter to Untermeyer that "Marx had the strength not to be overawed by the metaphor in vogue. . . . Great is he who imposes the metaphor." To change the shape of something, a writer must first know the shapes it has already been given. In that sense, to be a great poet, and Marx would surely count as one, is also to be a great scholar.

Anyone who uses language is accepting, even without knowing it, an entitlement and, with it, an obligation usually honored more by resentment than by gratitude. Words have a way of suggesting that they have already had an earlier, very likely a better life than any we propose to offer. And in reaction everyone likes, as it were, to "turn a phrase." By the turning, the troping of it, language can be made into a sign not of human subservience but of human power, though that power might also consist, as I argue in the final chapter, "Writing Off the Self," in the decision not to trope any further, to leave the world to its own changes, free of human intrusion, though this imagination of the world is, of course, itself a trope. At least some of the time, especially in playful conversation, everyone is a kind of poet without intending thereby to be a modernist, one who feels there is something special to recent times which compels him, in Eliot's phrase, self-consciously "to force, to dislocate if necessary, language into his meaning." Few social occasions are more gratifying than those in which conversational witticisms come by chance, when unintended jokes are like a gift hidden in the words we utter. So that while language makes limiting claims on any effort to express life, it seems at the same time to lend itself to human inventiveness, to incite or even initiate it by hints of its promiscuity, as in the mere slip of the tongue.

Literature goes the crucial step beyond this. It is the Olympics of talk and of writing, an Olympics which requires that the spectator actively compete in the games. Literature records itself, shows how its records might be broken, and how the assumptions of a given discourse or culture might thereby be challenged. Shakespeare is, again, the great example. He is amazingly dense but almost never turgid, except for special or comic purposes as in, say, *Troilus and Cressida,* and for the reason that while his dialogue proceeds in a manner completely natural to each of his characters, it manages simultaneously to fill itself with echoes and reverberations of which his speakers are mostly innocent. Those telling repetitions that anyone can hear in the casual talk of a friend—grist for the psychoanalytic mill—are transformed by Shakespeare into the exploratory shapings of an entire play. In Act V of *Julius Caesar*, for example, Antony berates Brutus and Cassius by saying that "your vile daggers/hacked one another in the sides of Caesar"—a gruesome bit of talk, and nastier than Antony realizes, since what he cannot know is that the word "hacked" had been given unusual prominence earlier in the play by Brutus himself when, in the conspirators' scene in Act II, he voiced opposition to Cassius's recommendation that Antony should also be assassinated. "Our course will seem too bloody, Caius Cassius," he argued, "To cut the head off and then hack the limbs." And he goes on to say that they should proceed like "sacrificers, but not butchers," that they should "carve him as a dish fit for the gods,/Not hew him as a carcass fit for hounds." Because of Brutus's earlier discriminations of "carving," "hewing," "hacking," "hunting," "cutting," and the like, the later accusation that his own dagger "hacked" with Cassius's inside the body of Caesar may strike the reader with a force beyond anything that Antony, even in the fullness of his contempt, could have wished for. The troping of terms creates significances that have far less to do with expressions of character than with the larger expressive intentions of the whole work. At such junctures Shakespeare himself is to be discovered within the deployments of his language. The troping of terms having to do with killing and bloodletting points to a central problem in nearly all of his tragedies and histories: how is it possible to kill, how to bleed or cause others to bleed, so that instead of making the time more gory and slaughterous it may instead be redeemed, as by the bleeding and killing of Christ? Can a butcher, that is, become a sacrificer? Can an assassination become a ceremony? How is it ever possible effectively to trope murder?

Literature makes the strongest possible claims on my attention because more than any other form of art or expression it demonstrates what can be made, what can be done with something shared by everyone, used by everyone in the daily conduct of life, and something besides which carries most subtly and yet measurably within itself, its vocabulary and syntax the governing assumptions of a society's social, political, and economic arrangements. Works of music, dance, paintings, filmmaking —any of these may be more enjoyable or affecting than a given work of Literature and may also, of course, exhibit comparable operations of genius. But none depends for its principle or essential resource on materials that it must share in an utterly gregarious way with the society at large and with its history. None can teach us so much about what words do to us and how, in turn, we might try to do something to them which will perhaps modify the order of things on which they depend for their meaning. To Literature is left the distinction that it invites the reader to a dialectical relationship to words with an intensity allowable nowhere else, which Technology, especially in the form of video, cannot offer in any sustained way, and which many kinds of writing are quite anxious to abridge. Despite its own affiliations with Technology, and perhaps because it feels guilty about them, Literature tells us not that we are in "the prison house of language" but that we are on parole.

Chapter 4

RESISTANCE IN ITSELF

The universal cataract of death
That spends to nothingness—and unresisted,
Save by some strange resistance in itself,
Not just a swerving, but a throwing back,
As if regret were in it and were sacred.

Robert Frost, "West-Running Brook"

EMERSON SAYS now and then that language might lead us back to human origins, that "language," as he says in "The Poet," "is fossil poetry." This implies that there are discoverable traces in language of that aboriginal power by which we invent ourselves as a unique form of nature. Frost in an Emersonian mood ends the poem "All Revelation" with a tribute to this human inventiveness:

Eyes seeking the response of eyes
Bring out the stars, bring out the flowers,
Thus concentrating earth and skies
So none need be afraid of size.
All revelation has been ours.

Stevens alludes to the same condition in "Sunday Morning," to a time when he hopes the "sky will seem much friendlier then than now/A part of labor and a part of pain . . ./Not this dividing and indifferent blue." Revelation is not up there, it is down here, and it is still going on. *Ours* in "All Revelation," as in other poems by Frost like "In Hardwood Groves" and "Rose Pogonias," is a play on *hours*. He means to suggest that human possessiveness, especially of the things it creates, is always haunted by temporality. Within the bravado of the poem, the word hints at the brevity of any generational claim or, for that matter, the claims of the human species itself, given its tiny measure within the vast reaches of time. All revelation is nonetheless "ours," for the present at least, and since we also invent the past it, too, is always presently available to us, to every newborn child, as the natal-sexual images earlier in the poem suggest, though the child might not ever become fully aware of the bequests made to it.

"Ours" does not refer, then, only to certain accomplished individuals, like poets, since any poet is only a facet through which the composite power of Man might prismatically show itself. Language is essential to the expression of this power, but it cannot ever fully represent it even in all of its accumulations. Man is still revealing himself to himself, continuously coming into being, continuously recreating in the present a past which the historic past itself cannot have known. That most Emersonian of movies, *2001*, takes all this impressively for granted, visually collapsing differences among past, present, and future by allowing the same motifs to recur in each projected period. Any merely localized expression soon reveals itself as eccentric, but the localization encourages corrective and creative efforts. These also can only be partial, and this process intensifies the desire to find something less momentary, more inclusive and essential. Literature is one expression of this desire, but like language, which is its instrument, it is to a great extent shaped by the order of things predominant in any given historical epoch. Its language, as Wordsworth remarks, is always subject to arbitrary associations. This condition does not change; neither does the human urge to create within and against its pressures.

It seems, then, as if human creativity depends for its incentives on the preliminary imagination of something that is simultaneously a support and an obstruction, something that will need eventually to be overcome, some representation of an already existing reality that probably *cannot* be overcome. Emerson has this in mind in his 1841 lecture "The Conservative." Arguing at one point against the party of innovation, he persuasively describes the relation in his work between "aspiration" and "antagonism," which are the terms he uses at the beginning of "Prudence," or, as he intimates, between the desire for originality and the obligation to tradition:

You who quarrel with the arrangements of society, and are willing to embroil all, and risk the indisputable good that exists, for the chance of better, live, move, and have your being in this, and your deeds contradict your words every day. For as you cannot jump from the ground without using the resistance of the ground, nor put out the boat to sea, without shoving from the shore, nor attain liberty without rejecting obligation, so you are under the necessity of using the Actual order of things, in order to disuse it; to live by it, whilst you wish to take away its life.

"The Actual order of things" is of course no more than a phrase. It conjures up some possible versions of social or historical reality that might then give significance to actions taken in response to it. It is a metaphor meant to describe those arrangements which excite cooperative or resistant energies. "The Actual order of things" can, as I have been showing, assume other similarly provocative titles like Technology, History, Tradition, Convention, System, Society. All of these tend to be characterized in works of literature, though with varying degrees of intensity, as constraints on Freedom, Imagination, Aspiration, Desire, Originality. However, in the process of completing itself, a literary text is apt to prove as inhospitable to any of these good things as are the bad opponents designated for them by literature. Literature cannot be expected openly to admit this, but often comes close. Indeed, the constrictive nature of literary texts is implicit in the admission found in nearly all of them: that they must work with traditions, forms, syntaxes that in themselves constitute an "order of things," and that their own claims to originality are at best the perpetuation of a merely enabling mythology.

The desire to originate began with the origination of ourselves, and even this was only a revision or transformation of whatever Else was there. The forever unrequited desire for originality is the evidence of its impossibility. Language is proof enough of this. Words are quotations,

so to speak, of the things they refer to; they can never be those things.
When Emerson says in "Prudence" that "we write from aspiration and
antagonism, as well as from experience," he means that while we aspire
to say something new, the materials at hand indicate that whatever we
say can be understood only if it is relatively familiar. We therefore
become antagonistic to conventions of language even though we are in
need of them. Indeed, the social and literary forms that ask for our
compliance were themselves produced in resistance to conventions of an
earlier time. Even in words that now seem tired or dead we can discover
a desire for transformation that once infused them. Any word, in the
variety and even contradictoriness of its meanings, gives evidence of
earlier antagonistic uses, and it is this which encourages us to turn on
them again, to change or trope them further.

Literature provides the texts where this most vitally happens, where
language is most alert to itself. The general relevance to literature of
such Emersonian conjectures is even more apparent should you choose
to discard his attendant vocabulary of "power" or "soul" or "Man" or
"nature" and think only of some of the actions I have already described
by which literary texts create meaning and form. Language represents
both an entitlement to say certain things and the evidence that we are
never done trying to say other things. This is apparent in the relations
among literary texts and also within any one of them. A literary text, as
is conspicuously the case in Shakespeare's plays, dramatizes the story of
its own struggle with the terminologies to which it has married itself.
Its struggle with language never ends, but like some marital arguments
can produce always greater density or complexity. Referring perhaps to
Eliot, but more likely to some composite of poets, Stevens says in "The
Creations of Sound": "Tell X that speech is not dirty silence/Clarified.
It is silence made still dirtier."

LITERATURE IS UNIQUE among the arts both because of its entire dependence upon language and because it exhibits an acute sensitivity to
language's own dependence on the history of its usage. I would say then
any poem, novel, play, or essay can be of lasting interest only if it reveals
a thoroughgoing inquisitiveness about its own verbal resources; it must
let itself discover as much as can be known about the previous uses of

its words. Shakespeare in *Romeo and Juliet* had to know Petrarch in order to distinguish the artificial from the true expressions of love, but he had also to know the Old Testament, so that when Lear sounds like Job there is no danger of our confusing the two. Literature's preoccupation with the past is of its essence, as is directly acknowledged by writers like Spenser and Milton and Pope, like Hawthorne and Proust. By allusions and echoes and mimicries, by punning and parody and a mastery of lingoes, literature makes the indentured state of its language into a recurrent subject. Gore Vidal's *Myra Breckinridge*, in its reformulations of the language of such late twentieth-century media as soap opera and video drama, discovers the submerged content of materials which Joyce, had he written *Ulysses* fifty years later, would have wanted to bring into the Circe episode.

The "inventor only knows how to borrow," Emerson says in "Plato." "Every book is a quotation; and every house is a quotation out of all forests, and mines and stone quarries; and every man is a quotation from all his ancestors." Unless writing is alive to its inheritances, it cannot of course do anything with them; it cannot transform them in a way that enhances their value; it cannot, in William James's phrase, "add to both the substantive and to the predicate parts of reality." This means, again, that only a very small portion of all that is written deserves to be called *literature*, though to say this will offend various factions who want to modify the term by putting racial, national, sexual, or political adjectives in front of it. To claim a literature for oneself is to acquire cultural power and conspicuousness, but first the literature has to have been written. In its absence, any group which aspires to have a literature will first have to assent to the fact that its production depends on literary traditions in large part the creation of writers who have unapologetically identified themselves as male, partriarchal, and patriotic. I am not approving but merely describing a situation which must be accepted by anyone who proposes to change it. And there is only one way to change it: by acts of writing which are designed to become a part of the traditions which the writing opposes. I am recommending an Emersonian antagonism to literature as the best, indeed the only, way to create it.

"Every book is a quotation" means that a book cannot be made up out of your head, that it can be summoned or seized only from a tradition in which you also find yourself, that it is always derivative. Eliot's famous remark that "immature poets imitate; mature poets steal" is its own best illustration, stolen as it was from Emerson's essay "Shakespeare." There he says of Chaucer, whom he calls a "huge borrower," that he steals "by this apology—that what he takes has no worth where he finds it, and the greatest where he leaves it. It has come to be practically a sort of rule in literature that a man, having once shown himself capable of original writing, is entitled thenceforth to steal from the writings of others at discretion." On the face of it, all this sounds a bit smug, as if literature were entirely a closed and self-generating system. It is because Emerson understands this as a real possibility that we have heard him at other points call upon criticism to "easily entertain the supposition of [literature's] entire disappearance," and why, again without fully articulating or even acknowledging the implications of his positions, he talks favorably about other kinds of art in a way that he could not possibly talk about literature.

How, for example, can his emphasis on the self-referentiality of literature—on literature as quotation, as borrowing, as theft—possibly be squared with the assertion in his essay on "Art" that "the reference of all production [is] at last to an aboriginal power"? I want here to add to the questions I have already raised about this passage. Emerson's nagging use of the phrase "at last" often suggests that he has gotten back to something prior even to human culture. Because it calls upon some power belonging to the human but as yet unacculturated species, artistic production, in what he calls "works of the highest art," can become "universally intelligible" and "restore to us the simplest states of mind." But if this were indeed ever possible for literature, then what I have called "the question of genius" would not exist; instead of being a partial expression of human genius, a literary work could fully represent it. In fact the notion of universal intelligibility is at variance with nearly everything he says about literary production and reception, no matter how theoretically true it may be with respect to other forms of artistic expression. Most of us who bother with "art"—so relatively few as to make the word "universal" sound supercilious—have on occasion experienced in a particular work a radiant sense of human glory, "a wonderful expression," as he says later on, "through stone, or canvas, or musical sound, of the deepest attributes of our nature," some "reappearance of our original soul." But he conspicuously does not refer here to literary composition. In the rest of the essay there is only a passing reference to a few writers, along with the remark that "the real value of the Iliad, or the Transfiguration, is as signs of power . . . tokens of the everlasting effort to produce, which even in its worst estate the soul betrays." His comments on "the universal intelligibility" of art apply to works which superficially can be taken in at a glance or a hearing, and not through the prolongations of words in sentences and paragraphs. Words could only encumber the "original soul" with historical and individual partialities, especially in a socially conditioned form like the novel, which Emerson particularly distrusted.

Emerson does not exclude literature when he says that "the reference of all production [is] at last to aboriginal power," but how is such power to be located or experienced even by those who can read, much less by those who, more "universally," cannot? If, as is the case, all language is quotation, if, further, every book is a quotation,[1] then where in this welter of quotation is there an opportunity for literary production to express "original soul" or "aboriginal power"? The answer, which brings us to the generative core of Emerson's own writing, is that this "power" and this "soul" manifest themselves in an instinctive antagonism to "quotation," in disruptions, variation, and tropings of it.

Thanks mostly to Foucault and his followers, the word "power" has become tiresomely recurrent in discussions of cultural forms or the order of things. It is nonetheless unavoidable in any consideration of Emerson. He uses it repeatedly, and he can be confusing about it both because he does not always indicate the kind of power he has in mind, whether it be individual or natural, and because he only reluctantly and intermittently admits that individual power is continuously threatened by that ineluctable power of nature called death. He knew, as did Dylan Thomas at his infrequent and Wordsworthian best, that we are literally made speechless by forces which also give us life, that "the force that through the green fuse drives the flower/Drives my green age" and that "I am dumb to tell the crooked rose/My youth is bent by the same wintry fever." In his obsession with power, Emerson is a philosopher-prophet of a discernibly American idea of progress, one that hopes to ignore

ruptures, deterrences, and fatalities, that will not submit to final reckon-
ings, to meanings ultimately arrived at. Though he sometimes acknowledges, as in "Experience," that "human life is made up of two elements,
power and form, and the proportion must be invariably kept," he
chooses just as often to see "life" itself as the constant expression of a
power in nature that is only further accelerated by any human resistance
to it. Transposed from nature to cultural or social existence, power then
becomes for him a process in which, ideally, the absorption as well as
the transformation of inheritance, the compliance with social system as
well as resistance to it are all so simultaneous as to preclude any permanent divisions, gaps, or interruptions. "Every thing," he writes in the
Journals for June 1847, "teaches transition, transference, metamorphosis: therein is human power, in transference, not in creation; & therein
is human destiny, not in longevity but in removal. We dive & reappear
in new places." Emerson is predicting the William James of *Pragmatism*
who, italicizing *engender,* says of the existent world that "man *engenders*
truths upon it." These provocative connotations are especially apt in the
case of Emerson, who could at times treat even the birth and the death,
at age five, of his firstborn son, Waldo, as a transitional event, part of
a creative mythology, forgetting how much he doted on his own and his
wife Lidian's little boy. To bring a new being into the world is, strictly
speaking, not an act of creation, as Emerson reminded himself, but of
transference, the transfer of already encoded materials into a new, on-
going combination. The inherited codes are instantly metamorphosed
by an act of engendering, and this act can be thought of less as an
individual and scarcely unique one than as an instinctual repetition of
biological-ancestral desire. Sexual-biological inferences of this kind can
be drawn from most theories of artistic creation, as I have shown on
other occasions,[2] so that in his exultations about artistic originality ("O!
In the virgin womb of the imagination the word was made flesh"),
Joyce's Stephen is doing no more than Paterizing Aquinas and St. John.
Thus, too, the barren landscapes in poems by Frost and Stevens represent, in the context of their other writings, an expression of a dreaded
depletion of generative energies, sexual and poetical, while the involu-
tions of Melville's *Pierre* result in part from his conflicted feelings about
the maternal-patriarchal nature of authorship, of bringing into the world

something new which will also re-present him. Literary production can be a privileged form of individualism, and yet for Emerson, as for all the writers I have mentioned in this book, the privilege is contaminated by the fact that it requires a language that has already been given birth and has many times over given birth to mutations of itself. It therefore continually proves to be an impediment to the self-realization it promises to assist.

The complex derivativeness of literature, or of any other form of life, substantially modifies Emersonian "individualism" and is at odds with the vulgar meanings assigned to the term. Consider the relation of Emerson, as he reports it, to the birth of Waldo, leaving until later his equally affecting and, it seems to many, peculiar response to the boy's death five years later. In an entry in his *Journals* dated October 31, 1836, he writes:

Last night at 11 o'clock, a son was born to me. Blessed child! a lovely wonder to me, and which makes the Universe look friendly to me. How remote my knowledge, how alien, yet how kind does it make the Cause of Causes appear! The stimulated curiosity of the father sees the graces & instincts which exist, indeed, in every babe, but unnoticed in others; the right to see all, know all, to examine nearly, distinguishes this relation & endears this child. Otherwise I see nothing in it of mine; I am no conscious party to any feature, any function, any perfection I behold in it. I seem to be merely the brute occasion of its being & nowise attaining to the dignity even of a second cause no more than I taught it to suck the breast.

Emerson here looks at his son, as he looks most of the time at himself: he is a "fact" to be studied. The child is less the incorporation of the father (or the unmentioned mother) than of something remote from both, belonging as much to the Universe within which it exists as a fragile and momentary form. "Now am I Pygmalion," he says a little later on. Anything a human being creates, a statue, a child, or a book, teaches him that it is not his alone; it comes also from the dead. The insistence on individual possession of such things, including self-possession, is for Emerson an immensely complex repetition of the original sin. This becomes dazzlingly evident when we put into conjunction a series of passages which he did not intend to conjoin and which reveal an obsessive concern that he himself, by the transgressive act of writing (and of parental possessiveness?) might be repeating the sin of the first parents. To begin with, there are his comments in *Representative Men* on the ambitions of Plato:

He has clapped copyright on the world. This is the ambition of individualism. But the mouthful proves too large. *Boa constrictor* has good will to eat it, but he is foiled. He falls abroad in the attempt; and biting, gets strangled: the bitten world holds the biter fast by his own teeth. There he perishes: unconquered nature lives on and forgets him. So it fares with all: so must it fare with Plato. In view of eternal nature, Plato turns out to be philosophical exercitations.

This sounds, at least superficially, like a derisive self-criticism of Emerson's own dream of world engorgement. Five years before the first version of this passage appeared in the *Journals,* he reported in October 1840, "I dreamed that I floated at will in the great Ether, and I saw this world floating also not far off, but diminished to the size of an apple. Then an angel took it in his hand & brought it to me and said 'This must thou eat.' And I ate the world."

Emerson's mind is so saturated in mythologies of origin and in the transits back and forth between human and mythic identities of the self that these two passages instead of contradicting one another are actually supplementary. That is, the man-as-serpent who bites into and strangles on the world is, though a representative of a fatal kind of individualism, also an analogue to Emerson himself during his dream of eating the world. Both figures are versions of Adam and Eve. He knew that "dreams are true to nature," as he writes in the *Journals* for April 1838, "& like monstrous formations . . . show the law. Their double consciousness, their sub- & ob-jectiveness is the wonder," and he therefore would not feel the need to say, especially in the privacy of his journals, that his dream is an example of what he calls "transference": of himself into Adam, Eve, and the Fall. He nearly always declines even in the essays to signal such shifts of identity because he is convinced, quite rightly it seems to me, that the shifts are more rather than less frequently the rule and ought therefore to be treated, along with dreams, as a quite natural, expected part of daily existence. Even as he dreams of eating the world it is not only the subject but the fact of dreaming which proves how, already within us, are residues of the first and all subsequent parents. The forbidden fruit is knowledge of the world; it is the desire to take the world into oneself, to make the created universe into a part of man and not the other way round. The Fall is already implicit in this desire because the desire could not exist if man had felt comfortably at one with the world. In his willful degree of otherness, his invention of individualism, man discovers also his consciousness of death. To have claimed Waldo as entirely his own on the basis of physical parentage would be to admit then and there, at his birth, that the eventual death of the son would remove him, and his father, from the links of existence. The child must exist instead as part of the everlasting phenomenon of the Cause of Causes. Father and son must not be merely incorporated.

These images of biting and eating, of engorging and strangulation, become all the more resonant when joined to an astounding entry in the *Journals* for January–March 1845: "Eve softly with her womb/Bit him to death." Since Eve, like Emerson and all of us, is mythologically of and from Adam, his death in her womb can be considered coincidental with our birth out of it. We are in every sense quotations of Adam, out of his side and out of her womb, and the mythic elaborations among these passages is a parable of the artistic, literary, and human "production" which we have already heard him describe in its relations to past and future. Indeed, because these journal fragments are joined not by Emerson but by me and do not therefore constitute a composed text, their accidental configuration illustrates how the human mind instinctively creates meanings by an insistent, obsessive cultivation of its own terminologies. Mythologizing is a fact of human nature. Frost's great dream poem, "After Apple-Picking," is another such parable of creation, Milton transcribed into a New English vernacular. Milton's "paradise within," a fortunate consequence of the loss of Paradise, is the place of dream, imagination, "transference" rather than "creation," a place already saturated with images of heaven, earth, and hell, of all animals and all flowers.

The publication of these images in poetry can be worried over, as it sometimes is by Coleridge and Wordsworth, as a further, aggravated assault on the natural world which has been left us, an attempt to violate its integrity by taking meanings away from it. Emersonians are sometimes equally worried, but they like to convince themselves that their work with language is also, as William James suggests, something that "works" *for* the world. Writing, that is, can enhance the mythological power which is also the due inheritance of writing. How, an Emersonian asks, do I invest the inheritance so as to increase it? How do I manage the estate of poetry so that besides being an heir I can also create some heirs? It is possible to be anxious about this, and also, as with Whitman, happily bumptious. "Crossing Brooklyn Ferry," for instance, allows him a natural geography for images of transit, forward and back, so that he is put inevitably in mind of future readers for the poem he is then and there composing: "The men and women I saw were all near to me,/Others the same—others who look back on me because I look'd forward to them,/(The time will come, though I stop here to-day and to-night.)" Stevens, most notable among Whitman's heirs, was, however, not so confident that he, in turn, would leave recognizable traces of his passage, which is the plaint, as we shall see, of "A Postcard from the Volcano." The hope that some trace of your part in life will remain to be discovered in the future presupposes a relation of past to present not unique to poetry. There is evidence of it everywhere one looks; it is part of practical economy in every form of human life. "Therein is human power, in transference not in creation, & therein is human destiny, not in longevity but in removal"—if this describes, as I maintain, the essential nature of literary production, it also describes more ordinary forms of human enterprise. "The common sense of Franklin, Dalton, Davy, and Black," Emerson says in "Nature," "is the same common sense which made the arrangements which it now discovers."

THESE EMERSONIAN mythologies of transmission and transformation are implicated, it seems to me, in the peculiar similarity of pattern by which words in various literary texts tend to work against as well as with one another. Typically, the words initially create an "order of things," as Emerson would say, an order very often meant to represent some allegedly actual structure in nature or society. "Shall I compare thee to a summer's day?" Go right ahead. But Shakespeare himself takes immediate exception: "Thou art more lovely and more temperate." "Happy families are all alike; every unhappy family is unhappy in its own way" is a proposition to which anyone might assent, though *Anna Karenina* proceeds to explore its limitations. Works of literature like to set an initial course for themselves which they intend to modify, challenge, or even reverse. Another way of putting it is that literary works develop an energy that is subversive not only of historical, social, and literary structures external to themselves, but of their own, internally generated rhetorical structures. The process is not, of course, so simple or so mechanically sequential as my attempt to summarize it might suggest. It can occur haphazardly throughout a work, as in that moment, well past the middle of "Self-Reliance," when Emerson impatiently dismisses his own title ("Why, then, do we prate of self-reliance? . . . To talk of self-reliance is a poor external way of speaking"), or when, as in Shakespeare, a word that at one point in a play occurs in the free flow of conversation will suddenly reemerge at another point with immense, hitherto unsuspected implications.

I am saying that one obvious characteristic of a literary text is that its words tend to destabilize one another and to fall into conflicted or contradictory relationships. Some writers, like Shakespeare, happily indulge in this situation and profit from it, while others, as we shall see in the case of Mark Twain in *Adventures of Huckleberry Finn*, are insufficiently alert to the resulting pressures that build up in a work and cannot then repair the damage eventually done to it, as by a fault line that can suddenly show itself in a formal garden. Emerson very often involves himself in contradictory uses of the same key word, but this only makes his work stronger, and for the reason that he manages to suggest that the contradictions are an inescapable consequence of mythologies necessary to the continuations of human culture as writing has made it known to us. Consider, again, his use of the word "power." It has a variety of meanings for him, and they can on occasion cancel one another out. In "Experience," for example, he first says that "life is a mixture of power and form and will not bear the least excess of either." Then, a bit further on, he says that "human life is made up of the two elements, power and form, and the proportion must be invariably kept." The problem is that while "power" having to do with "human life" can include and express the "power" belonging to "life" in general (life as synonymous with nature) it is also in an antagonistic relationship with it, and for the reason that death is an inevitable consequence of that larger "life" or "power." Indeed, it is only human life, and not life in general, that can be conscious of death.

To call this an example of deconstruction, of pointing out the way words eventually invalidate the meanings they propose for themselves, seems to me trivial, since most people are prepared to agree both that such contradictions are inherent to the mystery of human existence in time and to the very words by which we have imagined it, and, furthermore, that Emerson wants his writing to partake of this mystery. At nearly every point he knows what his writing is doing. In this particular instance he will leave the clarifications to others, and we will presently see how Frost accepts the challenge. In other instances he is quite capable, as in the passage just noted from "Self-Reliance," of precipitating a crisis over his own terminology. He loses his grip on the phrase "self-reliance" in order to show that it is dangerous to hold onto it, to trust for long in *any* formula. Emerson is especially appealing to me because, like his followers, and like such great predecessors as Chaucer, Shakespeare, and Milton, he never blames such difficulties as these on anything outside the writing. He is never superficially historical. Instead, he finds the difficulties already present in the words he uses because the words have been fashioned by beliefs, traditions, and mythologies which also make his writing possible. He never evokes some cultural or historical crisis of the moment in order to give his essential complications the quite unnecessary license and patina of a merely historical necessity. There is a resort to such tactics even in a writer so closely allied to Emerson as Wordsworth. In his Prefaces and Appendices, he argues that his language is subject to so many "arbitrary associations" that the poet is obliged to "melt these down for his purpose." To make matters worse, the reader may be incapable, he says, of "exerting, within his own mind, a corresponding energy," in which case the words in the poem, no matter how refashioned, will retain a shape inimical to the poet's intentions. By the same token, though far less persuasively, we have heard Eliot in "The Metaphysical Poets" propose that because of conditions peculiar to "our civilization" the poet "must be *difficult* . . . must dislocate if necessary language into his meaning." Some credit should be given to such historically rooted complaints no matter how often they are heard, but their very recurrence ought to suggest that literature has always displayed a degree of edginess or effortfulness or struggle with respect to the idioms it wants to use.

The importance of Emerson to this central issue is that when he says "we write from aspiration and antagonism, as well as from experience" he intends this to be true for all writing of whatever time and to suggest the *enabling* as well as the restrictive influence of particular social-historical arrangements. The "aspiration" comes in part from communal beliefs and assumptions, even to the extent, as he says in "Shakespeare," that "the generic catholic genius who is not afraid to owe his originality to the originality of all, stands with the next age as the recorder and embodiment of his own." Along with these entitlements, however, are the limitations they impose, until the very things which facilitate thought and expression begin, like an Emersonian "circle," to confine it. We eventually discover that the means of expression frustrate the liberating purposes of expression, that freedom makes us aware of Fate, which he defines in his essay of that title as "organization tyrannizing over character." For "organization" read "literary form" or syntax or grammar. It is in response to this situation that Emerson remarks, at the end of "Circles," that "the way of life is wonderful: it is by abandonment." But he scarcely means that we should give up, much less drop out. Rather, he recommends that we abandon one discourse for another, give up one tone of voice for another, change or trope the vocabulary that has also been found to be at least procedurally useful. By "abandonment" he essentially means "transition," not merely moving away from something familiar but toward something desired. Earlier in the same essay it is made clear that for him movement is paradoxically the fixed principle of life. With Frost he has confidence only in "momentary stays against confusion"; indeed the only "stays" which are not confusing *are* momentary. "Nothing," he says, "is secure in life but transition, the energizing spirit." The most enduring tradition is the effort to abandon it, as each season gradually abandons its hold on the world, knowing its turn will come again.

This sounds like rather more than enough for even the greatest works of art to cope with, and the results of such efforts as Emerson recommends are likely to exceed any perceived logic, to make shapeliness appear like vested interest, and to make authors and readers care as much for works that fail as in those that appear to succeed. It was self-exaltation, not self-pity, that induced Melville to say that he proposed to write books that would fail. Language encouraged by the present order of things can become so tenacious as to overwhelm any effort to revise, subvert, "dislocate," or "melt it down." Fate can overwhelm the impulse to freedom not only in the fable but in the form of a literary work, as it does in the case of *Adventures of Huckleberry Finn.* Besides giving us some indispensable clues as to the nature of literature, Emersonian tradition can make us acutely sensible of its failings, especially when the failings are the result of worthy ambition. It is in light of this that I want briefly to recall a contrast I first made in an earlier book, *A World Elsewhere,* between the situation of Mark Twain in *Huckleberry Finn* and the situation of Jane Austen in *Emma.*

Structurally, the problem for Emma is the problem for Huck; the difference consists in what the authors are able to do about it. Using the social-linguistic resources Jane Austen can make available to her, Emma can give a shape to her life that also fulfills her desires. She wants, as does Huck, to find an alternative to "civilized" confinements, and to this end she for a time involves herself in imaginative excesses, especially involving Harriet Smith, and in the sort of theatricalized behavior encouraged by Frank Churchill, an adult version of Tom Sawyer and his trickeries. Her indulgences in artifice make her on a crucial occasion indifferent to the hurt she inflicts on her social inferiors, especially Miss Bates. At this point of crisis and social fracture, however, she is able to recognize—and, more important still, Jane Austen is able to provide—a healing and healthy alternative from within her social group, the aptly named Mr. Knightley, a man of amiable directness and natural good manners.

Their marriage affirms Jane Austen's confident belief that the natural and the social need not be at odds, though even in a society as stable as hers such an affirmation is by no means easy to make. In Mark Twain it proves impossible, which gives some added piquancy to his remark, in *Following the Equator,* that "just that one omission alone"—of Jane

Austen's novels from the ship's library—"would make a fairly good library out of a library that hadn't a book in it." For several years, between 1876 and 1883, he was unable to bring *Huckleberry Finn* past the point, less than a third of the way through, where Huck reaches the crucial decision to give up Tom Sawyer's conformist kind of trickery and to resort instead to the rebellious trickery of the lie which saves Jim, a runaway slave, from capture. Structurally, the apology to Jim is equivalent to Emma's more delicate restitutions to Miss Bates after the Box Hill episode in *Emma*. Both Emma and Huck resolve to give up games and tricks that hurt other people, but this is precisely the point where Twain's novel gets into trouble. Why? Because in the first, placidly comic sections of the book, Tom's "tricks" are so elaborately identified with the idioms of adult exploitation that for Huck to give up "tricking" Jim or "playing the game" is to divest himself of a functioning vocabulary. This situation effectively silences the book as well as the hero. Out of a naïve nostalgia for the communities of his own childhood, Twain writes himself into a situation in which his hero has no way, except by soliloquy or silence, to express the inner being which his creator, his readers, and he himself have discovered. When the novel resumes, Huck has effectively disappeared from it, reduced to sulking and complacent gab, a mere hanger-on at Tom's "party" and in the mock "freeing" of Jim. Mark Twain's own bitterness and alienation are expressed for the rest of the book not through his hero but independently of him, in a kind of episodic survey of those conditions of riverfront society which have made Huck an inarticulate moper.

Huckleberry Finn is a particularly extreme version of a problem that besets a number of literary texts. It is a problem which Emerson explains and indeed wants to precipitate, even if this means the failure of a work or the disappearance of literature. Whenever an arrangement or "circle" threatens to hem in life, he recommends "abandonment," and this would especially be the case with novelistic structures which, in the interests of larger purposes, are notably repressive of human character. The problem is evident, though less starkly than in Mark Twain, in many other nineteenth-century works, English as well as American. That Dickens could write two different endings for *Great Expectations*, one happier than the other, is evidence, for example, of a kind of fracture deeply embedded in the book. His friend the novelist Edward Bulwer Lytton saw nothing the matter with recommending that the original unhappy ending be changed so that Pip and Estella could be reunited. In accepting Bulwer's advice—"I have put in as pretty a piece of writing as I could"—Dickens confirms the uncertainty of the book's direction, implicit from the outset in the style given to Pip as its narrator, a style which in the very first paragraph is far more socially accommodating, funny, and entertaining than any man could imaginably afford to be who has already passed through the horrendous experiences he is ready to talk about. His mode of speech is that of a theatrical entertainer or recitalist, a very clubbable fellow.[3] This is at least one case where the man who suffers is not the man who writes, or narrates, and Dickens wants us simply to overlook the discrepancy. He never takes it into account and neither do most readers who agree, as do I, not to press the issue too strenuously. It is nonetheless important to know when a novel has involved you in so risky a moral enterprise, and to note, once again, that works of literature very often cannot come to terms even with themselves, cannot heal the fissures they create, much less the ones we discover in our historical experience. To resort to Emerson's vocabulary, "the Actual order of things," on which the structure and rhetoric of a work may call for provisional support, can become so strong that it is then impossible to "disuse it," even in the interests of human possibilities which the writer wishes to endorse.

I WANT NOW to consider *Middlemarch,* a novel that claims to be fully cognizant of these problems in all of their historical ramifications. It is often credited, besides, with transcending them. Its author, who greatly admired Emerson's essays, met him in England in 1848 when he was famous and forty-five, she relatively obscure and twenty-nine. "She has a calm and serious soul," he said, and she wrote to a friend, "I have seen Emerson, the first *man* I have ever seen."

One sign of a great novelist, which George Eliot brilliantly exhibits, is the ability to recognize the technical difficulties experienced by immediate predecessors, like Dickens, and then to perceive them as more than merely technical, as evidences, instead, of some larger cultural dislocation. This is what Joyce does in *Ulysses,* and what *Middlemarch* manages to do with the apparent fact that human desire tends to fracture any of the formal arrangements within which it is expressed, to make the arrangements seem merely arbitrary. Besides being central to Emerson, this problem haunts such novels after Jane Austen as *Bleak House, Vanity Fair,* and *Jane Eyre,* all written within twenty years of the 1832 setting for *Middlemarch.* Of *Jane Eyre* Lawrence astutely observes that it verges on the pornographic; it cannot, that is, find a socially acceptable language, any more than can Mark Twain, for the human desires it feels compelled to represent. As he remarks in "Pornography and Obscenity":

Mr. Rochester's sex passion is not "respectable" till Mr. Rochester is burned, blinded, disfigured, and reduced to helpless dependence. Then, thoroughly humbled and humiliated, it may be merely admitted. All the previous titillations are slightly indecent, as in *Pamela* or *The Mill on the Floss* or *Anna Karenina.* As soon as there is sex excitement with a desire to spite the sexual feeling, to humiliate it and degrade it, the element of pornography enters.

Such evidences of the gap between social acceptability and desire, or between opportunity and aspiration, are especially evident to a writer like George Eliot, aware as she was that such disproportions are common to the lot of women in the nineteenth century. Her "Prelude" to *Middlemarch* announces this, and in a rhetoric which suggests how little she herself intends to be victimized by the plights of her heroines:

That Spanish woman who lived three hundred years ago was certainly not the last of her kind. Many Theresas have been born who found for themselves no epic life wherein there was a constant unfolding of far-resonant action; perhaps only a life of mistakes, the offspring of a certain spiritual grandeur ill-matched with the meanness of opportunity; perhaps a tragic failure which found no sacred poet and sank unwept into oblivion. With dim lights and tangled circumstance they tried to shape their thought and deed in noble agreement; but after all, to common eyes their struggle seemed mere inconsistency and formlessness; for these later-born Theresas were helped by no coherent social faith and order which could perform the function of knowledge for the ardently willing soul. Their ardour alternated between a vague ideal and the common yearning of womanhood, so that the one was disapproved as an extravagance and the other condemned as a lapse.

Her novel publicizes the failure of a variety of efforts, nearly all of them initiated by men, to create forms of coherence and knowledge, in the areas of medicine, social theory, mythology, science, even family planning. The historical frequency of their failure is attested to by the spectacle of Rome during Dorothea's miserable honeymoon there with Casaubon. It is a city of "suppressed transitions," whose "stupendous fragmentariness heightened the dream-like strangeness of her bridal life." The novel's only alternative to the "vast wreck of ambitious ideals" is to be found in George Eliot's presiding rhetorical presence, the warm and ennobling authority of her voice, especially when she is characterizing the limits of knowledge and the disastrous consequences of dogmatic judgment with nothing to guide it. Her homilies are irresistible, or, as we shall see, nearly so:

If we had a keen vision and feeling of all ordinary human life, it would be like hearing the grass grow and the squirrel's heart beat, and we should die of that roar which lies on the other side of silence. As it is, the quickest of us walk about well wadded with stupidity.

Opinions in novels, especially when expressed in prose so obviously pleased with itself, are not to be judged as either true or false, and in this instance there is a hint of ethical theatricality. Objections are not anticipated, and though she often sounds quite tentative, the narrator's authority is only enhanced thereby, as if she were already cognizant of any arguments a reader might want to make. The rhetoric is meant to silence us, though just short of the "other side of silence" where we would disappear altogether. It assumes that ordinary life is a matter not of surfaces, which is Emerson's position, as we shall see in a moment, but of depths, and, further, that the depths are pretty much inaccessible to the questions we normally ask. But if we agree that we have been made stupid by acculturation, then Eliot provides some comfort, for this is also said to be true of "even the quickest of us," including the novelist and novels, which are so conspicuously voluble as to be more than ordinarily insulated from "that roar that lies on the other side of silence." If we or if novels were keen enough we would see or hear something that would make language irrelevant, human differentiation and self-definition impossible.

Since this degree of complication would dissuade us from the force of what George Eliot is more obviously saying, she does not intend the passage to be taken as far as I have taken it. She wants simply to persuade us to take it easy, to be in no hurry to judge others, especially those in her novel, since we cannot know enough even about ourselves, only bits and pieces. Nor is she attacking novels, especially her own. Rather she is cautioning her readers not to jump the gun, not to presume to make judgments about matters whose complications she will reveal only in her own good time. And yet her rhetorical "far resonance" here and at other points compels her to say more than she wants to say. Her excess of meaning is a symptom of her eventual need to exert a degree of constraint that she would rather avoid. Furthermore, this evidence of insecurity in her own rhetoric is an indication that she might have something on her mind that her rhetoric cannot accommodate, intentions it could not sanction.

"If we write novels so," Henry James asked in his review of *Middlemarch*, "how shall we write History?" He was suggesting that the book is free of that novelistic arbitrariness he found so prevalent in Trollope, an arbitrariness scarcely restricted to modernist narratives. Consider, then, the apparently open, flexible, humanely managed plot of *Middlemarch*, the main facets of which correspond, presumably, to something in the life of the community, while its slow pace and the corresponding exertions of patience on the part of George Eliot and her reader induce a more than usual judiciousness and decency of feeling. All of these commendable things do indeed happen, but other things happen, too, things not usually considered so nice, but which are at the source of the energy that produced the book.

George Eliot wants to prevail upon the reader not to rush to judgment. Her efforts in this regard are tactically necessary if she is later to enforce judgments of her own, but they also express a desire she shares with Emerson and with Wordsworth before him: that her writing might effect the liberation of the reader from "our pre-established codes of decision," as Wordsworth phrased it in 1798. She endows Ladislaw, Dorothea's eventual husband, with virtues she hopes will reside in her own work. He is so free of social obligations that he seems to Mr. Brooke like "a kind of Shelley," and his avoidance of fixed positions enables him to shift his perspectives rapidly in obedience to emergent feelings.

When asked by Dorothea if he intends to be a poet, he gives an answer which the novel endorses but with which, as we will see, it will be unable formally to comply. He is uncertain about being a poet because, as he says, "To be a poet is to have a soul so quick to discern that no shade of quality escapes it, and so quick to feel, that discernment is but a hand playing with finely ordered variety on the chords of emotion—a soul in which knowledge passes instantaneously into feeling, and feeling flashes back as a new organ of knowledge." Dorothea's reply—"But you leave out the poems"—is not merely an implicit criticism of Ladislaw's Paterian aestheticism. It attests also to George Eliot's Emersonian awareness that writing, any verbal textualizations of feeling, actually endanger the process Ladislaw has in mind. Writing immobilizes the "instantaneous" passage between feeling and knowledge. *Middlemarch* as a text aspires to the condition, the transits and continuities, which Ladislaw describes.[4] But George Eliot appears early on to suspect the fate which awaits this aspiration—that it will fall prey to the work's organizational rigors; "An expense of ends to means is fate," says Emerson in "Fate," "organization tyrannizing over character."

There is, then, some considerable pathos in the conduct of George Eliot's narrative, and in the rhetoric by which she so frequently asks us to be cautious when reaching decisions about her characters or verdicts as to their guilt or innocence. Consider, in illustration, a moment very late in the book, at the beginning of Chapter Eighty-five, when she highlights a passage from Bunyan's *The Pilgrim's Progress*. This longest of the headnotes enumerates the verdicts of "guilty" brought against Faithful, with that special vehemence of those who are themselves culpable, by Mr. Malice, Mr. High-mind, Mr. Liar, Mr. Implacable, and others like them. By this time it has been borne in on us, perhaps more than once too often in passages like the ones we have just examined, that we are not to think of others, especially some certain others, too harshly, Mr. Bulstrode being the case at hand. The injunction may have begun to lose some of its power. Too many people, too many incidents have been the occasion for its evocation, and by this late chapter a reader is apt to have become less rather than more patient with Dorothea's obtuse incapacity to see that Casaubon is jealous of Ladislaw or that Ladislaw is in love with her, and to have become long since exasperated with displays of tolerance on behalf of the despicable Casaubon. What is to be learned with respect to him is not, I would say, the virtues of compassion and forbearance but the value of brute intuition. Celia was right to begin with, regardless of the fact that her objections include the way the gentleman eats his soup. It is to George Eliot's purpose to load the dice by contriving that the early objections to him should be so trivial that we can do nothing but dismiss them immediately, in favor of the author's hortatory admonition against "too hasty judgment":

If to Dorothea Mr. Casaubon had been the mere occasion which had set alight the fine inflammable material of her youthful illusions, does it not follow that he was fairly represented in the minds of those less impassioned personages who have hitherto delivered their judgments concerning him? I protest against any absolute conclusion, any prejudice derived from Mrs. Cadwallader's contempt for a neighboring clergyman's alleged greatness of soul, or Sir James Chettam's poor opinion of his rival's legs—from Mr. Brooke's failure to elicit a companion's ideas, or from Celia's criticism of a middle-aged scholar's personal appearance. I am not sure that the greatest man of his age, if ever that solitary superlative existed, could escape these unfavorable reflections of himself in various small mirrors; and even Milton, looking for his portrait in a spoon, must submit to having the facial angle of a bumpkin.

George Eliot, novelist with a novel to write, will take *her* revenge on Casaubon in her own good time, in the "big mirror" of her book. Meanwhile, she needs him around, and she is not above question-begging to keep him there. Quite aside from the fact that no one is talking about "the greatest man of his age" or John Milton, is it not to the point that, except for literary snobbery, neither of these worthies would necessarily be considered a fit candidate for the post in question: husband to a fresh, eager, lovely girl of eighteen? Whatever moral urgency there may be in the heavy sarcasm of such a passage, it is merely a cover, I suspect, for her more necessary literary tactics. She needs the solicited toleration because it is essential to the slow pace, the massive room for maneuver, in a novel that will require the simultaneous array, at some point, of interacting and representative social forces. The only quick judgments she allows are those derived from instantaneous compassion, and even these need the excuse that they result from prolonged intimacy, such as exists between Bulstrode and his wife.

And yet, boorish as it may sound, there is reason to insist that for all practical purposes—of getting married, of doing business, as distinct from reading novels—the "hasty judgments" made of Bulstrode and of Casaubon turn out to have been the right ones. We are brought to a question to which, in my view, the later novels of James would have to be even more rudely submitted. Of what practical good are the expenditures of feeling and intelligence which follow from her "protest against any absolute conclusion"? Must we not wonder what is gained by all the demonstrations of caution and compassion—demonstrations on the part of the heroine and of George Eliot—for a man who, in the progress of the novel, reveals himself as even more wretched than anyone supposed him to be? The book raises one of the central issues having to do with the so-called educated heart: of what use is it? What are the benefits of mature intelligence? I mean in George Eliot's sense of that phrase, which I take to be the sense also of most people who look into novels for exemplifications of intelligence.

These are questions that need to be asked of certain high-minded authors like Henry James and George Eliot and E. M. Forster. And after eighty-four chapters of *Middlemarch* and the opening of Chapter Eighty-five, the questions have become acute. One good way to begin dealing with the problem is to suggest that only second-rate writers are proud of their ideas. The great ones, like George Eliot, and the very good lesser ones, like Raymond Chandler, have in common that, like any accomplished technocrat, they exploit whatever is at hand for the good not of the reader's moral development but of the book's development. If, for the sake of the book, the reader must be persuaded that his or her soul is being saved, then so be it. George Eliot will set about to save it, even believe in saving it. But she will have done it all for the sake of the book. Let it be granted, in order to get on with the argument, that George Eliot's moralizing and instructive rhetoric do offer an education useful to the conduct of life outside as well as in her novel. It is, nevertheless, also a "trick" or a technical device meant to slow us up, allow her to slow up, to slow the narrative, to exonerate it for not providing certain pleasures, like Trollopean allegory, so that all the while it can provide room for things to happen that would be impossible if a different kind of intelligence were being promoted along with a different structure for making judgments. Her "protest against any absolute conclusion" can be read, without her intending or wanting it to be, as a protest in favor of her own ways of plotting and against those of earlier (and later) novelists. Judgments are delayed even when they become inevitable, and always by an appeal to our pity or understanding or by an induced appreciation of "necessary" complexity.

It is a measure of George Eliot's anxiety lest we rush past her toward a hasty and conclusive judgment of her people that, for all its length, the passage from *The Pilgrim's Progress* is only very tangentially appropriate to the situation of Bulstrode. In the paragraph immediately following the quotation from Bunyan, she in fact makes the point that Faithful is unusual in literature or history, in that though he is condemned he is "guiltless." As in the cautionary passage about hasty judgments of Casaubon, she again evokes the image of the "great" man who cannot measure up to simple expectations or moral absolutes: "That is a rare and blessed lot which some greatest men have not attained, to know ourselves guiltless before a condemning crowd—to be sure that what we are denounced for is solely the good in us." Again, while the subject here apparently has to do with guilt and judgment, it is simultaneously, and as importantly, about something else. She is flaunting the difficulties she has set for herself by creating in Bulstrode a character without a semblance of heroism or greatness and, at the same time, by putting him in a situation in which it is impossible to reach an "absolute conclusion"—narratively as well as morally. Because he "knows that he is stoned, not for professing the Right, but for not being the man he professed to be," Bulstrode is in a position which he cannot easily sustain. But in drawing attention to this, George Eliot means to remind us that Bulstrode's situation is more difficult to render novelistically than would be the equivalent one of more romantic heroes or of "greatest men," whose roles, like those of the kings in Shakespeare, are always inherently schizophrenic anyway.

No one will be surprised at this kind of self-advertisement who recalls the characterization of Casaubon or, even more, Lydgate, with his "spots of commonness":

Some gentlemen have made an amazing figure in literature by general discontent with the universe as a trap of dullness onto which their great souls have fallen by mistake; but the sense of a stupendous self and an insignificant world may have its consolations. Lydgate's discontent was much harder to bear: it was the sense that there was a grand existence in thought and effective action lying around him, while his self was being narrowed into the miserable isolation of egoistic fears, and vulgar anxieties for events that might allay such fears.

What George Eliot does to Lydgate here, with her fillip of sarcasm at the "amazing figure" of "gentlemen" with "their great souls," is what she elsewhere does to Casaubon and Bulstrode—all men of considerable, if quite different, public aspiration. By her rather edgy rhetoric of compassion she makes them at last indistinguishable from "later-born Theresas," while at the same time she pities them for the presumption that as males they might have been otherwise destined. The eventual fate to which she dooms them, that is, is the initial, the gendered fate of her heroic women.

Her attack on "the amazing figure in literature" is further enunciated in her essay of 1857 on the poet Young, "Worldliness, and Other Worldliness," where she brings to bear an implicitly Wordsworthian-Emersonian standard (though Emerson worried about living up to it) by which truth is associated with an immediacy of feeling for the objects around you. "In Young," she concludes, "we have the type of that deficient human sympathy, that impiety towards the present and the visible, which flies for its motives, its sanctities, and its religion, to the remote, the vague, and the unknown." If a sense of "stupendous self" is to be denied to women by force of historical circumstance, then they are fortunate in their deprivation, and by her novelistic techniques, she will help the men in her novel toward a similar improvement. The disparagement goes even further than that, and why not? It also denies the value of those consolations, following on the failure of heroic enterprise, which have traditionally been the province of men in history and literature. She proposes, and quite rightly I think, that heroic failure, and the solicitious admiration that attends it, are far easier to bear than is "discontent." As the Prelude to *Middlemarch* makes clear, "discontent" is the destiny of aspiring women, and George Eliot so contrives things that "discontent," rather than the glamour of heroic failure, gradually emerges as the destiny of all the men in the novel, except someone like Fred Vincy, who accepts his lot as a child-producing, beloved, and patronized husband.

By inference, she offers a radical critique of American epic fiction of the nineteenth century—hers, she admits, is the "home epic"—and of modernist posturings of the self as against so large an abstraction as "the culture" or "the system." It does not diminish her accomplishment as a critic of these, and also of English fiction acclaimed in her time—a critic *in* her novel, that is—to suppose that within the complex of her attitudes we hear also the accents of feminine revenge. It manifests itself not merely in the killing off, as noted by Sandra M. Gilbert and Susan Gubar in *The Madwoman in the Attic*, of the significant males in the book: Casaubon dies, Lydgate's death is reported, Bulstrode's in this chapter is rather theatrically imagined. It is even more significantly in evidence in those moments where her moral rhetoric, as I read it, is inextricable from novelistic techniques of plotting designed slowly and relentlessly to impose the domestication of life on everyone. Both the rhetoric and the plotting protest against "absolute conclusions" as if nature itself will not permit them, especially the nature of family life. All the failures of male ambition are transformed by women—think of the peripatetic psychiatric social work of Dorothea after Casaubon is out of the way—into modest forms of social reality, social accommodation. At the end Bulstrode finds it easier to imagine the "invisible pardon" of God than to settle things with his remarkable wife by telling her the whole story, so far as he understands it. He will apparently pay for her complete forgiveness only with his life: "Some time, perhaps—when he was dying—he would tell her all." Meanwhile, it is also suggested that because, like Dorothea, Mrs. Bulstrode cannot know certain things, or refuses to know them, refuses any "absolute conclusion," she is able still to nourish some fragile webs of connection with her family and thus with the Middlemarch community, into which she had introduced her husband in the first place. She so arranges it that Bulstrode sets up Fred Vincy as manager of Stone Court. The very scene of Bulstrode's crime and hence of his disgrace thus becomes the homestead of a happy marriage, clearly dominated by a wife whose many children will carry the benefit of Bulstrode's penance into an "inconclusive" future.

Middlemarch is among the strongest and most tough-minded novels ever written—surely it would long ago have been more widely recognized as such if a man had written it—and it should not be treated as if it were merely compassionate and high-minded. It is an effort to take command of the many different forces massed in English culture as George Eliot saw it at one of its most important junctures, the Reform Act of 1832; it is the work of a great strategist who knew how to mass and move her resources, how to use her troops and also when to sacrifice them. In its elaborate structural juxtapositions, its pacings and proportions of attention, its deployment of a vast proliferation of characters, scenes, and authorial ruminations, it is an example of technical mastery, and all the more for its ability to cover its tracks with a rhetoric opposed to the manipulative use of people and condescending to the human capacity for truly informed judgment.

This technical proficiency tells us as much about George Eliot as do her memorable passages about "hearing the grass grow and the squirrel's heart beat." In that particular instance, for example, it is clearly not the plight of grass or squirrels that is meant to concern you, or even whether, as a decent person, you are remorseful about your inability to get close to them. The passage is part of a put-together thing, a novel, and the question is why so much of its space is taken up with talk of this kind. What does she get out of it? What does it reveal about the encroachments upon her of the tactical requirements of her book? As a good pragmatist would say, do her rhetorical interventions *work*? I find them often extremely affecting, but not primarily because of the worthiness of their sentiments. Instead, they seem to me impressive evidence that she must repeatedly affirm her freedom from the increasingly restrictive structural demands of her own book. Her rhetoric is a struggle to escape the plight of those women of the nineteenth century who, as the book's Prelude explains, are denied the possibilities of "far resonant action," including far resonant rhetoric, and whose "spiritual grandeur" is "ill matched with the meanness of opportunity." She needs to show herself, as well as us, that she remains a free agent despite her own formal handiwork, and does so by a meditative aloofness from its confines. Given her historical grasp of the plights she is describing and her brilliant ways of getting around them, it is important to notice, however, that she inevitably does give in to novelistic requirements and arrangements. "By the end of *Middlemarch,*" as Leo Bersani puts it, "George Eliot's presence in the novel has become anything but 'incalculably diffusive.' She is making connections which the rest of the novel has trained us to see as naïve, unworkable novelistic connections. The subtle, almost indefinable influence of one life on other lives has been replaced by melodramatic conceptions of crime and rare circumstance. Thus fiction unexpectedly—and, I think, unintentionally—points to its own status as purely verbal artifice by the ways it demonstrates the persistence of significant structures in modern life."[5]

Like Emerson, George Eliot is disarmingly forthright about the problems she gets herself into and about their historical recurrence in all manner of human expression. They are problems of incoherence, of discontinuity, of the gap between, on the one hand, the desired expressions of a mind and, on the other, the words and forms into which that mind must turn itself if it is to leave some legible traces of its existence. For these very reasons, *Middlemarch,* no less than Emerson's essays, both popularly supposed to be repositories of saving or at least uplifting truth, are in fact warnings to those who hope "to reclaim a heritage" from literary works. Such a heritage is, at best, a heritage of trouble and trouble-making. What R. P. Blackmur in "Anni Mirabiles 1921–1925" says of the modernist literary episode—"it is almost as if to make trouble had become the creative habit of the general mind"—is true of the creative mind in general. No matter how articulately opposed to so-called systems, conventions, social arrangements, and technologies, no matter how expansive and loose it tries to be, literary form exists, as does language, in limitation. No artifact of culture can ever approximate "the one vast picture which God paints on the instant eternity." This "picture," evoked in Emerson's *Nature* at the very outset of his career, is different from the paintings in Rome which we have heard him criticize in "Art," and for the reason that its very inclusiveness leaves nothing for it to be compared to. "God" or "genius" or "divinity" or the "soul" are all forever in a state of "becoming"; they cannot be framed or bound or scheduled. Of "this universal tablet," this painting "on the instant of eternity," he says that we do not look at it microscopically; the soul "respects the end too much to immerse itself in the means." Alas, "means" are all we humans have at our disposal.

A distinction, usually assigned to Emerson's later writings, is apparent here, at the beginning of his career: in artistic as in all human production, the end which the soul cherishes, which at other times he calls its "desire for the whole," is to a great extent deformed by the "means" or the techniques of the medium through which it tries to express itself. To be subdued by "means" is to succumb to Fate, "organization tyrannizing over character." Emerson is no radical sentimentalist on the subject of form or organization or structures. These, too, as I will presently show, are partial expressions of "soul," of "desire raging, infinite; a hunger, as of space to be filled with planets," as he writes in "Montaigne." Organization, even to tyranny, is the urgent filling of space with representation of the self; it is necessary to the methods of creativity. That villainy in literature is so often associated with persuasive manipulators like Iago or Satan, Ahab or Chillingworth or Henry James's "governess," and that all of these exhibit something of the writer's own social acumen and verbal charm, is literature's attempt, I think, to exorcise its own demons. The entire career of Henry James leads him toward *The Golden Bowl*, where a maximum of rhetorical amplitude is combined with an ever more self-effacing imposition of control. His characters in that novel are devoured by his voice, which is why they mostly sound alike. Henry James *is* the turn of the screw, and he knows it, even while, as in the story of that title, he writes in apparent abhorrence of any gross efforts at governing. The efforts are instead ascribed to the governess herself or to the seriatim of narrators. The story is in effect about the impossibility of locating the source of the exquisite mental tortures that make the story itself so terrifying and exciting.

"Governing" was, appropriately, the fantasy that occupied James in an extraordinary way in the last months of his life, as he slipped in and out of delirium, his hands moving compulsively over the counterpane as if he were forever writing, while his secretary, Theodora Bosanquet, was on call should he wish to dictate. As we learn from Leon Edel's biography, he had been reading Napoleonic memoirs, and not long before had met various descendants of the Emperor. All of this so lingered in his confused mind that he dictated a letter to "Dear and most esteemed Brother and Sister," though both William and Alice (unless he meant William's wife) were long since dead, in which he majestically discusses the redecoration of the Louvre and the Tuileries and signs it "Napoleone," the original Corsican form of the name. In another letter he seems to imagine the James family as the family of Napoleon with himself as the conqueror of a transatlantic empire, which in a sense he was, and is ready to endow William and his wife, whom he addresses as "sister," with "a brilliant fortune": "I have displayed you as persons of great taste and judgment. Don't leave me a sorry figure in consequence but present me rather as your fond but not infatuated relation, able and ready to back you up, your faithful Brother and Brother-in-Law."

Having already argued that literature might be considered a form of technology disguised as an attack upon it, I am additionally saying that it is a form of cultural and imaginative imperialism. Since about 1850, except in a rare instance like Kipling, literature pretends nonetheless to be appalled by imperialist conquest of a political or military nature. I do not mean such a characterization to arouse neo-Marxist reflections on what strike me as belated discoveries as to the brutal efficiencies of literary form or the fact that English literature allows itself to be used for the projection of state power, as, conspicuously, in the social pacifications of India and in some of Shakespeare's history plays. Works of art confer an aura of grandeur, necessity, and excitement on their own performative necessities, while castigating equivalent performances in life. To create an ingenious plot, to control the action, to dispatch a character who gets too big for his role in the play or the novel, all this deserves the highest literary commendation, and while I cannot be supposed to applaud the same activities in historical life, I am suggesting that there is an intriguing if limited equivalence, and that this may be a clue to the kinds of human energy excited by the prospect in life of any efficient form or system.

Most writers want to be powerful, want to define the nature of the time they live in, to help establish a consensus on relations of cause and effect, to lay down the metaphors that define the age they live in. Writers also discover, as does any ambitious person, that such will to power is invariably frustrated, no less than are attempts to create a work of art that will make any further artistic innovation unnecessary. Indeed, every generation of writers, every writer for that matter, proposes to "make it new," and the best, the toughest and truest deflation of such cant is to be found in Emersonian tradition. As from one writer or one period to another, "make it new" can only mean something like this: please give me your activating power, your germinating power; meanwhile keep what you yourself have done with it, knowing that traces of it will appear in what will now replace it. Distinct from what most readers propose to find in works of the past, distinct from their meaning, their images, their historical consequentialities, and hidden away even in works which depict forms of life wholly unlike anything later generations recognize as their own, there can be found evidences of a kind of action, of doing, of movements that are forever young and yet as old as creation itself. Free from the usual banalities of criticism, Emerson remarks in "Nature" that "we talk of deviations from natural life, as if artificial life were not also natural. The smoothest curled courtier in the boudoirs of a palace has an animal nature, rude and aboriginal as a white bear, omnipotent to its own ends, and is directly related, there amid essences and billetsdoux, to Himmaleh mountain chains and the axis of the globe."

WHILE MOST WRITERS talk of being innovative, there is a particular urgency for innovation shared by Emerson and Wordsworth, by Whitman, Shelley, Stevens, and Ashbery, and, in the novel, from George Eliot to Joyce and beyond, and it is attributable to a supposition that even though artificial life is also natural, it was beginning more than ever before to obscure perceptible connections to "animal nature," or to whatever best describes the human power to renew itself. At issue, between Emersonians and modernists, is how best to confront or talk about this difficulty. Hawthorne, at least at the opening of his story "The New Adam and Eve," is expressing what I take to be more a modernist than an Emersonian position when he remarks that:

We who are born into the world's artificial system can never adequately know how little in our present state and circumstances is natural, and how much is merely the interpolation of the perverted mind and heart of man. Art has become a second and stronger Nature; she is a step-mother, whose crafty tenderness has taught us to despise the bountiful and wholesome ministrations of our true parent. It is only through the medium of the imagination that we can lessen those iron fetters, which we call truth and reality, and make ourselves even partially sensible what prisoners we are.

Emerson's "artificial life," that nonetheless has a recoverable spark of nature within it, is to be contrasted with Hawthorne's "artificial system," into which you are born a prisoner and resistance to which can only remind you of that fact. The difference puts Hawthorne on the road, though he frequently swerves off it, toward modernist conceptions of the total arbitrariness of form, while it points Emerson toward Frost and Stevens, and the latter's perception that "life is not free from its forms" and that in any case "imagination applied to the whole world is vapid in comparison to imagination applied to a detail" ("Adagia"). Emerson liked the freewheeling style of the lyceum of his time because it escaped the limits of genre, in this case of the pulpit sermon and the polite essay, and it let the speaker "dare to hope," as he says in the 1839 *Journals*, "for ecstasy and eloquence." A modernist like Melville, the predecessor of Joyce and Pynchon, felt the need to push further in the disruption of genres and of the social institutions that helped sustain them. *Moby-Dick*, no less than *Ulysses* or *Gravity's Rainbow*, is an encyclopedia of genres whose boundaries collapse into one another. Emerson favors disruptions, but his likely response to modernist versions, as against his own more inflected kind, can be inferred from his comment on Hawthorne's method in the *Journals* for May 1846 before publication of any of the novels: "Hawthorne invites his readers too much into his study, opens the process before them. As if the confectioner should say to his customers Now let us make the cake."

This stricture seems to me fair enough about a few of the stories, and its real importance is as a further clue to Emerson's impatience with the premeditations required of any novelist and, especially, with the degree to which the plots of novels propose to imitate social arrangements that are artificial to begin with. He reports in the *Journals* dated January–February 1841 that he picked up Sir Walter Scott's *Quentin Durward* to find a passage and

turned over the volume until I was fairly caught in the foolish trap & read &
read to the end of the novel. Then as often before I feel indignant to have been
duped and dragged after a foolish boy & girl, to see them at last married &
portioned & I instantly turned out of doors like a beggar that has followed a gay
procession into the castle. . . . These novels will give way by & by to diaries or
autobiographies;—captivating books if only a man knew how to choose among
what he calls his experiences that which is really his experience, and how to
record truth truly!

Even in forms like a diary, in which the writer himself is the principal
character and ostensibly writes to and about himself, it is difficult
enough, he suggests, to distinguish "that which is really his experience"
from those fabricated versions which have been made to seem real by
art, not to mention social custom. But while Emerson, like any writer
one can think of, likes to sound off about the differences between what
is real and natural and what is not, he is especially worth listening to on
the subject because he admits that part of what is most amazing about
human creativity is precisely its capacity to nullify such distinctions.
When he insists that "artificial life" is also a part of nature, he is
expressing some measure of tolerance for novels and for the kind of life
they depict. In fact, six years after his complaint about *Quentin Durward*
(which is also an admission of how compelling he found it), he objects
to Thoreau in an 1847 *Journals* entry for "railing at the novel reading."
"Novels, Poetry, Mythology must well be allowed," he writes, "for an
imaginative being. You do us great wrong Henry T. . . . The novel is
that allowance & frolic their imagination gets. Everything else pins it
down."

Emerson's objections to literary artifice, as it is embodied in the novel,
is only to artifice that seems to him self-indulgent, over-insistent, uncompromising, nascently modernist. He complains about an excess of formal
contrivance, and it is precisely a matter of degree that distinguishes
Emersonian practice from the more provocatively obvious calculations
of form and technique in modernist writing, a writing where, as he says
of Hawthorne, the author invites readers "into his study," opens the
process before them.

The Emersonian explanation would go something like this: while everything made by human beings is "artificial," it always bears a trace, nonetheless, of "aboriginal nature," of "the essential man," to which, as he says in "Self-Reliance," only "great genius" can return in any full force. Even minor artistic production gives evidence of nature's pervasive, insinuating presence. "The real value of the Iliad, or the Transfiguration, is as signs of power," to recall his essay "Art," and he goes on to locate some of the same evidences even in inferior works of any kind. Everything is part of a creative flow or torrent, an image I will discuss in a moment, and any work of art is a surge within the flow, "billows or ripples they are of the stream of tendency; tokens of the everlasting effort to produce, which even in its worst estate the soul betrays." Consider that word "betrays." It catches an inescapable contradiction in the effort of man to make his presence known to the world and to himself. The double sense of "betrays" is evidence that we are bound within a process by which any act of human creation, any assertion of human consciousness is simultaneously a showing forth of life and a cheat upon the potentialities of life. He can imagine the disappearance of literature because he is confident that in place of it some alternative structuring of life will emerge. It is an imperative of human nature, or of nature that is a part of our being human, that we leave traces of ourselves and of our time on earth, and these, when measured against the human reality still to be discovered, are in danger of being mistaken for waste. No matter how much you may oppose "artificiality" or artifact, human beings are determined to create them and to leave them lying around. It is "ghastly" to carry on about the accumulations; Emerson used that word, along with "powerful," to describe *The Scarlet Letter,* and he might have said the same of *Moby-Dick* if he had read it. It is "ghastly" to let the accumulations tyrannize your work, as if your own methods cannot modify the systems, including the allegorizations and typologies, that at any historical juncture might seem to dominate life.

Emerson, and Emersonians generally, are a species of radical conservative, a term used to describe himself by the most conspicuous Emersonian of the present time, Norman Mailer. Beginning with *Advertisements for Myself* in 1959, Mailer's writings are laced with Emersonian doctrine, and most of his positions will be familiar to any reader of William James, who would have better understood than have most of Mailer's contemporaries his complex infatuation with criminals and criminal behavior. It is consistent with this tradition that Mailer feels no obligation to acknowledge it. He and any predecessors share equally in the same origin. His novel *Ancient Evenings* continues the vast meditation begun in *The Prisoner of Sex* on the mystery of origins, on intimations in individual life that you are the reincarnation or "quotation" of someone else from some other time, and on the relation of origins and inheritance to literary (and sexual) creativity. Asserting in *The Prisoner of Sex* that "in the seed of Christianity was the origin of technology" (though technology precedes Christianity by millennia), Mailer like Emerson wants to look beyond Jesus so that he might "begin to believe . . . that the marrows and sinews of creation were locked in the roots of an amputated past." About the only sure evidence of that past now exists for him in "the hieroglyphics of the chromosome (so much like primitive writing)." And while Mailer involves himself actively in political issues, as did Emerson with slavery and William James with American imperialism, and while he uses, as do they, a vocabulary of revolution, none of them can or wants to imagine a revolution except one that might change human consciousness through the revolutions or tropings of words. The basis for truly decisive change in the real world cannot, that is, be imagined in the terms provided by what Emerson calls in "Self-Reliance" the existing "communities of opinion." The revolution worth pursuing is the continuous act of turning and overturning the page. I describe their position, but also agree with it, as against the infatuations of those who imagine a more direct relation between literary and political action. Any "revolution" that goes on to establish itself, in a book or in life, would "betray" the revolution.

Not surprisingly, Emerson, no less than William James, has some difficulty explaining what he means by individual human "acts," since even while an act might reveal an individual human presence, it is at the same time submerged in the continuities that flow through it. This raises once again the question of human genius, and I address it here, as in Chapter 1, as a problem in Emersonian vocabulary, especially as this has to do with thinking about literature. Since human consciousness initiated a separation of the human mind from the "flow" of nature, a separation called "culture," how can expressions of that consciousness, especially in such a fabricated structure as literature, also in any way be an expression of nature? Analogously, how and why should an individual whose very knowledge of himself depends on "communities of opinion" set out to resist or transform those communities? How does anyone's idea of himself ever get into words when the act of writing always "betrays" its distance from the experiences the words propose to represent? This peculiar situation is frequently described by Emerson, Thoreau, and Whitman as a problem of "doubleness"; it was quite specifically connected to literary composition by Wordsworth in Book II of *The Prelude*, where, as with the Emersonians, doubleness is also accompanied by a feeling that he is outside of his body:

> A tranquillising spirit presses now
> On my corporeal frame, so wide appears
> The vacancy between me and those days
> Which yet have such self-presence in my mind,
> That, musing on them, often do I seem
> Two consciousnesses, conscious of myself
> And of some other Being.

Emerson's writing, even more than Wordsworth's, proceeds from this sensation of self-detachment and self-monitoring, of being suspended over various versions of yourself that can become, in any passage of talk or writing or recollection, superimposed one on another. You are forever elsewhere as you go about your daily business. This is especially the case if the business is writing, which is almost invariably about moments other than the present moment of composition. You are present at some earlier version of yourself that stretches back to ghostlier demarcations, beyond the "frame" or limit of your bodily life. The self can, however, be located here and now, not by reflection but, so far as Emerson and William James are concerned, by virtue of "acts." These acts are variously named—"resistance," "antagonism," "transition," "abandonment." None has to do with compliance. They are *re*active to any particular mode of expression, even the one you yourself might have chosen, if it threatens to fix identity or to locate it in some socially accredited idea of the human. Indeed, Emerson comes perilously close at times to calling for the disappearance of that idea—which is the general subject of the next chapter.

That is, Emerson sometimes pushes the oppositional nature of individual self-definition, which is everywhere implicit in his work, to the extremity reached in "Fate," where he tells us that "if truth come to our mind we suddenly expand to its dimensions, as if we grew to worlds. . . . This insight throws us on the party and interest of the Universe, against all and sundry; against ourselves as much as others." It is easy enough to imagine being "against ourselves" on behalf of something greater or more valuable to the future, as in the sacrifice of one's life for another or for one's family or country. However, this capacity is ours only because, from our very origins, we defined ourselves not on behalf of but in opposition to the Universe, insofar as it is governed by something called "God" or the "flow" of nature. Our human beginnings were an abruption of that flow. Emerson seems willing now and again to forget this—as is Thoreau, especially in his *Journals* [6]—as if hoping that we really do still have a chance to rejoin the current of "life," a chance to start inventing ourselves afresh and all over again, as if we were part of a "perpetual inchoation." That phrase, from "The Method of Nature," stunningly summarizes what seems to him the productive logic of life and, for that matter, of literature. Weakly translated it means that form consists in acts of beginning, acts so continuous as to obliterate the boundaries of any one of them. "Perpetual inchoation" would also therefore have the unfortunate effect of obliterating us.

The wholeness we admire in the order of the world, is the result of infinite distribution. Its smoothness is the smoothness of the pitch of the cataract. Its permanence is a perpetual inchoation. Every natural fact is an emanation, and that from which it emanates is an emanation also, and from every emanation is a new emanation. If anything could stand still, it would be crushed and dissipated by the torrent it resisted, and if it were a mind, would be crazed; as insane persons are those who hold fast to one thought, and do not flow with the course of nature.

The confusion occurs near the end, in the equation of "mind" with some object that resists the torrential flow. It allows an inference that Emerson usually avoids because he finds it so dangerously seductive: it is implied that in order not to be crazed by holding on to one thought, the mind must "flow with the course of nature." It must, for all practical purposes, disappear. And yet, as I have just pointed out, nearly everywhere in Emerson the movement of mind from one idea to another is described not as a flow at all but as an act, a transition and therefore an evidence of distinctly human will and power. Indeed it is usually an antagonistic movement by which the mind counteracts its tendency to inertia. "The mind goes antagonizing on," as he says in "Experience." The mind is anything but submissive, and its contributions to the flow called life consist of resistances that help accelerate the forward motion. What Emerson wants to say here, at least consciously, is expressed in Frost's "West-Running Brook." The poem is a direct "emanation" from this passage of Emerson's, and deserves, by clarifying it, to be called a "new emanation." It is among the most profound expressions ever given to the immensely intricate Emersonian linkages of origins, actions, and creativity:

> "Speaking of contraries, see how the brook
> In that white wave runs counter to itself.
> It is from that in water that we were from
> Long, long before we were from any creature.
> Here we, in our impatience of the steps,
> Get back to the beginning of beginnings,
> The stream of everything that runs away.
> Some say existence like a Pirouot
> And Pirouette, forever in one place,
> Stands still and dances, but it runs away;
> It seriously, sadly, runs away
> To fill the abyss's void with emptiness.
> It flows beside us in this water brook,
> But it flows over us. It flows between us
> To separate us for a panic moment.
> It flows between us, over us, and *with* us.
> And it is time, strength, tone, light, life, and love—
> And even substance lapsing unsubstantial;
> The universal cataract of death

That spends to nothingness—and unresisted,
Save by some strange resistance in itself,
Not just a swerving, but a throwing back,
As if regret were in it and were sacred.
It has this throwing backward on itself
So that the fall of most of it is always
Raising a little, sending up a little.
Our life runs down in sending up the clock.
The brook runs down in sending up our life.
The sun runs down in sending up the brook.
And there is something sending up the sun.
It is this backward motion toward the source,
Against the stream, that most we see ourselves in,
The tribute of the current to the source.
It is from this in nature we are from.
It is most us."

It is important to notice that an Emersonian can belong to "the party
and interest of the Universe" even "against ourselves" without subscrib-
ing to a First Cause or Prime Mover. In a characteristic locution Frost
says only that "there is something sending up the sun," only "something." It is the "something there is that doesn't love a wall" in "Mend-
ing Wall"; it speaks (or does it?) through the scythe in "Mowing":
"Perhaps it was something about the heat of the sun,/Something, perhaps, about the lack of sound." This is philosophical skepticism indistinguishable from the lilt of country talk. It is Frost's intention that the
"truth" should exist exactly *there*, and not in Big Talk. "Something"
lurks inconspicuously in our speech, a mystery on the tip of our tongues,
on the very surfaces of our lives. Looking intently into a well in obedience to the promise that truth is to be found at its bottom, Frost sees
only

. . . a something white, uncertain,
Something more of the depths—and then I lost it.
Water came to rebuke the too clear water.
One drop fell from a fern, and lo, a ripple

Shook whatever it was lay there at bottom,
Blurred it, blotted it out. What was that whiteness?
Truth? A pebble of quartz? For once, then, something.

That last sentence, which gives the poem its title, can be voiced in a
number of ways, all of them relaxed; portentousness has been ruled out
not only by its syntax but by the gentle mockeries of ominous sounding
words in the lines that precede it. Emersonians like to be at odds with
those whom William James calls "intellectualists," people who prefer to
think of truth as something already waiting to be discovered, something
with a capital letter, not followed, as in Frost, by a question mark.
Intellectualists associate truth with depth, with some richness to be
found there, an inference from the word "profound," which, besides its
association with the word "fund," can mean "to fathom," as in *Moby-
Dick*, where another kind of whiteness comes from the deep. The idea
of *depths* is a fabrication of hidden riches, and it can sometimes dissuade
those who believe in it from coping effectively enough with the surfaces
of life. "Intellectual tasting of life will not supersede muscular activity,"
Emerson insists in "Experience," "life is not intellectual or critical but
sturdy." And he then goes on to a further disquisition on "surfaces," not
having to do in this instance with the "smoothness" of nature, imagined
as a flow of water, but with social-cultural life, imagined as some combination of skating-pond and workplace:

We live amid surfaces, and the true art of life is to skate well over them. Under
the oldest, mouldiest conventions, a man of native force prospers just as well as
in the newest world, and that by skill of handling and treatment. He can take
hold anywhere. Life itself is a mixture of power and form, and will not bear the
least excess of either.

It is impossible to come to terms with this passage because Emerson
himself is unable to. On the one hand, it sounds exuberant about the
"man of native force" who can "take hold anywhere"; on the other, it
admits that all he has to cope with are "surfaces," and that it makes no
difference whether his situation is culturally encrusted or culturally bare.
I am less interested, this late in my inquiry, in his ideas of power, action,

and resistance to constraint than in an undertone of lassitude, amounting to self-derision. About a quarter of "Experience," published in *Essays: Second Series* of 1844, can be traced to the *Journals* for 1842, and its ideas are familiar from "The American Scholar" of 1837 and from "Self-Reliance" and "Circles" in *Essays: First Series* of 1841. The changes in these few years are a matter not of ideas but, as Frost would say, of the way he now carries himself toward them. It sounds as if his confidence in the efficacy of human "force" has become a source of irritation, as if he were discovering shallows in his own rhetoric. The death of five-year-old Waldo from scarlet fever and Emerson's skepticism about the reality of grief and the necessity of mourning, though obviously relevant to whatever he says in "Experience," are nearly always improperly magnified in order to suggest that the essay marks a decisive turn in his life and work. The fact that he himself alludes to the death of his son only briefly in the opening pages and then drops the subject does not, of course, prove that he is not obsessively concerned with it. His bitterness and bereavement are evident enough in his letters and his *Journals*. But as I have just indicated, the essay is committed, and with no important variation of meaning, to the terminologies of the earlier work, and I want to show why it is important to recognize that the death of his son—preceded as it was by the deaths of his first wife, Ellen, at age nineteen in 1831, of his often deranged brother Edward in 1834, and of his favorite brother, Charles, in 1836—only makes more apparent to him a dilemma already evident in his definition of selfhood, his conception of how someone indicates his presence in the world.

He did not need the wasting loss of a son to make him wonder about his disengagements from others and from himself, a concern that began with his very first entries in the *Journals* in 1820 and which he shares with Wordsworth and with such childless figures as Thoreau and Whitman. In *Essays: First Series*, he describes "intellect" the way he has already described the new-born infant in its crib: "Intellect is void of affection, and sees an object as it stands in the light of science, cool and disengaged. The intellect goes out of the individual, floats over his personality, and regards it as a fact, and not as *I* and *mine*." The "self" on which Emerson chooses to rely exists only in transitions. Identity is discernible to him in acts of antagonism directed against the already formulated, against your own previous utterance, "against ourselves as much as others," as he says in "Fate," if it proves to be in the interests of the Universe.

It is disconcerting to be taken at your word, and appalling when, having for so long insisted that you do not find yourself in your own body, you also find that the offspring of that body has in fact vanished into "the wholeness we admire in the order of the world" ("The Method of Nature"). Keep in mind that Emerson means everything he says. Imagine a father and a writer who, having called for the disappearance of literary texts because they inhibit "original genius," must in addition be satisfied to lose the text originated by his married body, lose it to the whim or force of nature. What can he then confidently leave to such a universe as a trace of himself? The question is especially acute when he must count as among the mere surfaces amidst which we live the very words on which his rhetoric depends, like *life, power, form, convention,* and *nature.* It may be, as he observes in "Plato," that intellect is superior to nature because it "made and maketh" it, but it can only do this because intellect is to begin with "interpenetrated by the mind that made nature," and us. How does one mourn the deaths and disappearances from within a process that does not acknowledge them, even if the loss is of a child of whom he writes in the *Journal* for June 1840, "My little boy grows thin in the hot summer & runs all to eyes & eyelashes"?

Even under conditions not so ruthless, Emerson has great difficulty finding a rhetoric to support the positions he advances, positions having to do with the whole phenomenon of human, including literary, production, and with questions of origin, action, and traces. The passage about "surfaces" is a particularly vivid example of his difficulties. He cannot, for example, clearly locate the "surfaces" he alludes to, and for the reason that he intends that they should include and therefore abolish their defining opposite, which is the idea of "depth." You can both skate on his surfaces and handle them; you can be "in" them, "on" them, or "under" them. None of the verbals—handling, treating, taking hold— refers to an object, because all objects, including such words as "life," "power," and "form," are surfaces only to be manipulated. The terms he confidently falls back on have to do entirely with actions, like skating, handling, holding. William James will eventually turn the Emersonian dilemma into an exhortation on behalf of American pragmatism. Leading up to one of his famous references to the "cash-value" of words or ideas, he notes that

the universe has always appeared to the natural mind as a kind of enigma, of which the key must be sought in the shape of some illuminating or power-bringing word or name. That word names the universe's *principle*, and to possess it is, after a fashion, to possess the universe itself. "God," "Matter," "Reason," "the Absolute," "Energy," are so many solving names. You can rest when you have them. You are at the end of your metaphysical quest.

But if you follow the pragmatic method, you cannot look on any such word as closing your quest. You must bring out of each word its practical cash-value, set it at work within the stream of your experience. It appears less as a solution, then, than as a program for more work, and more particularly as an indication of the ways in which existing realities may be *changed (Pragmatism)*.

Emerson could not mourn for long the deaths of sons and lovers, of Waldo or of Ellen, because his work from the beginning has already celebrated the fact that the Universe—and he, Emerson, who is on its side—can afford to be indifferent to the human presence even while being enhanced by it. The human presence can make itself felt only by and in its actions, even while the results of those actions, the texts and other bodies it produces, will be obliterated by the power it is trying to interpret. If Frost in "West-Running Brook" offers a gloss on a great visionary moment in "The Method of Nature," Emerson's other son and heir, Wallace Stevens, does much the same for "Experience" in "A Postcard from the Volcano," a poem about the pathos of human creation and inheritance. Its first line beautifully suggests that the children who might casually pick up "our bones" from among the wastes of the world have without knowing it also picked up our bones within themselves; parts of their bodies are parts of nature, parts of us:

> Children picking up our bones
> Will never know that these were once
> As quick as foxes on the hill;

And in that autumn, when the grapes
Made sharp air sharper by their smell
These had a being, breathing frost;

And least will guess that with our bones
We left much more, left what still is
The look of things, left what we felt

At what we saw. The spring clouds blow
Above the shuttered mansion-house,
Beyond our gate and the windy sky

Cries out a literate despair.
We knew for long the mansion's look
And what we said of it became

A part of what it is . . . Children,
Still weaving budded aureoles,
Will speak our speech and never know,

Will say of the mansion that it seems
As if he that lived there left behind
A spirit storming in blank walls,

A dirty house in a gutted world,
A tatter of shadows peaked to white,
Smeared with the gold of the opulent sun.

Stevens will leave behind him a poetic estate, an oeuvre, that will look like a ruined mansion even to his instinctively artistic heirs, those "Children/Still weaving budded aureoles." *Still* can mean "always"; these children, to recall Emerson's "Art," are expressing that "everlasting effort to produce, which even in the worst estate the soul betrays." Appropriately they weave "aureoles," circles of light, imitations of the sun which is an image central to Stevens and to Emerson. The sun is called *opulent* not simply because it is golden but because Stevens's poetry has enriched it, first by disposing of its encumbrances, its old names, and then by giving it a new one, as in "Notes Toward a Supreme Fiction":

> There is a project for the sun. The sun
> Must bear no name, gold flourisher, but be
> In the difficulty of what it is to be.

Flourish is from the Latin word for flower or bloom or bud, so that in making the aureoles "budded" Stevens intends, no less we may recall than William James, that his children should follow his example.

All these Emersonian children recreate the sun out of a heritage not of tropes already made, of which they are innocent, but out of the better heritage of troping itself and of the entitlements they find in the things of this world. Stevens's poetry is imagined as "A dirty house in a tattered world." This is not as sad as it might be, because, as he says in "The Creations of Sound," "speech" is "silence made still dirtier." Further changes in what he has left, by inheritors like the poets Ammons, Ashbery, and Hollander, will make it dirtier still, and more valuable, "smeared with the gold of the opulent sun." Poetry has arranged to smear the world with its bequests. "I bequeath myself to the dirt," Whitman says near the end of "Song of Myself," "to grow from the grass I love,/If you want me again look for me under your bootsoles." He means, with Stevens, that even if his poetry is never again read, he has left something behind in the look of things, left what he felt at what he saw, evidence that he did something to the world. Ashbery is directly in the line of Whitman and Stevens when, in the conclusion of "Street Musicians," he writes:

> Our question of a place of origin hangs
> Like smoke: how we picnicked in pine forests,
> In coves with the water always seeping up, and left
> Our trash, sperm and excrement everywhere, smeared
> On the landscape, to make of us what we could.

Obviously these linkages and lineages are not ingeniously plotted by poets or by critics like me. They are hard evidence that genius does in fact move in ways attributed to it by Emerson. At the same time, however, no writer of genius, least of all Emerson himself, can ever wholly stifle the human complaint that he must disappear into the very things he has helped create, and all the more inevitably because he copied, borrowed, or stole most of them. The writing of literature in this vein quite naturally induces the supposition that the very idea of Man, of the individual, of the self, ought to be done away with altogether. That is the subject of the next and final chapter.

WRITING OFF THE SELF

HOW WOULD YOU LIKE TO DISAPPEAR?

P ROPOSALS TO DO away with the self—which has nothing to do, of course, with the physical extermination of people—are nearly as old, in the history of writing, as efforts to represent it. With considerable variations, such proposals are found in Virgil, Dante, and Spenser, Bacon, Milton, and Racine, Mallarmé, T. S. Eliot, and Lawrence, Artaud, Stevens, Beckett, and Pynchon. You may recall that Wordsworth proposed in 1815 to "melt down" the "arbitrary associations of language," such as govern the existence of social man at any given time, in order to discover something he calls "Man." This is only somewhat less radical in its implications, though much quieter in tone, than the later call from Nietzsche, Foucault, and others for the disappearance of the human altogether, at least as it has chosen to recognize itself in Western culture. It is no more, in their view, than an exhausted, discredited invention, which nonetheless makes it impossible to conceive, as yet, of what might follow after it.

The question of whether or not the abolition of the human is a good or a bad idea is not to be decided by a show of hands. We should try instead to understand why the idea occurs to so many writers popularly supposed to speak for the preservation of human culture, and why, also, the idea itself is so immensely difficult to substantiate or hold onto. Indeed, its ultimate significance may reside in its resistance to formulation in language, which, first and last, is the only way it can hope to get formulated. My title for this chapter is therefore a kind of pun, suggesting that you must depend on the self even as you try to write it out of existence. The idea of human evaporation, when it is put into writing, is oxymoronic, at once sharp and foolish, partly for the reason, again, that the idea exists in language and nowhere else. Joined to a rhetoric of persuasion, it finds itself uncomfortably adapting to those very aspects of a cultural discourse—and therefore to human assumptions that make that discourse intelligible—which it wants to erase. Once this problem is recognized, the situation becomes still more complicated, since there are then several different and quite legitimate ways of responding to it. Some may decide that it is a mere academic issue and of no practical consequence. Others might argue that the rhetorical difficulty involved in writing off the self is only one more laudable evidence that human reality, as it has so far been invented, is irreplaceable and therefore "true." Still others, and I count myself among them, see the problem more opportunistically as a chance in these instances to analyze language in order to learn something about its limitations as a cultural artifact. This involves locating points of rhetorical stress or discontinuity, moments where the language, and the cultural presuppositions that empower it, seem to thwart rather than facilitate an idea.

There is immense value in discovering these moments of edginess. We become better able thereby to measure how much in our present circumstance can be usefully worked upon and how much is perhaps irremediable. We determine the extent to which it is possible to "make the verge of to-day," as Emerson enjoins us to do in "Circles," "the new centre." In none of this is there a promise, even a recommendation, of revolutionary change. There is only a sense of possibility larger than any we could entertain if we merely accepted the "verge" as a necessary boundary.

I propose here to listen to what is going on in a variety of passages and to reveal some similarities and differences among European, Ameri-

can, and English invitations to do away with the human self. Even in
the most brash instances it will become obvious that no matter how
urgently a writer may wish to do away with the human as a cultural fact,
there are unavoidable problems even in framing the proposition. For one
thing, it would appear that there are as yet no alternatives to the idea
of the human; there is no "new" role into which it might enter that is
not somehow coherent with the one it would be disowning. Following
from this, we return to the likelihood that it is impossible to write
anything without in the process salvaging some part of existent humanity, and this is apt to be the case especially where writing betrays its
obligations to an inheritance it is trying to reject.

With such provisos in mind I want to proceed by first glancing rather
briefly at the most frequent and historically revered kind of human
self-extinction, one that in Western thinking represents an especially
good way to go. You may, that is, see the desirability of your own end
—in this case including the end of your physical being—in expectation
of a better hereafter; you surrender the self and the will in hope of saving
what is called the soul. Instances are to be found in Dante, Spenser,
Milton, or T. S. Eliot, and there is always along with it a predictable
recreative or countermovement. Self-disposal becomes a prelude to redemption. The human disappears only to reappear in some "better,"
spiritual form; there is an extension rather than a break in narrative
continuity, in the so-called "story of man." As a later comparison between Stevens and Frost will suggest, allegiance to narrative continuity,
along with the refusal to break it off, is one indication of the degree of
a writer's loyalty to existent ideas of the human. Christ in his death and
resurrection is the central example, and it has provided a revered para-
digm for Western conceptions of narrative.

This Christian mode helps clarify other kinds of self-eradication that
are more culturally embattled, especially so when they are represented
in writing. I will therefore be on the lookout for signs of stylistic stress,
evidences of the trouble a writer can get into as a consequence of his
own rhetoric. I will be listening to the *voicing* of the idea of self-
eradication, as we turn first to Foucault and Nietzsche and then, with
glances at a few others, to a group beginning with Emerson and including William James, Henry James, Sr., Stevens, and Frost. Superficially,

at the level merely of ideas—which I have been distinguishing from the way the ideas are held or carried by the words used to express them— the European contingent is very like the American, in that neither necessarily assumes a creative countermovement to human dissolution, at least of the sort that can broadly be called Christian. Neither expresses any sustained concern for the human soul as an entity or as a projection of the self into an after-life. It follows, too, that both are implicitly critical of the concept of narrative continuities, the mythos of narrative. Nonetheless, I will eventually want to suggest a distinguishing difference between the European and American writers, and I will locate it in style, in voice or manner. The Emersonian group, as compared to what can be called the Nietzschean, tends to suggest that cultural formations, no matter how imposing, can be manipulated or transformed in ways sufficient to the individual, perhaps by so small a subversive gesture as joking or punning on institutionalized terminologies. There is no need for any radical social or cultural upheaval in order to liberate the self from inherited ideas that contain him. In Emerson and his affili- ates, culture is treated less as a burden or impediment than as an oppor- tunity, as we have seen, for troping, for turning over or overturning, for twisting out of shape whatever comes to you by way of inheritance. This matter of voice and of tone—of how language is modulated for the ear—is central to the argument I will try to make. I will be show- ing how passages of writing, even as they call for self-erasure, unavoid- ably also call attention to the self as a performative presence in the writing.

FOUCAULT AND NIETZSCHE

I BEGIN WITH a well-known passage from the end of Foucault's *The Order of Things,* the title in 1970 of the English translation of *Les mots et les choses* of 1966. I quote in English because while keeping in mind an admonition Frost borrowed from Shelley—that poetry is all that is lost in translation—I am satisfied that what I will say about the passage, and about a subsequent one from Nietzsche, could be said also of the original:

If those arrangements [of knowledge] were to disappear as they appeared, if some event of which we can at the moment do no more than sense the possibility—without knowing either what its form will be or what it promises—were to cause them to crumble, as the ground of Classical thought did, at the end of the eighteenth century, then one can certainly wager that man would be erased, like a face drawn in sand at the edge of the sea.

These are the accents of someone who feels that he has already exposed and categorized the forces of civilization with extraordinary tactical skill. He has good reason to think so. In the preceding text he has set out to discover the "arrangements of knowledge" by which man of the present dispensation was brought into being, so that he can now at least "sense" how the arrangements might disappear, and, as he says, he can "certainly wager" on the immense results of this disappearance. There is in all this an audible excitement, a Nietzschean excitement. But there is also something from Marx, which, even as it inferentially constricts Foucault's vision of human dissolution, also substantiates the Utopian zeal with which he proposes it. Arrangements or structures reveal themselves, as Marx would have it, principally at the moment and in the act of breakdown. Thus the *episteme* of the Classical period—those rules of discursive formation that would govern what can be said even by parties in dispute—became recognizable as such only when, by breaking apart, they revealed how unnaturally they had been put together. This began to happen, according to Foucault's calendar, when, around 1790–1810, the Classical period was to be replaced by our present order of things. This new epistemic order is now in its turn, and for the first time, becoming visible to us as it, too, begins to collapse, to expose its design through its fractures.

Though these periodizations are by his own testimony quite approximate and are blurred still further by Foucault's later work, they nonetheless provide here and throughout his writing a license for the rhetorical assurance, the peculiar mixture of urbanity and flourish with which he customarily writes about the disappearance of man, of modern man. Foucault's voice would just as soon hurry him off the stage, though he cannot predict what will follow, and he regards his polemical accent as an obligation, for reasons made clear in a 1967 interview:

When one is dealing with the Classical period, one has only to describe it. When it comes to the modern period, however, which began about 1790–1810 and lasted until 1950, the problem is to free oneself from it. The apparently polemical character [in his writing about the modern period] derives from the fact that one has to dig out a whole mass of discourse that has accumulated under one's feet. One may uncover with gentle movements the latent configurations of earlier periods; but when it is a matter of determining the system of discourse on which we are still living, when we have to question the words that are still echoing in our ears, which become confused with those we are trying to formulate, the archeologist, like the Nietzschean philosopher, is forced to take a hammer to it.[1]

It was not until "L'ordre du discours," the 1977 Appendix to the American edition of *The Archeology of Knowledge,* that Foucault fully conceived of "event" as the emergence into visibility of subterranean and circuitous discursive formations. But even in *The Order of Things* the word "event" is seldom used as conventionally as it is at the end of the book. Which is to say that whether we are reading early or later Foucault, "arrangements of knowledge" do not emerge from what is normally meant by an "event," but only from astonishingly complex and devious movements within a culture. Since nowhere in Foucault are "arrangements" meant to appear in consequence of an "event," a reportable happening, they cannot, except rhetorically, disappear as a consequence of one. The word "event" at the conclusion of *The Order of Things* is intentionally provocative. So is the melodramatic suspense induced by a phrase like "at the moment," as if the reader is tensely holding onto the book in expectation of a happening. We are to be rhetorically persuaded that history unfolds with a kind of conventional narrativity, even though he has been intimating at this early stage something he will insist on in "L'ordre du discours" and thereafter: that such narrativity is designed to obscure the real "events"—those movements or forces that are given no place in what is commonly called the "story of civilization." The sequential narrative of historical events is really a form of repression for Foucault, but he suspends this recognition when, as at this point, he is enjoined by polemical purposes. Emerson in this, as in other respects, anticipates Foucault, as when he remarks in "Experience," "How easily, if fate would suffer it, we might keep forever these beautiful limits, and adjust ourselves, once for all, to the perfect calculation of the kingdom of cause and effect. . . . And yet he who should do his business on this understanding, would be quickly bankrupt. Power keeps quite another road than the turnpikes of choice and will, namely, the subterranean and invisible tunnels and channels of life. It is ridiculous that we are diplomatists, and doctors, and considerate people: there are no dupes like these."

Let me make clear that I am not attacking Foucault or being fussy about the brief passage I have quoted from his writing or arguing against its ideas. Instead, I am trying to investigate the status of the writing at a point where the author has chosen to excite the reader and himself with the notion that man is to disappear along with, let it be noted, his ability to represent himself. It is important to register the oddity and instability of this particular moment, measured against not only our ordinary disposition but Foucault's own customary procedures. The oddity here is highlighted by the specific figure with which the passage, and the book, is brought to a close: the comparison of a man to a face drawn in sand. The voice stretches this comparison, doubles it, so to speak, until the face is not only drawn in sand but drawn at the edge of the sea. It is close to hackneyed, and the more effective for being so. This could be the sand of Arnold's "Dover Beach," allowing for the pebbles; and the edge of that sea could mark the spot where, supposedly, we crawled out in an evolutionary movement now to reverse itself. But Foucault does not here or anywhere else suggest the end of a physical species. He calls rather for the end of those particular organizations of knowledge which are responsible for the invention of man and, in consequence, for his self-regard, his desire to become the object of his own study and reflection. It is therefore important that the object marked at this point for destruction is actually a drawing of man, a self-representation.

Noteworthy for my purpose is that, in its maneuvers with language, the voice here is quite deferential to the "human," to traditional human tastes, to fairly standard literary conventions. Inferentially, the passage depends on the community of assumptions it all the while designates for extinction. Again, I am scarcely criticizing Foucault for doing this.

Writing cannot entirely escape its own conventions, and in such an instance as this it might just as well use them despite the attendant contradictions. Indeed, Foucault's own mastery as a writer—he was one of the greatest of his time in France—reflects his sense of the immense historical power of which writing is capable. He wants to show how, in the modern period, it has substantially codified and controlled, how it can actually create human self-consciousness. By comparison, a face of man drawn in sand would be quite simply executed; it would, for one thing, offer far less evidence of the trappings of human artistic exultation than do Foucault's elaborate sentences. If the face "drawn" by Foucault's words were actually to be "erased," then so would any justification for writing as eloquently as he does here. Indeed, this spectacular scene of erasure cannot, according to the logic of the whole book, even occur as an "event" in history. It cannot occur in the sands of time. It could hope to occur only in the *act* of writing, reading, speaking, in some momentary change of discourse.

What is to be said of this? Perhaps we can get closer to the phenomenon by looking now, and more briefly, at a passage in Nietzsche that anticipates Foucault. It appears in a posthumously published fragment written in 1873, "On Truth and Lie in an Extra-Moral Sense":

In some remote corner of the universe, poured out and glittering in innumerable solar systems, there once was a star on which clever animals invented knowledge. That was the haughtiest and most mendacious minute of "world history"—yet only a minute. After nature had drawn a few breaths the star grew cold, and the clever animals had to die.

One might invent such a fable and still not have illustrated sufficiently how wretched, how shadowy and flighty, how aimless and arbitrary, the human intellect appears in nature. There have been eternities when it did not exist; and when it is done for again, nothing will have happened. For this intellect has no further mission that would lead beyond human life. It is human, rather, and only its owner and producer gives it such importance, as if the world pivoted around it. But if we could communicate with the mosquito, then we would learn that it floats through the air with the same self-importance, feeling within itself the flying center of the world. There is nothing in nature so despicable or insignificant that it cannot immediately be blown up like a bag by a slight breath of this power of knowledge; and just as every porter wants an admirer, the proudest human being, the philosopher, thinks that he sees the eyes of the universe telescopically focused from all sides on his actions and thoughts.

Spatial images abound here, images of miniaturization, expansion, telescoping. What they suggest is plain enough: man, especially what Nietzsche calls the intellect of man, is no more significant in relation to the cosmos than is a mosquito in relation to the air in which it floats. Each is solipsistically assured that it is the center of the world. It might be said both of man and the mosquito that they are "wretched," "shadowy," "flighty," "aimless," "arbitrary"—and doomed. And yet anyone would be embarrassed to offer commentary on matters already made abundantly obvious. Images so reiterated and redundant call for translation only for someone too dull witted to read the passage to begin with. Instead, the images refer us backward to their source, to the inferably imperious will and energy of the author. We are free to decide either that this voice is haughtily contemptuous of its auditors, or that it assumes auditors who, like itself, do not need to be persuaded of human insignificance. In either case the energy of the voice brushes dissenters to one side, if, indeed, it even bothers to acknowledge their possible existence. So that the spatial images, far from communicating anything important about the ratio of man to universe, refer instead to a speaker who, in imagining the end of man, is expansively enthusiastic, someone above and beyond mosquito-man. Rhetorically, he is in a position much like Foucault's. For while it might be argued that of the two Nietzsche is far more sweepingly dismissive, and that Foucault addresses himself not to all of "history" but only to the latest in a series of epistemic dispositions, the fact is that neither of them proposes that there is waiting for the species any form of self-representation other than the one they want to get rid of.

When writing arrives at such intransigence as we encounter in these passages, readers often succumb to an anxiety peculiar to the Arnoldian aspect of Anglo-American literary culture. They start worrying about the dangers of modernist or radical or uncompromising rhetoric. Are we not, it is asked, is not civility, is not civilization itself imperiled by this rhetoric? The answer is no. And for the reason, in part, that writing and reading should be regarded as one kind of experience among many and that for most people a number of other experiences are far more frequent and affecting.

It has to be said, of course, that writing is unique because of the extraordinary degree to which, when it is done with any semblance of genius, it calls for examination and for re-examination, the degree, that is, of its calculated solicitation. But for that very reason writing on a page reminds us that it is not the same thing as life on either side of it—life before anyone looks at the writing and after anyone stops looking at it. Writing exists in a mutually modifying but very confused, accidental, and varying relation to other usually less calculated, less examined, and comparatively messier experiences of life. Writing and reading are not related to history in an ideal, direct, glamorous, and potentially perilous transaction. Those who like to think that they are, and who therefore worry about what literature might do to "other people," invariably show thereby that they are themselves ignorant of the mediations and distractions that are a part of all writing and all reading.

What to some must therefore seem especially disturbing about Foucault's or Nietzsche's sort of writing is that it blatantly proposes to be indifferent to *any* sort of life that might exist in a tangential relationship to it. They sound altogether oblivious to the claims of daily, muddled, time-ridden existence, and to the values of historical inheritance or perpetuation, values recognized elsewhere in Foucault and, for example, in Nietzsche's often quoted "On the Use and Misuse of History for Life." Their apparently destructive relish when it comes to cultural institutions is generated by the fact that on the European, as compared to the American scene, these institutions still have enormous presence and ubiquity. I refer to the much more developed apparatus in Europe for the preservation of cultural experience, the burden, in some places, of fifteen centuries of it, including the visible presence, as part of the ordinary architectural landscape, of medieval religious structures. The kind of programmatic, hammering enunciations that go with the Nietzschean-Foucauldian position is something not needed in an American writing that proceeded brilliantly enough in default of precisely those cultural artifacts whose absence was cause for complaint, as we have seen, in Henry James, in James Fenimore Cooper, and even in Emerson. The difference, putting it rather crudely, is that on the European side is a tendency to link human disappearance to a cleansing historical apocalypse or, in Foucault's case, an emergent Utopianism, while the American tendency is usually more private, focused far more on language and thus on modulations and punning. Instead of the prospect of historical eruption, Emersonian writers offer something closer to quotidian self-erasure.

I have been probing these passages less to discover what they are saying, since that is obvious enough, than to determine how the sounds they make might impinge on various kinds of readers. What can this writing do to us? What should it do? In what ways may it be taken? What kind of sense does such writing make when it confronts the forms of life, to borrow a phrase from Wittgenstein, in which readers customarily find themselves? The possible varieties of response are a measure of important cultural and historical differences, and some of these can be accounted for by words like "European" or "English" or "American." Some but not all differences, since there are many variations within each of these categories. An American critic like Lionel Trilling, for example, conditioned by what seemed to him the authentic historical pressures within a New York intellectual coterie that flourished in the 1940's and 1950's, seems to have been influenced not at all by an earlier American tradition that goes from Emerson to William James to Stevens, Frost, and, with Marxist admixtures, to Kenneth Burke. All of these in their turn have been far more influential than Trilling on such near contemporaries of mine as John Hollander, Harold Bloom, Stanley Cavell, George Kateb, Richard Rorty, and Sacvan Bercovitch. And since the Emersonian legacy, in my interpretation of it, predicts, even while it offers an effective alternative to, the French writers who are most influential on contemporary theory—Derrida, Foucault, and Lacan—critics like Paul de Man and Leo Bersani are not less "American" merely because they show European affiliations.

When I use the term "American" I refer, in any case, not to something out of New York or the Vanderbilt University of the Southern Agrarians but out of Concord. More specifically, I refer to a way of reading things which Emerson induces in us, rather than to any ideas or attitudes abstracted from a reading of him. The passages from Foucault and Nietzsche are for me not an invitation to think about "the

Abyss" but to think about the way style—during the time one is attend-
ing to it—can make the possibility of self-eradication seem exhilarating
or culturally beneficial. I do not normally feel this way about these
possibilities; I do not, in fact, normally think about them at all. The
rhetorical audacity of Foucault or of Nietzsche is achieved by specific
efforts with language, and the effortfulness is telling evidence that each
is aware of the resistance in language to any of the cultural changes they
recommend. Their stylistic predicament and opportunity was anticipated by Emerson when, in "Circles," he cautioned against getting
too excited even by what he wryly calls "an abyss of skepticism":

Every ultimate fact is only the first of a new series. Every general law only a
particular fact of some more general law presently to disclose itself. There is no
outside, no inclosing wall, no circumference to us. The man finishes his story,
—how good! how final! how it puts a new face on all things! He fills the sky.
Lo! on the other side rises also a man, and draws a circle around the circle we
have just pronounced the outline of the sphere. Then already is our first speaker
not man, but only a first speaker. His only redress is forthwith to draw a circle
outside of his antagonist. And so men do by themselves. The result of to-day,
which haunts the mind and cannot be escaped, will presently be abridged into
a word, and the principle that seemed to explain nature will itself be included
as one example of a bolder generalization. In the thought of tomorrow there is
a power to upheave all thy creed, all the creeds, all the literatures, of the nations,
and marshal thee to a heaven which no epic dream has yet depicted. Every man
is not so much a workman in the world, as he is a suggestion of that he should
be. Men walk as prophecies of the next age.

Step by step we scale this mysterious ladder: the steps are actions; the new
prospect is power. Every several result is threatened and judged by that which
follows. Every one seems to be contradicted by the new; it is only limited by
the new. The new statement is always hated by the old, and, to those dwelling
in the old, comes like an abyss of skepticism. But the eye soon gets wonted to
it, for the eye and it are effects of one cause; then its innocency and benefit
appear, and presently, all its energy spent, it pales and dwindles before the
revelation of the new hour.

Whatever their differences, Emerson, Nietzsche, and Foucault allow
us to infer two things: first, that what they say in their writing is

ephemeral, and, second, that to the very degree that what they want to say *can* be said, their language carries some degree of endorsement from the culture they live in, the culture they also resent. The implication is that what is able to be understood between writer and reader is already superannuated. To try to get beyond that limit, to draw a new circle, will seem, for a time, an act of extravagance, of hyperbole. And it is as hyberbolic writers that Emerson and Nietzsche are customarily read, even though they are asking not to be read that way. They ask to be taken literally, and that, of course, is most difficult to do. Something they want to say needs to be said, but the historical condition of language cannot without contradiction sustain what needs to be said. Nonetheless, it is still that "something" which should concern us, especially its tribulations in language. It is paradoxical that a writer should call for the obliteration of man as we know him while exhibiting the need for man's approval and approbation, and it is paradoxical that a reader should agree to the necessity for self-obliteration using as his guide the mental faculties and educated feelings that are objects to be done away with. The objects have been turned into provocations for their own destruction. The value of the proposals consists in the paradox to which language, and the culture which inhabits language, has exposed them.

This effort to talk about the end of human beings is a clue, in fact, to one of the astonishing attributes of human beings—the capacity to accept, if only for a moment, the argument that its own kind is an impertinence. The effort testifies to the human desire at least sometimes to elude any definition of the human, and this explains in part why Nietzsche and Foucault are necessary figures whether one agrees with them or not. When Nietzsche says that with the end of man "nothing will have happened," the "nothing" will include his having said so, his testimony that this is true, his writing. At last he is really talking, as is Foucault in his sand image—as is Emerson nearly everywhere—about erasing his own rhetorical discourse. In that sense the writing is, to look forward to Stevens, "nothing that is not there and the nothing that is."

I am by now pleading a case. Try not to get stuck in the inexorable paradox that occurs in attempts at writing off the self. Try instead to literalize, to believe what is being said, and to take responsibility for the belief. Only then will it be possible to recognize something still more significant than the paradox: to recognize in such writing not the negation of the human but a brave putting forth of a kind of human feeling that is *un*sanctified and *un*sponsored. Those who want merely to stop at the paradox are on the way to hoping that arguments for the end of the human are not really serious, that they are, instead, only another trope in an ancient human enterprise by which customary ideas of the self are enhanced, as in the Christian enterprise for the salvation of souls. But to get excited by the prospect of the end of man—the extinction, again, not of a genetic, biological species but of our invention of the human—is just as "noble" as getting excited by projects for the continuation of man in his present form, enhanced or spiritualized. It could be argued that the more drastic of the two possibilities—the desire for self-obliteration, with no preconceived image ready to receive whatever is left—reveals a more invigorating impatience with the repressive consequences that attend the traditional work of redemption. We are asked, then, to get excited about a future which will be brought about by our own extinction; we are enjoined to do this by a rhetoric which is itself, along with its cultural vestiges, also to become extinct. ("There have been eternities when [the human intellect] did not exist; and when it is done for again, nothing will have happened.") Those animals which have before called themselves human will in some new form have become immune to this style of persuasion, immune to style itself, deaf to any language shaped by the pressures of a discarded historical reality, including notions about the nature and proper uses of the body.

These are tough propositions, and if they have nothing to do with the after-life of the soul, they have no truck either with programmatic ideas about the future scheme of things on earth. Projections of that sort, for Emerson or for Foucault, can be no more than the product of elements already in place, a creation out of the present dispensation and therefore an extension of what allegedly needs to be done away with altogether. When Foucault on Dutch television was invited by Noam Chomsky "to imagine a future society that conforms to the exigencies of human nature as best we understand them," his refusal was wholly within the logic of his positions and, though he would not have known this, within the spirit of Emerson's "New England Reformers."[2]

The desire for self-obliteration must, it seems, be utterly divorced from particular expectations, free of those "arrangements of knowledge" which created human beings in their present definition. What we have before us, then, is evidence that human beings can exercise a capacity to wish themselves radically other than what they are, to wish themselves evacuated from those "arrangements of knowledge." It is possible to do this, furthermore, without the comfort either of religion or of the so-called false needs produced by the conditions from which humans are, it is hoped, to be released. Thus, while Nietzsche and Foucault are far more concerned with cultural than with individual evaporations, the very extremity of their position enables us to come to a new appreciation of the more local and personal acts of self-disposal in, say, Emerson or Thoreau, Pater or Ruskin, Lawrence or Stevens, aspects which have been ignored or suppressed in the interest of accommodating everything they say to the overall humanistic tendencies necessarily exhibited in their work and in the work of their interpreters.

American Examples:
William James, Henry James, Sr., Emerson

Favoring what he calls the "floating" as against the "block universe," William James, like Emerson, foregoes any supports for the self that are extrinsic to its own workings. The self occurs *to* you; it is discovered *by* you only as and when it "works," and it is to be continuously rediscovered. This poses a semantic problem, since even to refer to the "self" implies that it is "there," that it exists prior to the naming of it. Hence, the dazzling complication of that moment in the essay "Self-Reliance" when, in exasperation with his own title, Emerson asks, "Why, then, do we prate of self-reliance? . . . To talk of reliance is a poor external way of speaking. Speak rather of that which relies, because it works and is." The "self" can rely only on those workings which in turn reveal it; its identity can therefore never be fixed or solidified. As he will say in "Circles," "There is no outside, no inclosing wall, no circumference to us." James intended to be more radically skeptical than Emerson, and this sometimes prevented him from recognizing the extent of his indebtedness. The passage just quoted from "Circles" finds its close equivalent in *Pragmatism,* when, having said that "all 'homes' are in finite experience," he goes on to say that "finite experience as such is homeless. Nothing outside of the flux secures the issue of it. It can hope salvation only from its own intrinsic promises and potencies."

But how, then, can we account for ourselves except in the most fragmented ways? How explain a person's sense of his own coherence? In trying to explain the human feeling of "continuity," James once again follows but does not acknowledge the Emerson who wrote in "Self-Reliance" that "power ceases in the instant of repose; it resides in the moment of transition from a past to a new state." In "A World of Pure Experience," he writes that "what I . . . feel simply when a later moment of my experience succeeds an earlier one is that tho they are two moments, the transition from the one to the other is *continuous" (Essays in Radical Empiricism).*

James's obsession with action and with being active was not of merely philosophical or Emersonian derivation, however. He had *made* himself, as we have seen, into a compulsively active man. His philosophy of action, like Emerson's, derives in part from the hysteria of the incipiently melancholic, the potentially invalided or emotionally-sexually incapacitated male, conspicuous examples of which in American letters are Parkman, John Jay Chapman, Hemingway, and Mailer. Given what is known about James into early middle age, his emphasis on the mobility and impermanence of self-definition is a response, both terrified and heroic, to threats of insanity and inanition that lurked in his own and also in his father's personal experience. There is, for example, the famous trauma, referred to at the end of the Prologue, which he ascribes in *The Varieties of Religious Experience* ("The Sick Soul") to an anonymous Frenchman, but which according to William James's son Henry was experienced by James himself in 1870: "I went one evening into a dressing-room in the twilight to procure some article that was there; when suddenly there fell upon me without any warning, just as if it came out of the darkness, a horrible fear of my own existence." The fear immediately enters into a species of combination with the image of an epileptic patient he had seen at the asylum, "like a sort of sculptured Egyptian cat or Peruvian mummy, moving nothing but his black eyes and looking absolutely non-human. . . . *That shape am I,* I felt, potentially." At the time William had no wife, children, or confidant to look to for solace, and while his father in similar circumstances could turn to his wife, Mary, William kept to himself, not reporting the crisis until *Varieties* was published in 1902 and even then ascribing it to someone else. As Howard Feinstein puts it, "William saw his mother as the most prominent person in his world who failed to recognize the awful truth personified by the sinister, implacable inmate." The distance between his own and his father's situation is that while Henry, Sr., could, in his panic, evoke "God," William could only say that "this experience of melancholia of mine had a religious bearing."[3]

But no faith in "God" preserved the father from discovering that the self could suddenly disappear, and with it the idea even of its necessity. In 1844, when William was two, Henry James, Sr., living in England, had a vision of "some damned shape squatting invisible to me within the precincts of the room, and raying out from his fetid personality influences fatal to life." Commenting in *Society the Redeemed Form of Man*, published in 1879, under William's supervision, the elder James admits that "it was impossible for me . . . to hold this audacious faith in selfhood any longer. When I sat down to dinner on that memorable chilly afternoon in Windsor, I held it serene and unweakened by the faintest breath of doubt; before I rose from table, it had inwardly shrivelled to a cinder. One moment I devoutly thanked God for the inappreciable boon of selfhood; the next, that inappreciable boon seemed to me the one thing damnable on earth, seemed a literal nest of hell within my own entrails."

Subsequently, he describes listening, while taking a water cure, to "the endless 'strife of tongues' about diet, and regimen, and disease, and politics, and parties, and persons" and, in once again cursing "the sense of selfhood," he remarks "how sweet it would be to find oneself no longer man, but one of those innocent and ignorant sheep pasturing upon that placid hillside, and drinking in eternal dew and freshness from Nature's lavish bosom."[4] This desire to surrender the self in return for the placidity of animal life—or, in William James, for its possible intensities—has an interesting analogue in Nietzsche's "On the Use and Misuse of History for Life," where man is said to envy the animals in the field for their lack of historical awareness and to become, in so doing, momentarily and sporadically in touch with life in a nonhistorical way.

In view of all this, and of what is made known in Jean Strouse's fine biography of the tortured existence of Alice James, a passage from a letter written by William to his wife from London in 1889 becomes still more remarkable. Despite its brevity it catches his highly idiosyncratic and appealing accent. As against every reason to be frightened by the prospect of looking at a nonhuman shape and admitting *"that shape am I,"* he recounts with boyish pleasure that "the best thing by far which I saw in Brighton, and a thing the impression of which will perhaps outlast everything else on this trip, was four cuttle-fish (octopus) in the Aquarium. I wish we had one of them for a child—such flexible intensity of life in a form so inaccessible to our sympathy." In response to something I once said about these sentences, Anita Kermode observed (in *Raritan: A Quarterly Review,* Winter 1982) that the apparition of the four cuttle-fish, with what she calls "the bald, domelike, infantile head, the blankly staring infantile eyes," might have evoked for him the four children of William and Alice James (children, it could be added, from whom he is also at the moment separated by a barrier of water). "Perhaps William approached the glass of the aquarium," she writes,

expecting to observe non-human presences, and was surprised to find that glass like a mirror, reflecting, however, not a humanistic but a human presence. It called to mind his children, but the thought of a child was a thought of himself, or a wish about himself, escaping from accessible form. But not from containment! A covert message, flashed to his wife: Spare me your sympathy, and your designs on my body, but do please maintain an environment which continues to take care of me! It's possible to read that passage, then, as an imaginary act of retrieving or reclaiming one's body from the humanizing designs that have taken possession of it—including marriage and fatherhood—but if so, it's done very tactfully and surreptitiously.

Habitual ideas of the human are thus eluded, not transcended, and in a manner so easygoing as to indicate in James no very particular allegiance to the human image and no desire, either, to reject it. It comes as it will come. He is, quite clearly, excited by what he has seen ("a thing the impression of which will perhaps outlast everything else on this trip"), and yet he communicates this excitement without any sort of grandstanding. His desire to reproduce himself in the shape of a cuttle-fish is part of his characteristically affectionate but unsentimental view of the oddity of being human. He can say, therefore, in *A Pluralistic Universe*, that there is a "conscious self of the moment . . . the present *acting* self," but at the same time he questions the very existence of "the really central self" as a constituent belonging in or to an individual. "Just as we are co-conscious with our momentary margin," he writes, "may we not ourselves form the margin of some more really central self in things which is co-conscious with the whole of us? May not you and I be confluent in a higher consciousness, and confluently active there, tho we know it not?"

When James writes in this way it is with an unabashed and contented calm oblivious to the likelihood that what he is saying will appear strange or extraordinary or disturbing to his readers. The human is placed at a kind of margin or interface with the cuttle-fish, and this happens almost by accident or chance, as if it could therefore happen at any time. There are many such stylistic moments in the Emersonian line, not only in Emerson himself and in Stevens, but also in Thoreau, as in the chapter of *Walden* called "Spring," where he asks, "What is man but a mass of thawing clay?"[5] or in Whitman's "As I Ebb'd with the Ocean of Life" where "I too but signify at the utmost a little wash'd-up drift,/A few sands and dead leaves to gather,/Gather, and merge myself as part of the sands and drift." There is nothing italicized in these words, nothing is made to sound unaccustomed in the prospect of self-dissolu-tion, the stripping away of human attributes in order to arrive at some quite unaccustomed condition of "thought." There is no suggestion, either, as there so often is at comparable moments in Wordsworth, that the experience is to have the utilitarian purpose of building up one or another acceptable human faculty.

In illustration I turn now to the transparent eyeball passage from Emerson's *Nature*. I do so for the very reason that most readers are quite bored with hearing it cited or alluded to. Redundancy of interpreta-tion has induced a more than ordinary inattentiveness to the problems posed in the passage as these have to do with any effort at writing off the self:

Standing on the bare ground,—my head bathed by the blithe air, and uplifted
into infinite space,—all mean egotism vanishes. I become a transparent eye-ball;
I am nothing; I see all; the currents of the Universal Being circulate through
me; I am part or particle of God. The name of the nearest friend sounds then
foreign and accidental: to be brothers, to be acquaintances,—master or servant,
is then a trifle and a disturbance. I am the lover of uncontained and immortal
beauty.

Emerson's transcendental claims here—or, to be more exact, the
claims of the figure he calls "the idealist"—are necessarily weighted
down by the sounds of a countervailing social contract with his readers,
his "acquaintances," as they can be called, on the occasion of his writing to and for them. They may be a "disturbance" to him, and yet his
way of recounting the experience is designed to keep him closely in
touch with them. He refuses, however, to promise them anything beyond the experience, anything humanly or socially useful. He is content to be suspended at what we have heard James call a "momentary
margin."

In this mood Emerson resists all attempts at translation into terms not
of his own contrivance. He does not claim even to have originated
anything; and being "transparent" he cannot be turned or troped or
traced in any direction. The represented event on that bare common is,
indisputably, only something that *has* happened, something always prior
to the reporting of it; but so, in fact, is the writing itself as mere script.
It had to have been written down in the past in order ever to be presently
available to us. Until the moment when we look at it, writing cannot
be said to exist any more than does the reported event. The writing is
created by the act of reading, and, first and finally, all that really happens
in this or in any other passage *is* reading and writing. As actions, reading
and writing are always occurring *now*, and when they are not going on
they cannot be said to exist. The experiences both of reading and of the
writing it creates are more real, more present to consciousness, than are
any prior circumstances that might have given rise to them. Our read-
ing-writing brings into existence a moment in which we are actively
there, but it is also a moment in which self-present identity is reportedly
lost. For that reason we can say that man and not-man are in a simulta-

neous, occurrent state, that the one cannot ever be severed from the other.

This is, to repeat, an inquiry into those passages where human beings are eradicated or temporarily displaced or transformed into shapes not recognizably human. More significantly, it is an inquiry into what human readers can make of such passages. So far, I have been concerned with the degree to which writing can register these extraordinary occurrences sometimes with ideological purpose, as in Foucault and Nietzsche, and sometimes, as in William James and Emerson, with an exhilaration that exists within ordinary movements of life that are not made available to ideology. "Ordinary life" is imagined as if it were not less but, because extemporized within and also against existent forms, immeasurably more than the result of some "arrangement of knowledge." Emerson and James, on the one hand, and, on the other, Foucault and Nietzsche, are therefore up to different things, but neither pair —and this is the important point—will participate in the tradition by which self-eradication is a mere prelude to the re-entry of an enhanced self into already existing "arrangements of knowledge." Whether it be Emerson or Nietzsche, James or Foucault, a nonideological process or an ideological one, it is presumably possible to experience such an interlude without calling for any of the religious and humanistic sanctions at work in the life around it and without contributing to these sanctions. It is possible to confer value on moments of transformation or dissolution without looking ahead toward a narrative of fulfillment. The moment is endowed with something as vague as wonder or beauty, empty of the desire to translate these into knowledge.

CRITICAL DIFFERENCES

WHAT, IT MAY be asked at this point, is all the bother about? Why explore this issue at such length and with such elaborate attention to mere details of its expression? The argument could, indeed, be much briefer and much simpler if I merely wanted to propose that one idea of the human should prevail over the other. In fact, I am recommending as a moral virtue the recognition that this issue is of necessity opaque.

Those who think that the customary (including Freudian) idea of the human is a necessary and laudable one have a long Judeo-Christian tradition on their side. This convinces them that they make eloquently clear sense even in their self-doubt, though what they say is often quite unclear to those who do not share their assumptions. By contrast, these others—who think the idea of the human is questionable or that it should be done away with—can, as I hope to have shown, get into serious trouble whenever they try to express this conviction.

I am therefore concerned with a model case of how writing, how language can involve us in stylistic hassles that have ultimately to do with our vision of what human life is supposed to be like and how we ought to think and talk about it. I contend that the human presence takes on an unaccustomed and admirably vital form in the very process of denying that presence, and, further, that this is a factor in literature that has been mostly shied away from. Even in its present, often highly skeptical mood, criticism almost always argues in a quite simple either/or fashion —either for the idea of the human, as traditionally conceived under a mostly Judeo-Christian aegis, or in opposition to it. And the opposition usually argues that the "self" which is discovered in language necessarily begins to dissolve there, since language has no fixed or ultimately rationalizing terms. One could therefore say of the self what Emerson says in "Circles": that "every ultimate fact is only the first of a new series," and that "there is no circumference to us."

The alternative possibilities—of discovering a form of the human which emerges from the very *denial* of its will to become articulate, or of looking at a landscape from which the familiar human presence has been banished and of enjoying this vista without thinking of deprivation —these are options few readers seem willing to take, even when the writing invites them to do so. Apparently the human presence must be a humanistically conceived one or at least give evidence that it wants to be. Trained as we are to read books and to look at film and dance as if the question of the human presence, humanistically and therefore narrativistically enacting itself, were really not a question at all, the absence from a text of what are called "human beings" is generally considered lamentable. So much so that some writers will insist, even against the evidence of their own work, that such beings really are *there* or ought to be there. The recent introduction by Thomas Pynchon to his collection of short stories called *Slow Learner* is a nearly ludicrous example of this. A novelist who has powerfully demonstrated why so-called "full" or "real" characters cannot be available to him decides retrospectively, and under the cultural pressure of humanistic criteria, to turn on his own early writings and complain that it is insufficiently populated by such figures.[6] Similarly, though the acquisitions of socially accredited selfhood are treated with exuberant hostility in the novels and poetry of Lawrence, it is nearly always assumed that the difficulties this entails for the reader are resolved by translating his writing, sometimes with support from Lawrence's own rhetoric, into programs for human improvement. And where, as in the poetry of Stevens, there is a frequent reduction of selfhood to the so-called First or primary idea, readers tend to ignore the evidence in some of his best poems that he wants the human will to remain unactivated by this reduction.

In line with this I will now make a further distinction between two great poets, Frost and Stevens. The distinction has considerable bearing on the conduct of criticism, especially as it concerns the vexed issue of voice and presence in literature. For both poets a sense of "nothingness" or a condition of vacancy is one of the likely experiences of daily living. It may be "an illusion that we were ever alive," says Stevens in "The Rock"; there may be a "design of darkness to appall" says Frost in "Design." The difference is that Frost seems more often to have contrived this perception in order that he may then ostentatiously resist it. His poems tend again and again to break away from the condition of "barrenness" by means of some abrupt, syntactically and formally signaled change of tone: "They cannot scare me with their empty spaces," or so he says in the last stanza of "Desert Places"; and when, as in "A Leaf-Treader," falling leaves "tapped at my eyelids and touched my lips with an invitation to grief," he manages at the end to put them underfoot: "But it was no reason I had to go because they had to go./Now up, my knee, to keep on top of another year of snow." He is instructing not his real knee but his poetic feet. Emerging from a poem of strong anapestic tendency, the line becomes a steady march of mostly monosyllabic iambics that allow for just a slight anapestic resistance with the word "another." The verse form recommends a form of human conduct.

Frost's intimated presence is a *performing* presence. Indeed, the poetic
calculation here is so measured for its effect, so bald and unapologetic
as to suggest that poetic maneuver, no less than seasonal change, is allied
to the workings of nature.

Frost shares Emerson's conviction that the act of writing can imitate
forms and forces attributable to the natural world. His winter landscapes
are allowed to become more threateningly aggressive than comparable ones in Stevens because he is confident of support for his retalia-
tions; he has precedents on his side and can trace these even to the
sequence of the seasons. If, in the natural course of things, the self is
faced with erasure, as imaged in the fall of leaves or snow, then it will
also happen in the nature of things that the leaves will be trodden
underfoot; that the snow will melt; that the logic of survival will
be affirmed. His figurations of voice are thus very often indistinguishable from a faith in the inevitability of narrative developments, as in
"The Onset":

> Always the same, when on a fated night
> At last the gathered snow lets down as white
> As may be in dark woods, and with a song
> It shall not make again all winter long
> Of hissing on the yet uncovered ground,
> I almost stumble looking up and round,
> As one who overtaken by the end
> Gives up his errand, and lets death descend
> Upon him where he is, with nothing done
> To evil, no important triumph won,
> More than if life had never been begun.
>
> Yet all the precedent is on my side:
> I know that winter death has never tried
> The earth but it has failed: the snow may heap
> In long storms an undrifted four feet deep
> As measured against maple, birch, and oak,
> It cannot check the peeper's silver croak;
> And I shall see the snow all go down hill

In water of a slender April rill
That flashes tail through last year's withered brake
And dead weeds, like a disappearing snake.
Nothing will be left white but here a birch
And there a clump of houses with a church.

I am concerned here not with the Miltonic syntax of the first stanza, which also incorporates echoes of Francis Thompson's "The Hound of Heaven," or with the degree to which this poem refers to Frost's Scottish Presbyterian heritage. Instead I want to call attention to his characteristic way of treating self-obliteration ("as if life never had begun"). He very often imagines it as a snowfall which obliterates signs of life, especially communal life, around a farm or village. The snow is "gathered," as if by design. It might remind us of "the storm bred on the Atlantic" in Yeats's "A Prayer for My Daughter," where it is compared to "the great gloom" in the poet's mind, a Coleridgean "dejection," some portentous threat to creative possibilities. Frost tells us at the opening of the first stanza that this snow is "always the same when on a fated night," and he may therefore only be cheering himself up when he opens the second stanza with the assertion that "all the precedent is on my side." It is a very questionable claim. "Fated nights" are a precedent, too, and they are conspicuously not on his side. It is true that "winter death has never tried/The earth but it has failed." And yet, as the suspense of that enjambment reminds us, "winter death" has also tried men and succeeded in overwhelming them. The transition from stanza one to stanza two, from "fated" death to "precedents" for the renewal of life, is the expression of a Jamesian will to believe not because of but in spite of the evidence that the belief is chancy.

We know these "precedents" thanks in part to poetry. I do not mean merely that poetry often records the changes of season; I mean that its very structure may mimic or be obedient to ideas of narrative development that are implicit in the idea of the seasons. In moving toward a conclusion, for example, most poems prefer to imitate the benign and promising sequence from winter to spring, from death to some form of rejuvenation. A nice instance is Wordsworth's "To————, in her Seventieth Year":

Such age how beautiful! O Lady bright,
Whose mortal lineaments seem all refined
By favoring Nature and a saintly mind
To something purer and more exquisite
Than flesh and blood; whene'er thou meet'st my sight,
When I behold thy blanched unwithered cheek,
Thy temples fringed with locks of gleaming white,
And head that droops because the soul is meek,
Thee with the welcome snowdrop I compare;
That child of winter, prompting thoughts that climb
From desolation toward the genial prime;
Or with the moon conquering earth's misty air,
And filling more and more with crystal light
As pensive evening deepens into night.

The ancient Lady, delicately holding on to life, nonetheless paradoxically combines—in Wordsworth's comparison of her to a snowdrop, the earliest of spring flowers—both the end of winter and the beginning of spring. She is dying into life. It is the image itself, or, more specifically, Wordsworth's contrivance of it, that prompts in the poet "thoughts that climb/From desolation toward the genial prime." The poet's self-consciousness of the process suggests that his poem, as much as the woman, is an example of generative maturity. Frost is seldom so ruminative as Wordsworth or Stevens when it comes to the "death" or deprivation of the self. Though he might seem to submit to the drift of a season or a climate, he is generally more anxious than they to ally himself with resistances to drift. And while Stevens is not immune to the charms of seasonal sequence or of the passage, say, from night to morning, he is usually more interested in the half light of dawn or twilight or the starry sky. He is more skeptical than Frost about reassurances held out by poetry or the passage of time or the conventions of narrative restitution. Barrenness or bareness, so-called reduced circumstances, exist for him less in a time sequence, with implications of escape and rebirth, than in space, space to be explored and contemplated, space in which the human figure more or less disappears.

Very often in Stevens the inactivation of the will is not seen as

necessarily a deprivation. The will does not exhibit even that self-regard-
ing fear which needs to be overcome, according to Schopenhauer, if one
is to experience what he means by the "sublime." (In the process of that
experience, as Schopenhauer describes it, a human being becomes conscious of objects hostile to the expression of the will. But "by a free and
conscious transcending of the will and the knowledge relating to it," he
is then able to contemplate these objects passively and without fear,
"raised above himself, his person, his will, and all will.")[7] Beginning
tentatively in his earliest volume, *Harmonium,* Stevens concerns himself
with the process by which we encounter or imagine some elemental
reality. It was not, however, until nearly twenty years later, in 1942, that
he called this reality the First Idea, a term used earlier by Charles
Peirce.[8] In a letter about *Notes Toward a Supreme Fiction,* the most
summary of his long poems, he writes: "If you take the varnish and dirt
of generations off a picture, you see it in its first idea. If you think about
the world without its varnish and dirt, you are a thinker of the first
idea."[9] This is in fact a quite lackadaisical definition, and for something
better we must turn to the poem itself, a section entitled "It Must Be
Abstract":

> How clean the sun when seen in its idea,
> Washed in the remotest cleanliness of a heaven
> That has expelled us and our images . . .
>
> The death of one god is the death of all.
> Let purple Phoebus lie in umber harvest,
> Let Phoebus slumber and die in autumn umber,
>
> Phoebus is dead, ephebe. But Phoebus was
> A name for something that never could be named.
> There was a project for the sun and is.
>
> There is a project for the sun. The sun
> Must bear no name, gold flourisher, but be
> In the difficulty of what it is to be.

The sonorities of "purple . . . umber . . . slumber . . . autumn . . . umber" are playfully repetitive to the point of ridicule. The ridicule is directed beyond the god Phoebus or his superannuation and toward those of us who need to be told, at this late date, that gods do die and that we should let them. The funereal rotundities that announce the death are in themselves a species of poetic junk left over from some older project for the sun—the ever-recurring effort to discover and name a center for the universe, a godhead. Nor is there greater deference shown toward more current versions of the same thing, attempts to find new gods; this, like previous efforts, will only create new circumferences, to recall Emerson's essay "Circles," the title of which is a trope for the sun. These will, in turn, be superseded by others, and so it goes.

We are invited to wonder, with William James in *Pragmatism*, if "behind the bare phenomenal facts . . . there is *nothing*." "The sun/ Must bear no name," the ephebe is told. And yet there can be no escape from naming; it is what human beings *do*. Thus, the poet, himself an ephebe once, a poet in early manhood, is unable to follow his own edict: he proceeds, in fact, to give a new name to the sun. He calls it "gold flourisher," a phrase discussed at the end of the previous chapter. It is thus offhandedly suggested that the genesis of gods is simply an irresistible consequence of the human compulsion to use words. The "difficulty of what it is to be" is not resolved by poetry; the "difficulty" is created by poetry. Poetry prevents us from seeing "what it is to be." We are again back to Emerson, where in the process of breaking a "circle," or a confinement, we inescapably, and with an experience of only momentary liberation, create new ones.

It is important to distinguish between the predicaments posed by some of Stevens's poems—of imaginative impoverishments, of winter landscapes in the mind—and the style with which he renders them. The style, as in the relaxed title of one such poem, "The Man Whose Pharynx Was Bad," often suggests that he feels no unmanageable urgency about deprivations. And about the "difficulty" of things, as they pass in his poetry from one conceptual frame into another, he is mostly sardonic. Though he can believe, for example, that the "thing" is free of "rotted names" (in "Man With the Blue Guitar") the freed "thing"

is then shown to be merely on its way, in transition, to further subjuga-
tion under still another name.

To reduce anything to a First Idea is not, then, to arrive at "nothing,"
or at the "thing" itself, since the very idea of the "thing itself" is a great
poetic invention, a trope pretending not to be one. It is to arrive, rather,
at another fabrication and the fiction, discussed in the Prologue, that any
word can ever lay claim to being "first" or before anything else. Because
of this there is always for the poet, as Stevens imagines him, an unsatisfi-
able aspiration, the dream of an impossible possibility: to see something
without having to name it, without having to think about it, to see it
without having to re-create it, to see it as would a transparent eyeball,
with no sense of its dependence on the human will. This, it might be
recalled, is Emerson's dream of "genius": to know a world without
knowing it as a text.

That there should be such an intercourse with "things," cleaner or
more real than any permitted by language, truer and more honest than
language allows—this would appear to be an ambition utterly at odds
with the poet's calling. It is nonetheless an ambition especially strong
in Emerson and his descendants, an intensely private, cold, astringent
desire, as we learn from "Experience," where it is said that "the life of
truth is cold and so far mournful; but it is not the slave of tears,
contritions and perturbations. It does not attempt another's work, nor
adopt another's facts." This ambition is part of the poet's wry joke on
himself and on the reader, who is to some extent always the imagined
product of the poet's language. Frost is capable of such joking, and to
a retaliatory degree, especially on those who want to trust to his folksi-
ness. It looks beyond an audience of persons and toward some ideal
audience composed by and in other poems, like so many monitoring
stations in space.

It is not possible always to know when a great poet feels in a poem
as if the mastery he is flaunting to the world is really, so far as he is
concerned, a betrayal of his true calling, or when, as measured against
his local intentions, his mastery may seem to him to have counted for
little. Such feelings are, I suspect, especially strong in Stevens after
Harmonium, and there are hints of it everywhere in his work. His
rhetorical tactics are frequently tinged by self-mockery, and he seems to

me at his best not within the relatively neat structures of a poem like "The Idea of Order at Key West," masterful though it is, but in the more meandering, ruminative opacities of poems like "The Rock" or "A Rabbit as King of the Ghosts" or "Two Figures in Dense Violet Light" or the haunted and haunting "The River of Rivers in Connecticut." He writes at such times as if obeying random instructions of a consciousness released from any clear sense of itself, as if the comfort and pleasure his verse affords have less to do with sentiments or beliefs than with the casualness of his hold upon them and with the inadvertent discovery, as in "The Rock," that belief may adhere to forces mysteriously inherent in nothingness, "as if nothingness contained a métier." He is impoverished and opulent, embattled and relaxed, as in a daydream, rather than by an act of will. Even when the rhetorical shifts in his poetry are distinctly calibrated, they tend to induce a sense of drift, of exploratory meanderings, as one feeling dissolves into another or both are held together in a sort of suspended animation.

I am trying to describe the most difficult and impressive achievement of the poetry as I read it, while recognizing that many dazzling poems, like "Tea at the Palaz of Hoon," are altogether more self-assertive, and that at certain moments of extreme self-doubt Stevens will, like Frost, announce his presence with a stoic doggedness, as in the section of "Notes Toward a Supreme Fiction" entitled "It Must Give Pleasure": "There is a month, a year, there is a time/In which majesty is a mirror of the self:/I have not but I am and as I am, I am." With a few exceptions, criticism tends to favor this latter response to a crisis of selfhood, and in large part because it is among the most common of critical assumptions that structures are *meant* to develop in this direction, that persons are *meant* to "find" themselves. However, the assumption takes no account of evidence that if read just a little differently, some of the most revered poems in English, especially by Stevens, ask us instead to be content with a calm, contemplative receptivity to prospects of human dispersal.

I confess to being pleased by this receptivity and, when faced with uncertainties as to my own existence, feeling temperamentally in favor of relaxation rather than self-assertion, of drift rather than aggressive deployments. Partly for this reason I am reluctantly at odds with Harold

Bloom, a critic in whose work I take the most admiring interest. It will be obvious to readers of Bloom that there are many affinities between us, but I do not trivialize the differences when I call them temperamental. What else could they be? As the most ardent of Emersonians, Bloom would agree with the assertions in "Experience" that "temperament shuts us in a prison of glass which we cannot see" and that "on its own level, or in view of nature, temperament is final." William James is again taking a lead from his forebear when he declares in *Pragmatism* that "the history of philosophy"—and surely this cannot be less true of literary criticism—"is to a great extent that of a certain clash of human temperaments." So that while Bloom has an avidity, as do I, for moments of self-fracturing and self-dissolution, he likes to treat them, as I do not, as enormous crises and potential catastrophes. He therefore nearly always looks in a poem for a correspondingly strong reaction, a recoil, some confirmation that the self, as the humanistic tradition conceives of it, finally must, does, and indeed should find a way to reassert its power. He allows for a remarkable degree of psychic repression in Stevens, but he assumes that if, in such circumstances, the human will fails to intercede, then the alternative need not, as in my sense, prove to be benign or liberating, and must instead result inevitably in what, in his book *Wallace Stevens: The Poems of Our Climate*, he calls "the reductive fallacy." That fallacy consists, for him, in the belief that "the ultimate truth about us is, by definition, the worst that can be said about us," namely that we are destined for "destruction," "ruin," the "worst."

This belief is, he feels, humanly unacceptable, and it probably is. But to suppose that it is the predominant or irresistible way to think about reductiveness is to imagine only one scenario or narrative, wherein the prospect of self-eradication, pushed to a point where it touches some imaginary root nerve of the will, then rebounds, projecting us back into a reconstitution of the self and of a habitable world. Perhaps most people do like to think about destitutions in life and in literature in just this way, as if the worst returns if not to laughter then at least to something plottable. What is left out of this version of life and of literature is the recognition that we are not required to think of loss or reduction or self-dissolution as if it were synonymous with deprivation. Why may it

not be exhilarating? Why may not reduction be associated in and of
itself with exploration and gain? part of some search for a world prior
to the human presence and subsequent to it? a world where the very
issue of dependence as Schopenhauer imagined it—are we dependent
on the world? is it dependent on us?—is at least temporarily annulled?

There are glimpses of such a world in Emerson's "Fate," for example,
where he observes that "we cannot trifle with this reality, this cropping-
out in our planted gardens of the core of the world," and in the *Journals*
for 1847 where he says that "we wish to get the highest skill of finish,
an engraver's educated finger, determination to an aim,—and then—to
let in mania, ether, to take off the *individual's interference* [my italics]
and let him fly as with thunderbolt." Nor can a process of reduction,
when linked inexorably to some form of reconstitution as both cause and
justification, embrace the daring of writers more equivocating than
Emerson, like Ruskin, with his sporadic desire to see the universe unpeo-
pled and himself invisible. Disputing a letter addressed by Carlyle to
Emerson, Ruskin says that:

In the beginning of the Carlyle-Emerson correspondence, edited with too little
comment by my dear friend Charles Norton, I find at page eighteen this—to
me entirely disputable, and to my thought, so far as undisputed, much blameable
and pitiable, exclamation of my master's: "Not till we can think that here and
there one is thinking of us, one is loving us, does this waste earth become a
peopled garden." My training, as the reader has perhaps enough perceived,
produced in me the precisely opposite sentiment. *My* times of happiness have
always been when *nobody* was thinking of me. . . . My entire delight was in
observing without being myself noticed,—if I could have been invisible, all the
better.[10]

The narrative of reduction-rejuvenation to which Bloom subscribes is
one which I think Emerson or Ruskin would often find uncomfortable,
more so, oddly enough, than would other writers who, to Bloom's Emersonian displeasure, insulate the possibilities of reductiveness within
Christian orthodoxies and disciplines. Bloom's essential vision is of cultural catastrophe, and it is as if individual self-rescue operations from the
catastrophies of the imagination afford him a kind of exemplary but

never wholly reassuring comfort. In his criticism he often prefers poems and interpretations that represent some moment of spiritual, psychic, and poetic crisis in a writer, especially when any of these prove to be obedient to a corrective movement, or at least to the prospect of one. The drama of reduction or dissolution to "firstness" is construed by him as a "crisis," when in my view it could just as likely be an expression— momentary in its effect, exploratory in its aim, sometimes enlivening— of what it feels like to envision human disappearance. Bloom, with brilliant results, dedicates himself to the local energies at work in particular uses of language, and if he can be called a humanist in a traditional sense, he is also a masterful critic determined that humanism should make its presence known by movements in language, by the tropings of poetry, including the tropings of voice. When he finds evidences of a humanistic crisis he therefore inevitably expects to find also evidences of what he calls at the beginning of the Stevens book a "crossing." "A crossing within a crisis-poem, like a poetic crisis, is," he writes, "a process of disjunction, a leaping of the gap between one kind of figurative thinking and another."

In its adduced psychological or aesthetic consequences, however, this idea of "crossing," with its Freudian implications, is quite unlike what I have described as the Emersonian ideal of "transition." It is little different, in fact, from what in an older, religious vocabulary would be described as the struggle for personal salvation. And if a poem fails to give clear enough signals of this, Bloom will then infer it by placing the poem in the gravitational pull of other poems where it can more prominently be found. The poetic kinesis he describes is not therefore dissimilar to movements in religious poetry where one first descends "Into the world of perpetual solitude,/World not world, but that which is not world"—to quote the Eliot of "Burnt Norton" in one of his more disappointing puns about movement and abstention from movement in a world that whirls—and then supposedly ascends into a new form potentially more worthy than the original one. This sequence goes back from Eliot through Milton to Spenser in Book II of the *The Faerie Queene*, to Dante and the Bible, and it has sexual analogues, again out of Dante, in the treatment of buggery in Lawrence and, with often witty speculativeness, in Mailer, notably in *Ancient Evenings*. Buggery could be called "an attempt to get into Christianity by the back door," to recall a remark of Eliot's on Baudelaire. Bloom has reasons for not greatly admiring Eliot, so that in adducing this connection between them I am suggesting that his commitment to "crises" and "crossings" is so resolute as to involve him in alliances he himself does not want to make.

This dogmatism about restitutive movements becomes especially apparent when certain poems by Stevens cannot, to his satisfaction, dramatize within themselves a "crossing," or such an assertion of poetic will against deprivation as can be found in "An Ordinary Evening in New Haven." Take as a well-known and conveniently brief illustration "The Death of a Soldier":

> Life contracts and death is expected,
> As in a season of autumn.
> The soldier falls.
>
> He does not become a three-days personage,
> Imposing his separation,
> Calling for pomp.
>
> Death is absolute and without memorial,
> As in a season of autumn,
> When the wind stops,
>
> When the wind stops and, over the heavens,
> The clouds go, nevertheless,
> In their direction.

Bloom offers a paraphrase of the poem which adheres strictly to the notion of the First Idea, or rather to his particular version of it:

But what has the First Idea, or an idea of Firstness to do with the poem, "The Death of a Soldier"? Stevens seeks what is not possible, in a tradition that goes back to Homer yet never has gone beyond Homer. He seeks to see earliest what the death of a soldier is. His reduction is fourfold:

1) The soldier falls expectedly, in and by seasonal contraction; this is the

primal *ethos*, the soldier's character as it is autumn's, and so a limitation of
meaning.

2) The soldier is not and has no part in Christ; he will not rise, after three days,
separated from the common fate and requiring celebration.

3) Any death, by synecdoche, is as final in itself and beyond language as is an
autumnal moment of stasis.

4) That is, any death is also without consequence, in the context of natural
sublimity; for us, below the heavens, there is stasis, but the movement of a larger
intentionality always goes on above the heavens.

To begin with, this account attributes a clarity of movement to the
poem that it does not exhibit. Instead, the voice drifts away from the
narrative and argumentative assertiveness of the first two stanzas and
solicits the reader to meander with it. Beginning with line eight ("As
in a season"), the poem passes into something like reverie, and though
the speaker retains some of his exactness, with that careful "nevertheless," the poem by now is in the service of developments that cannot
be talked about with the finality of such earlier lines as "Death is
absolute and without memorial." Consider what happens to the phrase
"As in a season of autumn." At first it sounds simply like an illustration
of the inevitable "contraction" of the seasons, of human life, and especially of the life of a soldier. It is then repeated, but with a qualification
that releases it from its relatively inert metaphoric function. An apparent clarification turns out to have been only a partial glimpse of something. "As in a season of autumn," becomes "As in a season of
autumn,/When the wind stops," and then becomes something still
more extended, "As in a season of autumn,/When the wind stops
. . . and, over the heavens,/The clouds go, nevertheless,/In their direction." Apparently there have been some introspective wanderings behind the ostensible forward movement, prompted by the repetition of
earlier phrasing, and as a result a metaphor for the contraction of human
life comes gradually to include, really to induce its opposite—a movement in the heavens that has a life of its own. By repetitions and
reiterations that are a characteristic feature of Stevens's poetry, we are
encouraged almost imperceptibly to forget any story of human death
and to find ourselves within a movement that has no story, a movement
not in time but in some prospect of space.

The reader's attention is shifted here by maneuvers and echoes that lull rather than alert attention. If the results are powerful, it is by restraint on any human urge to *figure* in the scene, either as a presence or as a tropist. Stevens has phased the poem into a mood wherein the human will, instead of registering its supposedly inherent resistance to self-dispersal, simply relaxes into it. Any Frostean self-assertion in the second half of the poem would here sound impertinent. So, too, would be any reminder that we have been reprieved from willfulness. Instead, the experience of stasis on the ground, as the wind stops, is simultaneous with the experience of seeing clouds which are moving "nevertheless," oblivious to our more local sense of things.

Except in a few instances, like Stevens's last poem, "Of Mere Being," Bloom objects to such a loss of human will, and where the loss does occur, where the human recedes in the presence of powers independent of it, he manages, like most other critics, to correct the balance by exerting his own will in and on the poem. This often takes the form of aggressive readings of particular words. In this case he does odd things with the phrase "over the heavens." It is taken to mean "above the heavens," surely a reading so forced as to be impelled by a larger motive. By placing the moving clouds "above the heavens," whatever that could mean, he is able to ascribe to them what he calls "a larger intentionality" and, more important, to make that intentionality inaccessible to the poet and the reader. It can only be a "larger" intentionality, however, if you want to assume a smaller one, activated by it and in competition with it—some intention of the human will. And if, instead, that human will really is in recession, then, so far as Bloom is concerned, it may participate in the peculiar effect on the ground but not in anything going on "above" the heavens.

This is not a small distinction, though it may sound like one. If the human will is not to assert itself in the poem, then for Bloom it is thereby deprived, in a "reduced" world, of contact with the sublime. But why cannot the sublime be experienced precisely by the relaxed indifference of the will? That is what this poem, like many others by Stevens, aspires to: a represented and enhanced experience wherein everything on the ground and "over"—that is, "across"—the heavens is occurring all at once, an experience wherein this simultaneity is rendered in a manner beautifully placid, devoid of contradiction and friction. The clouds need have nothing to do with "the movement of a larger intentionality," but rather with the marvelous *absence* both of "larger intentionality" and of the smaller intentionalities of the human will. These latter include the enshrined equations of "autumn" to human "death," when there may as easily be no connection between them at all. Those clouds move "nevertheless," and it is their freedom from having to mean anything at all that amazes and delights us. Meanwhile, the human presence, asserted earlier in a phrase like "three-days personage," is, by implication, dissolved into the scene, like the dead soldier.

The poem is at peace with its own reductiveness and never compromises it by suggesting that it is only preliminary to the will's effort at reconstruction. This makes Bloom uncomfortable with the poem, and also with the kind of pleasure Stevens himself claimed to be offering in another equally familiar one, "The Snow Man":

> One must have a mind of winter
> To regard the frost and the boughs
> Of the pine-trees crusted with snow;
>
> And have been cold a long time
> To behold the junipers shagged with ice,
> The spruces rough in the distant glitter
>
> Of the January sun; and not to think
> Of any misery in the sound of the wind,
> In the sound of a few leaves,
>
> Which is the sound of the land
> Full of the same wind
> That is blowing in the same bare place
>
> For the listener, who listens in the snow,
> And, nothing himself, beholds
> Nothing that is not there and the nothing that is.

"The worst reading possible . . . of this poem," according to Bloom, "is the canonical one we received from Stevens himself, when he said in a letter: 'I shall explain "The Snow Man" as an example of the necessity of identifying oneself with reality in order to understand it and enjoy it.' "[11] Bloom's effort to dislodge this reading depends on coercive ascriptions of meaning to two words at the expense of the drift of the whole poem:

"Being" in Stevens can live with the First Idea, but at the price of ceasing to be a "human" being. The listener, reduced to nothing, remains human because he beholds something shagged and rough, barely figurative, yet still a figuration rather than a bareness. This "nothing" is the most minimal or abstracted of fictions, and yet still it is a fiction.

The so-called figuration of "shagged" and "crusted" is on the face of it exaggerated, especially since the rhythm of the poem calls no particular attention to them. The attribution of human feeling to the wind—"misery in the sound of the wind"—occurs exactly in the middle, at line eight, and the punctuation of the one sentence which comprises the entire poem has the effect of blurring distinctions between, on the one side, the human perceptions allowed in lines one to the middle of seven, and, on the other, the perceptions thereafter ascribed to the snow man. Obviously some distinctions need to exist or there would be no point in blurring them, and it may be that the words "crusted" and "shagged" are quiet evidences of this necessity. But the syntax discourages us from pausing on them. The two halves of the poem are reflections of one another by virtue both of repetitions of words and of echoings of sound. Structurally the poem is identical to "The Death of a Soldier" and many other poems by Stevens in which, reversing the narrative line we could expect in a poem by Frost, there is instead a slackening out of the self, an expiration into passivity. We are allowed to think of misery in the wind but we are also invited *not* to think of it; it is possible for a human to be like a snow man and also not to be like one. The human partakes of the nonhuman by a process intended to seem imperceptible, so that whatever slight effort at configuration may exist in the first half is left behind, without nostalgia, when we get to the second.

In Bloom's account there is a kind of desperation to locate in this poem the "crossings," the evidence of will in the form of rhetorical shifts, which were even more difficult to find in "The Death of a

Soldier." To the point, indeed, where he sounds ready to give up on the latter poem entirely, though not before hearing an "undersong" which I cannot be alone in finding inaudible. Commenting on his own paraphrase, he remarks that it

omits what matters about the poem, which is rhetorical gesture, tonal *askesis*, dignity of a minimal *pathos*, excluding lament. Yet what it most omits is the poem's undersong, which is its *logos* or crossing. Rhetorically, the poem intimates that any such earliest seeing of a soldier's death is dehumanizing, intolerable, not to be sustained. This brief poem is almost all *ethos*, all contraction; the human in us demands more of a poem, for us, and where *pathos* is so excluded a death-in-life comes which is more that of the poem's shaper, speaker, reader than it could have been of the fictive soldier before he fell.

This is a rather startling break in critical decorum. If the soldier is, indisputably, "fictive," how can he suddenly be endowed with a real historical life? And why? Apparently so that he might testify against the authenticity of the poem itself. What Bloom offers here is not so much a reading or even a "misreading." Rather, it is a plea "for us," on behalf of "the human in us," in the soldier, and in Bloom. The plea, denied by the poem, is posed and answered by the critic's prose. His prose supplies the pathos or will to power over fate to which the poem refuses to rise. It is in fact to concede too much to say that the pathos is absent, since it is absent only if we first assume that it ought to be there. Instead, the poem asks us to countenance a refusal of grief; it refuses to grieve for a dead soldier and, more significantly, it refuses to grieve for our lost selves. We become transparent to the world, Emerson's great eyeball.

Stevens, it need hardly be said, is not finding some benign way to carry out the project of Nietzsche or Foucault. Rather, with Emerson he shows that if the individual is bound by Fate, then freedom is one of the characteristics of Fate. The poem, the act of writing going on in the poem, is itself the audible and inferably visible evidence of that freedom. The performance of and in the poem is a sign of human power even while the enacted experience has to do with the relaxation, even the abandonment of that power. Part of what I find admirable about this aspect of Stevens is accounted for by James Guetti in his book *Word-*

Music. Mostly about the aesthetics of narrative, the book makes Frostean claims for auditory rather than visualized tracings in language, for
reading more with the ear than with the eye. About Stevens he writes:

> This relation between Stevens's argumentative sequences and the images that
> they ultimately achieve thus involves a simple but crucial distinction for literary
> theory, a distinction between sequences whose results follow from their intelligi-
> ble process and are produced by the reader's continuing that process within and
> beyond them, as opposed to sequences whose results are discontinuous with their
> process and are produced only by the breaking off, the exhaustion of that process.
> . . . In his poetry . . . the exhaustion of the more rational, imaginative powers
> seems always—much less negatively—an exercise of mind that readies us to
> participate in a different sort of perception and energy.[12]

Some readers will object that to proceed in this manner is a guarantee
of philosophical indifference. And what Guetti proposes is not, I think,
wholly adequate to some of the great poems of Stevens and of Western
literature which in fact subscribe in their movements to the humanistic
dialectics that also govern the criticism that has been written about
them. But any criticism is partial, and the virtue of the critical practice
recommended by Guetti is that, more than most, it enables us to see
clearly into the odd and wayward possibilities of writers like Stevens and
into those same possibilities as they struggle for attention—how frequently we are perhaps not yet capable of recognizing—in all writing.

In view of this, Guetti does his position a disservice, I think, when
he joins in the current fashion which denies to Stevens (and Emerson)
the title of philosophical poet, though he may only be expressing his
impatience with the ways in which the title was previously bestowed on
him. To applaud a poet's capacity to generate noncognitive images "out
of the exercise and exhaustion of argumentative sequences" is to make
him, I would suppose, into a profoundly philosophical poet in the school
of Emerson no less than of Wittgenstein. Any poet is philosophical who
excites questions about the career of the words he is using and who
thereby requires us to ask about our own careers within the "circles" of
the language we use. This is notably the case with Stevens, for whom,
as for his Emersonian colleagues, the self-dissolving or deconstructive

tendencies inherent in language are taken for granted and without anxiety. If these tendencies are sometimes preliminary to a reconstitution of the self, they are at other times merely a precondition which allows the self to become a passive observer of its own alternatively crescive and transparent possibilities.

"I AM A VICTIM of neurasthenia and of the sense of hollowness and unreality that goes with it,"[13] William James wrote to his friend G. H. Howison, a professor of philosophy at the University of California, and I suspect that some version of this, as an enhancement of experience and of thinking, however painful and terrifying, is to be found in the other writers I have been discussing in this chapter. James's "will to believe" proceeds from the necessity not for affirmed selfhood and, from the author of *A Pluralistic Universe*, not for unity. It comes instead from a desire simply to know *how* one is to live while facing, as he says in *The Varieties of Religious Experience*, into the "pit of insecurity beneath the surface of life." Against the doubt of existence, one does not posture a "self" but only a "belief," and not even a belief in the self so much as a belief in life. "Believe that life *is* worth living," he advises in *The Will to Believe*, "and your belief will help create the fact." So far as any human self goes, it may be willed into and willed out of existence without loss of consciousness or loss of subjective life, and any act of belief, in the self or in its dissolution, is no more than a modification in the stream of thought. Quoting from Benjamin Paul Blood, an American philosopher, poet, and mystic who, in 1874, wrote *The Anaesthetic Revelation and the Gist of Philosophy*—a book expressing a belief in pluralism based on the use of anaesthetics—James allowed into his own text an eloquence rhapsodic even for him: " 'Reason is but one item in the mystery; and behind the proudest consciousness that ever reigned, reason and wonder blushed face to face. The inevitable stales, while doubt and hope are sisters. Not unfortunately the universe is wild,— game-flavored as a hawk's wing. Nature is miracle all; the same returns not save to bring the different. The slow round of the engraver's lathe gains but the breadth of a hair, but the difference is distributed back over the whole curve, never an instant true—ever not quite.' "[14]

It is fitting that as James came to the end of his life one of his last essays, "A Pluralistic Mystic," was a tribute to his friend Blood, at the conclusion of which he writes: "Let *my* last word, then, speaking in the name of intellectual philosophy, be *his* word:—'There is no conclusion. What has concluded, that we might conclude in regard to it? There are no fortunes to be told, and there is no advice to be given.—Farewell!' " If this is an echo of Emerson in "The Poet" or "Nature" or "Experience," it is an echo that reaches toward the Stevens who says in the "Adagia" of *Opus Posthumous* that "the poet represents the mind in the act of defending us against itself."

NOTES

1. Quotations from Emerson's *Journals* will be identified within my text by date of entry. The dates Emerson gives in the *Journals* are sometimes exact, by a date of the month, but his practice was haphazard, and in many cases the date has had to be approximated by his editors, and designated only by the month or months of a year. Most of my quotations from the *Journals* can be found in the excellent selection edited by Joel Porte, *Emerson in His Journals* (Cambridge: Belknap Press, Harvard University Press, 1982). All of them can be found either in the sixteen volumes of *Journals and Miscellaneous Notebooks of Ralph Waldo Emerson*, William Gilman et al., eds. (Cambridge, Mass.: Harvard University Press, 1960), or in Edward Waldo Emerson and Waldo Emerson Forbes, eds., *The Journals of Ralph Waldo Emerson*, 10 vols. (Boston and New York: Houghton Mifflin Co., 1910–1914).

2. See in this regard the remarkable book by John Hollander, *The Figure of Echo* (Berkeley: University of California Press, 1981), and his essay "Originality" in *Raritan: A Quarterly Review*, II, 4 (Spring 1983), pp. 24–44.

3. For a discussion of how Emerson imagines a connection between sexual

activity and the activity of writing, see Joel Porte, *Ralph Waldo Emerson: Representative Man* (Cambridge, Mass.: Harvard University Press, 1978), pp. 225–46; also, Eric Cheyfitz, *The Trans-Parent: Sexual Politics in the Language of Emerson* (Baltimore: Johns Hopkins University Press, 1981).

4. I refer to James Cox, "Ralph Waldo Emerson: The Circle of the Eye." One of the best essays on Emerson written in the past decade or so, it can be found either in *Emerson: Prophecy, Metamorphosis, and Influence*, edited by David Levin (New York: Columbia University Press, 1975), or in *Modern Critical Views: Ralph Waldo Emerson*, edited and with an introduction by Harold Bloom (New York: Chelsea House, 1985).

5. For his discussions of the historical antecedents to Shelley's theories of language, I am indebted to William Keach, *Shelley's Style* (New York: Methuen, 1984); for an account of the possible influence on Emerson of Guillaume Oegger, see John Irwin, *American Hieroglyphics* (New Haven: Yale University Press, 1980); also Hans Aarsleff, *From Locke to Saussure* (Minneapolis: University of Minnesota Press, 1982).

6. See David Bromwich, "Edward Thomas and Modernism," *Raritan: A Quarterly Review*, III, 1 (Summer 1983), pp. 101–23.

7. See *Raritan: A Quarterly Review*, II, 2 (Fall 1982), pp. 114–27. I refer specifically to D. W. Winnicott and his discussions of "transitional objects" both in *Playing and Reality* (London: Tavistock, 1971) and in *The Maturational Processes and the Facilitating Environment* (London: Hogarth Press, 1972).

8. For a discussion of the importance to Emerson of the so-called higher criticism, which subjected the Bible and Christianity to the techniques of comparative study, see Julie Ellison, *Emerson's Romantic Style* (Princeton: Princeton University Press, 1984). See also Barbara Packer, "Origin and Authority: Emerson and the Higher Criticism," in Sacvan Bercovitch, ed., *Reconstructing American Literary History* (Cambridge, Mass.: Harvard University Press, 1986), pp. 67–92.

9. Though he has so far ignored Emerson, Richard Rorty offers the best account of the effect of pragmatic practices on philosophical vocabulary, in *Consequences of Pragmatism* (Minneapolis: University of Minnesota Press, 1982).

10. Quoted in G. Hartley Grattan, *The Three Jameses* (New York: New York University Press, 1962), p. 192.

11. Thomas A. Goudge, *The Thought of C. S. Peirce* (New York: Dover Publications, 1950), p. 25.

12. Goudge, p. 26.
13. See Howard Feinstein, *Becoming William James* (Ithaca, N.Y.: Cornell University Press, 1984).
14. This entry can be found in Henry James, ed., *The Letters of William James,* 2 vols. (Boston: Little, Brown and Co., 1926), I, pp. 145–48.

Chapter 1

1. The importance to Emerson of the idea of "abandonment" is discussed by Stanley Cavell: "An Emersonian Mood" and "Thinking of Emerson" in *The Senses of Walden* (San Francisco: North Point Press, 1981).
2. Harold Bloom, *Agon: Towards a Theory of Revision* (New York: Oxford University Press, 1982), p. 170.
3. I am alluding to John Irwin, *American Hieroglyphics* (New Haven: Yale University Press, 1980).
4. Donald Pease is particularly good on this issue in "Emerson, Nature, and the Sovereignty of Influence," *Boundary 2,* 8:3 (Spring 1980), pp. 43–74.
5. R. P. Blackmur, *The Lion and the Honeycomb* (New York: Harcourt, Brace and Company, 1955), p. 34.

Chapter 3

1. One of the most impressive examples of Leavis's critical prowess is his tortured meditation on the limitations which attend Eliot's genius as a poet, *The Living Principle* (New York: Oxford University Press, 1975), pp. 155–264.
2. Bromwich, as cited in Note number 5 to the "Prologue." Thomas's comments on Pound can be found in the collection of his critical writings edited by Edna Longley, *A Language Not to Be Betrayed* (New York: Persea Books, 1981), pp. 116–23.
3. Richard Poirier, "Watching the Evening News," *Raritan: A Quarterly Review,* II, 2 (Fall 1982), pp. 1–9.
4. David Ferry, *The Limits of Mortality* (Middletown, Conn.: Wesleyan University Press, 1959).

Chapter 4

1. I do not discuss Emerson's 1859 lecture "Quotation and Originality" because it merely repeats ideas more interestingly developed in his earlier essays.
2. See my review of William Pritchard, *Frost: A Literary Life Reconsidered* in *The New York Review of Books* xxxii:7 (April 25, 1985), pp. 33–35.
3. See Robert Garis, *The Dickens Theater: A Reassessment of the Novels* (London: Oxford University Press, 1965).
4. George Levine's discussion of *Middlemarch* was extremely helpful at this point in my argument. See his book *The Realistic Imagination: Fiction from Frankenstein to Lady Chatterley* (Chicago: The University of Chicago Press, 1981), pp. 291–316.
5. Leo Bersani, *A Future for Astyanax: Character and Desire in Literature* (Boston: Little, Brown and Co., 1976), pp. 65–66.
6. See Sharon Cameron, *Writing Nature: Henry Thoreau's 'Journal'* (New York: Oxford University Press, 1985), especially Chapter Two, "The Language of the Journal," where she observes that because in Thoreau "human nature is a force in the self over which it has no control, it is kin to that larger force from whose unruliness Thoreau chooses not to distinguish it" (p. 37).

Chapter 5

1. The interview, given in 1967, can be found in Raymond Bellour, *Les Livres des autres* (Paris: l'Herne, 1971), pp. 23–32.
2. There is an account of this incident in Fons Elders, ed., *Reflective Water: The Basic Concerns of Mankind* (London: Souvenir Press, 1984). It is discussed in Edward Said, *The World, the Text, and the Critic* (Cambridge, Mass.: Harvard University Press, 1983), pp. 246–47.
3. For a detailed account of how different were the reactions of father and son to this collapse of selfhood, see Howard Feinstein, *Becoming William James*, pp. 243–45.
4. There is a fuller account of these episodes in F. O. Matthiessen, *The James Family* (New York: Alfred Knopf, 1947), pp. 160–66.
5. Such moments of self-dissolution in Thoreau are discussed in Sharon Cameron's, *Writing Nature: Henry Thoreau's 'Journal.'*

6. See my review of Thomas Pynchon, *Slow Learner* (Boston: Little, Brown and Co., 1984) in *London Review of Books*, VII, 1 (January 24, 1985), pp. 18–20.

7. R. B. Haldane and J. Kemp, eds., *The Works of Schopenhauer* (London: Routledge and Kegan Paul, 1983), vol. 1, p. 261.

8. For the idea of "firstness" in the works of Charles Peirce see Justin Buchler, ed., *Philosophical Writings of Peirce* (New York: Dover Publications, 1980), especially Chapter Six.

9. Holly Stevens, ed., *Letters of Wallace Stevens* (New York: Alfred Knopf, 1966), pp. 426–27.

10. E. T. Cook and Alexander Wedderburn, eds., *The Works of John Ruskin* (London: Library Edition, 1903–1912), vol. XXXV, pp. 165–66. See also Jay Fellows, *The Failing Distance* (Baltimore: Johns Hopkins University Press, 1976), pp. 158–87.

11. The letter from which Bloom is quoting is dated April 18, 1944, and can be found in Holly Stevens, ed., *Letters*, op. cit., p. 464.

12. James Guetti, *Word-Music: The Aesthetic Aspect of Narrative Fiction* (New Brunswick, N.J.: Rutgers University Press, 1980), p. 45.

13. Henry James, ed., *The Letters of William James* (Boston: Little, Brown and Co., 1926), II, pp. 22–23.

14. The passage quoted by James is from B. P. Blood, *The Flaw in Supremacy*, published by the author (Amsterdam, N.Y., 1893). See also Matthiessen, *The James Family*, op. cit., pp. 227–28.

INDEX

About the Author

RICHARD POIRIER was born and raised in Gloucester, Massachusetts. After graduating from Amherst College, which also awarded him an honorary degree in 1978, he took an M.A. at Yale, was a Fulbright Scholar at Cambridge University and then went to Harvard, where he received a Ph.D. He has taught at Williams, Harvard, Stanford, and Berkeley, and is currently Marius Bewley Professor of American and English literature at Rutgers University. Mr. Poirier is the founder and editor of *Raritan: A Quarterly Review*, a former editor of *Partisan Review*, and a director and chairman of the Selection Committee of the Library of America. At various times he has been on the executive board of PEN, a member of the Nominating Committee for the National Medal of Literature, a consultant to National Public Radio, a director of the National Book Critics Circle, and a director of the English Institute. He has been the recipient of the American Academy and Institute of Arts and Letters achievement award in literary criticism and is a member of the American Academy of Arts and Sciences. His books include *The Comic Sense of Henry James; A World Elsewhere: The Place of Style in American Literature; The Performing Self: Compositions and Decompositions in the Languages of Contemporary Life; Norman Mailer*, in the Modern Masters Series; and *Robert Frost: The Work of Knowing*. Mr. Poirier lives in New York City.